ADVOCATING
LIBRARIES

Advocating Libraries

Essays presented to

ROBERT CRAIG

Robert Craig
OBE BA MA MCLIP Hon FCLIP

ADVOCATING LIBRARIES

Essays presented to
ROBERT CRAIG

Edited by
Rennie McElroy, Brian D. Osborne,
Alan Reid and Alan G. D. White

2002

Published in Scotland in 2002 by
CHARTERED INSTITUTE OF LIBRARY AND INFORMATION PROFESSIONALS
IN SCOTLAND
1 John Street, Hamilton ML3 7EU
Scotland

Design by GSB (Edinburgh)
Printed by Bookcraft

ISBN 0 954 1160 2 X

CONTENTS

FOREWORD

I was only at the awards dinner of the British Academy of Film and Television Arts in London's Grosvenor Hotel because, at the last minute, a government minister had found it necessary to attend a parliamentary debate and left an empty place at the table. Robert Craig sat opposite me. The pate gleamed softly in the suffused lighting, the hands worked gently at the rituals of the pipe-smoker and the genial beam of the man who has eaten well sat on his face. We watched the spotlight fall on Lord Puttnam as the announcement was read out.

> … And the nominations for the BAFTA Interactive Entertainments Awards in the Learning Category are: George Lucas, Steven Spielberg and the Scottish Library Association.

Robert Craig, first Director of the Scottish Library Association (SLA) – and now of its successor, the Chartered Institute of Library and Information Professionals in Scotland – and founding Director of the Scottish Library and Information Council (SLIC), could quietly revel in the fact that he and his team had pulled it off again. Of course, we came second to Spielberg, but if a man is to be judged by the company he keeps, Robert Craig had just moved that judgement to a new level. Heineken man may reach parts others don't, but Lagavulin man reaches parts others can't even imagine.

It has been fashionable for more than a decade to denigrate the term 'librarian' and to look for synonyms which we hope might allow our professional skills to be valued for the importance they have in an information society, rather than being pigeonholed at the mere mention of the word. Never a dedicated follower of fashion, Robert Craig has preferred to take the fight to the enemy, to celebrate the role and skills of the librarian and to ensure that librarians have become central and indispensable to everyone, from government ministers to showbiz gurus.

Curiously, Robert has not himself spent a large part of his career as manager of a major library, but has instead embraced a role as a hugely effective advocate for all libraries. He has revolutionised the advisory structure in which libraries in Scotland operate. He has made libraries, the SLA and SLIC credible and influential with local and national politicians and senior institutional managers. He has acted as an advisor to government. And he has created a larger, more potent network than many an accomplished politician, many a senior industrialist.

His focus has always been on practical achievements and getting things done, usually working discreetly in the background to ensure that the skills of librarians, the members of SLA and SLIC, are recognised and used to support local and national initiatives. He has been able to show how libraries can contribute to issues on existing political and managerial agendas and success in this has helped him to place other library issues on the same agendas. He has led both the SLA and SLIC to the heart of information technology development, where he has ensured that the focus has extended to much more than hardware. At least one government minister has been heard to use the word 'metadata', in the right context and with apparent understanding.

In April 2002, the Scottish Library Association became the Chartered Institute of Library and Information Professionals in Scotland – the new organisation resulting from the merger of the Library Association and the Institute of Information Scientists. The new organisation meets the challenge of new opportunities with an extended membership, still under Robert Craig's sure and steady guidance. This is a time both for reflection and for looking forward.

It is also a time for recognising outstanding service and achievement. The Scottish Library Association has often been fortunate in those who have served it, but never more so than in the case of Robert Craig, whose contribution has been, and remains, peerless. So this year, as the Scottish Library Association changes its name and broadens its scope, we dedicate these essays to Robert Craig with appreciation, thanks and affection. This very readable *Festschrift* is meant to reflect the breadth of his interests and achievement. It includes personal reflections and anecdotes, as well as professional essays, and is a simple expression of the pride and the gratitude that individual authors and editors, his fellow librarians and the Association at large have for Robert. No one ever better fitted Burns' view that 'the man's the gowd for a' that'.

Derek Law
President, Scottish Library Association (until March 2002)
President, Chartered Institute of Library and Information Professionals in Scotland
(from April 2002)

Spring 2002

INTRODUCTION

I t was with unanimous acclaim and warmth, but more or less idly, that the editors of this book reflected, early in 2001, upon Robert Craig's work and achievements as the first full-time Director of the Scottish Library Association and the founding Director of the Scottish Library and Information Council. And it was quite casually that the idea of composing and publishing this collection of essays in his honour was first aired. Stuart James, President of the Scottish Library Association at the time, liked the idea and declared that the project should go ahead. Then, quite suddenly, we had to make it happen!

As subjects for the essays, we chose topics and areas of library and information work to which Robert Craig has contributed and where his influence has been felt – where he has 'made a difference'. Those who, looking at the contents page of this book, reflect that we didn't omit much, may draw the natural conclusion.

As contributors, we invited people who have exercised responsibility and earned some reputation in library and information work. They are people Robert knows, with whom he has worked and for whom he has respect and liking. They are all busy people. It is a measure of the regard in which Robert Craig is held that it was not difficult to convert invitations into acceptances.

We gave the essayists only a short, outline brief and wide scope to interpret it; they were not constrained by a close prescription. Hence, the occasional overlap between essays, the occasional difference of view that can be discerned. That said, the essays exhibit much more consensus than conflict, confirming a commonalty of view about what are the important issues and the preferred solutions. We extend our warm thanks and appreciation to all the essayists, for contributing and for bearing editorial demands with good humour.

Between the composition of the essays (September 2001 to February 2002) and their publication, the Library Association concluded its merger with the Institute of Information Scientists and changed its name in April 2002 to CILIP: the Chartered Institute of Library and Information

Professionals. The Scottish Library Association became the Chartered Institute of Library and Information Professionals in Scotland. So, a book commissioned by one organisation is published by another. But much of the work discussed in the book was done for and by organisations called the Scottish Library Association and the Library Association. Therefore, we have retained these former styles in the text, but have referred to CILIP and CILIPS in the preliminaries, the contributors' biographies and where it is essential to understanding.

We offer here our own affectionate tribute to Robert Craig, in addition to those extended by the essayists and by the President of CILIPS.

Rennie McElroy, Brian D. Osborne, Alan Reid, Alan G. D. White
Editors

Spring 2002

Part *One*

BIOGRAPHY

The present generation of Scottish librarians may not need the help of a biography to appreciate Robert Craig and his work, but we hope that this book may circulate furth of Scotland and that its insights and analyses may be of value in other places and at other times. So, it seems right to offer a view of the person and the career, the character and the achievement.

This first essay discusses Robert Craig, the person, and goes some way to explaining what he has achieved, and how. If the essay is occasionally elliptical, the reader must forgive two writers – one a colleague of long standing, the other a brother – who sought to protect their subject's privacy, while still informing and entertaining. The subject himself would have insisted upon it, had he been given the chance!

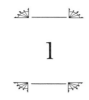

1

Robert Craig

Andrew Miller and Loudon Craig

R obert Craig has not only had a distinguished career, he is also one of those rare individuals whose work and influence contribute significantly towards defining their professional times.

One of three brothers, Robert was born on 2 July 1943. Euan, the youngest, went on to become a successful businessman. Loudon, also a librarian, was Director of Community and Leisure Services with Falkirk Council before his retirement in the late 1990s. From his father, a Master Baker, Robert inherited honesty, determination and an almost limitless capacity for hard work. From his mother came his imagination and iron will.

Although born in Hamilton, Robert and his brothers were brought up in the north Lanarkshire village of Newarthill. Nothing in Robert's life has been ordinary and that quality of 'difference' started very early. Robert had and has a prodigious memory. By the age of four, he was word perfect in *Tam o'Shanter* and had already started school. Attending Newarthill Primary, he successfully sat his eleven plus examination at the age of ten. A month after his eleventh birthday, he was in his first year at Dalziel High School, Motherwell. Six years later, a few days before his seventeenth birthday, he left that school with university entrance qualifications. Robert's rector at Dalziel and an important early influence was James K. Scobbie. Another Scobbie, this time William (James K's librarian brother), would be a significant influence later in Robert's career. But we are moving forward too quickly. Let us draw breath and go back to 1960.

The Craig family had moved to Hamilton. Robert, 17 years old, was leaving school and, despite the rector's advice, had decided against university, but did not know what he wanted to do with his life. James K. Scobbie arranged for him to meet a prospective employer and, like Charles Dickens before him, Robert became a court shorthand writer. Five years later, in 1965, he made one of his best decisions and married Ann. By this time, although he was, by reputation, one of the best shorthand writers in the country, Robert knew that this was not what he wanted to do. Around this time, librarianship had gone from one of several new career possibilities to a short list of one and so, in 1966, with Ann's wholehearted support, he accepted a post as a library assistant with Hamilton Burgh Library. Like others before him, he passed through the double doors of the library in Cadzow Street, under the carved inscription that declares, 'Reading maketh a full man'. The building dates from 1904 and, like Andrew Carnegie buildings elsewhere, was ornamented by quotations. Above the issue desk another quotation read, 'Wisdom is more precious than rubies'. Over the next 36 years, Robert would not only confirm the personal accuracy of the first quotation, but also demonstrate again and again that he is a man of wisdom and common sense.

In Hamilton Burgh Library he learned the rudiments of his profession, for, in the way of burgh libraries, everything was present in that one building – lending services for adults and children, reference services, accession room, local history collection, branch library administration and extension activities. Robert quickly realised that this job was not another false start, but the beginning of something he really enjoyed, wanted to do and was good at. To progress, he needed professional qualifications. This time there was no doubt. Encouragement was not needed. As soon as he possibly could, he went to university.

As a student of librarianship at the University of Strathclyde, Robert put the solid professional foundation from Hamilton Burgh Library to good use, winning the Kelso Memorial Prize for Bibliographic Studies, as well as the prize for best overall student performance.

Returning to Hamilton Burgh Library from university, Robert soon realised that expansion and development opportunities in an already developed burgh system were, to say the least, limited and that promotion would be slow. He started to look around for bigger and better opportunities. Diagonally across the street from the Burgh Library, at 4 Auchingramont Road, was the headquarters of Lanark County Libraries. The County Librarian at that time was the late, great W.B. Paton. Under his guidance the whole service buzzed with achievement. Challenges were met head on and overcome. Staff morale was high and talent was everywhere. The system was an incredible nursery, nurturing, developing and releasing some of the best librarians Scotland has produced. Robert and his contemporaries still regard the man and his service as a professional high point never again equalled in the generation following the Scottish local government reorganisation that consigned Lanark County Libraries to history. Never was the phrase 'centre of excellence' more deserved, or more accurately applied. When an opportunity for advancement materialised in Lanark County, Robert's application was swiftly and successfully dispatched. Never were an organisation and an individual more ideally suited. Robert Craig's career in librarianship had properly begun.

We move on. It is now five years since Robert Craig decided on a career in librarianship and just over two years since he joined Lanark County Libraries as a newly qualified librarian. Let us imagine we are reading the *Bellshill Speaker* for Friday 2 October 1970. There are three main stories on its front page. Their headlines are: 'There's been a hole at his back door for eight months', 'Moderator's visit will take in Bellshill area' and, complete with photograph, 'New librarian takes over':

> Mr Robert Craig, ALA has recently been appointed Bellshill District Librarian. Twenty-seven year old Mr Craig is a native of Newarthill who now resides in Hamilton. He is married with a young daughter. … Before coming to Bellshill Library, he worked with the County Council's Mobile Library Service and also spent time as Librarian-in-Charge at Bailleston and Blantyre libraries.

Robert's managerial, organisational and people skills had been quickly recognised and utilised, being honed and developed through a range of professional experience unheard-of today. After Bellshill, he took charge of the service's circulation system. This was a job more suited to a skilled transport manager than to a librarian, but Robert handled it as if he had worked for Eddie Stobart for years.

It was at this time that Robert worked most closely with the redoubtable W.B. Paton, then County Librarian. This occasionally could develop into a Pythonesque situation. In the County Librarian's office there was a large walk-in cupboard. W.B. Paton had the disconcerting habit of asking you to come to a morning briefing session, beginning the meeting, then disappearing into the cupboard, never to appear again for the rest of the meeting. You were, to all intents and purposes, talking to yourself and listening to his disembodied voice coming from behind an open door. If you have ever tried to have a detailed and sometimes technical conversation with yourself, you will know how difficult it is to remain cogent and coherent. Fortunately, another feature of this office was a long window and, if you stood in the middle of the room, you could see yourself clearly reflected in the glass. It was a common sight to pass the County Librarian's open door and see senior managers staring out the window, apparently talking to themselves. We are convinced that it was in this way that Robert developed the presentation and delivery skills that made him so successful as a lecturer and platform speaker. But again, we are getting ahead of ourselves.

Again, the scene changes. Robert was now the father of a boy as well as a girl. The 1975 reorganisation of Scottish local government was just around the corner. W.B. Paton had retired, William Scobbie had succeeded him and Robert, having set up the successful Bell Education Resource Centre for Teachers, pulling together in one place material for teachers in a rich variety of print and non-print formats, had been appointed Depute County Librarian. Along with William Scobbie, he oversaw the smooth winding down of Lanark County Libraries and the equally smooth creation of a separate school library service. It was ten years since he had decided on a career in librarianship. He was about to obtain a BA degree from the Open University. He was 32 years old.

After the local government reorganisation, Robert was appointed Principal Educational Resources Librarian for Strathclyde Region's Glasgow Division, where he established the Woodlands Teacher Centre. Again this was a service, unique certainly in Scotland, much appreciated by its users and it set the foundation of Robert's acknowledged major contribution to the creation of a credible library service for schools.

By 1978, he was looking for new challenges and he changed professional direction somewhat to become a lecturer in the University of Strathclyde's Department of Librarianship and Information Studies. His subjects included public library management, international and comparative librarianship and historical bibliography. His first hand experience of front-line librarianship let him speak with considerable authority, but he was not one to be overly authoritarian or pedantic. His students recognised his benevolence. They still speak of enjoyable lectures, delivered in a deceptively casual style and illustrated with mnemonic anecdotes. At this time, Robert was also showing an increasing interest in professional association matters. He was elected Chairman of the Youth Libraries Group and also a member of the Council of the Scottish Library Association (SLA). Only a short time later, he became a member of that Council's then Executive Committee. In 1980, he became that rare individual, an 'ALABAMA', having obtained an MA degree from Strathclyde to complement his professional qualification, ALA and his Open University BA. In 1981, he was elected Honorary Secretary of the SLA.

It had taken years of lobbying by the SLA to persuade the Library Association to fund the appointment of a full-time paid officer based in Scotland to look after the interests of librarians working in Scotland. When approval was finally given, the search was on to find the right person for the job. In 1984, it was Robert Craig who emerged from the selection process to become the first Executive Secretary (now, Director) of the Scottish Library Association and, of course, the yardstick by which all future holders of the post will be measured. No one on the interview panel has ever had cause to regret their decision. Robert Craig has developed the post and its responsibilities to the great and lasting benefit of the SLA membership across the broad spectrum of libraries and librarianship in Scotland.

While Robert's background and experience would serve him well in his new executive position, it was totally uncharted territory. Although the role had clear guidelines, just how the post would evolve was his sole responsibility. At the time, Robert saw himself as having four main areas of activity. He had to service the SLA Council and its committees; he had to promote library and information services to other organisations; he had to promote the SLA to its membership; and he had to be the link between the SLA and the Library Association. He is on record at the time as saying that promoting the SLA to its membership had the greatest importance, because the perception of many individual members was that the work of the SLA bore little relevance to their day to day concerns. In retrospect, the area in which Robert Craig has proved himself to be more than capable was one not even mentioned in those far-off days – the political arena. Robert had already realised that if the Association did not deliver what it promised; if it was not well regarded in political circles; if it did not earn its spurs – then there would be little or no future for librarianship in its broadest sense. He was now in a position to do something about this; and he had the talent to make it happen.

Between the ages of five and ten years, Robert and his brothers attended brethren meetings every Sunday. It was here that he heard, for the first time, people who could work an audience with the skill and subtlety of a Mozart sonata. Who, with word and gesture could make you laugh, cry, applaud, or sit in silent admiration. Above all, these speakers connected with their audience. They spoke with clear, honest conviction and were believed. Robert Craig has this talent and uses it well. He draws people into his world, individually or in groups, and they become willing participants in it. He is someone whose company and opinions people seek. He has never lost 'the common touch'. He connects with people. He is one of the great marketplace professionals, publicly and privately proclaiming his conviction in the continuing relevance of libraries and librarianship in tomorrow's society and convincing the country's 'movers and shakers' of this truth by delivering on his promises, time after time.

Networking within the system established a good working relationship between the SLA and the members and officers of the Convention of Scottish Local Authorities (COSLA). A working group of librarians and local government representatives was invited, under the aegis of COSLA, to examine Scottish public libraries and in 1986, produced standards for public libraries. These standards were updated in 1995 and were complemented by standards for college libraries and for school libraries. They were and are envied by many librarians and their representatives throughout the UK.

One of the main recommendations of the public libraries report was that a Scottish Library and Information Council (SLIC) should be established. This would be the focus of Scottish library and information activity across the country. So SLIC came into being, recognised from the beginning as the advisory body to Scottish Ministers and the Scottish Executive on library and information matters. At a stroke, the library and

Andrew Miller and Loudon Craig

information community gained a political arm which, in its advisory capacity, had ready access to the decision-makers in central and local government. Membership of SLIC is available on payment of an annual subscription to all organisations which maintain library and information services. Currently, all Scottish local authorities (representing public and school libraries), universities, further education colleges, health boards and trusts, and the prison service are in membership. SLIC's Management Committee is chaired by a prominent public figure and includes representation from all sectors of its membership base and from the Scottish Executive. The success of SLIC has cemented year by year a cordial and effective working relationship with the Scottish Executive and has paved the way to mutually beneficial initiatives. SLIC has no shortage of ideas and invariably has quick-start projects on the shelf that just need funding, while the Executive sometimes has funding looking for projects. The dependability of SLIC in the management of its affairs and the compounding success of its initiatives has persuaded the Executive to use SLIC as a medium for directing grant-aid to recognised priority areas of library and information work. Robert Craig has been Director of SLIC since 1991 and the inspiration and driving force in guiding its affairs.

For many years, Robert Craig has organised the SLA's Annual Conference with its associated trade exhibition. At one time, the Conference was an opportunity for professional librarians to give papers to other librarians. Gradually, Robert made changes in keeping with his strategies for widening the profession's outlook and influence, extending his range of speakers to include chief executives, politicians and educationists. As the Conference's reputation grew, these high profile speakers were easily persuaded to appear on the programme. They were comfortable with the organisation of the Conference and Robert's talent for 'whipping in' delegates who might otherwise have been distracted by rival attractions of the Conference venue. These delegates provided a lively and stimulated audience. These speakers, with their own reputations in mind, had to learn a bit about libraries before writing and presenting their papers. And they learned even more in the mostly convivial discussions which could go on long after the formal sessions had closed. Mindful also of his responsibilities to the membership in general, Robert saw that a Branch and Group Day was established during the Conference. Soon, its programme had to run parallel sessions to meet the demand for inclusion from a rich variety of professional focus and special interest groups. Over the years, due in no small measure to Robert's guiding hand, the Scottish Library Association's Annual Conference has gained a world-wide reputation for professional quality, social and political relevance and matchless Scottish hospitality.

Neither did Robert overlook the international dimension. A good relationship was forged with the Association des bibliothécaires français, the SLA's French sister association, and annual reciprocal visits have been made to each other's conferences. Many individual friendships have also been formed. An active interest has been maintained with the International Federation of Library Associations and Institutions (IFLA) and its annual conference. In 2002, the IFLA Conference is being hosted by Great Britain, in Glasgow, in recognition of the 75th anniversary of the foundation of IFLA, in Scotland, in 1927. Robert Craig was tireless in promoting, first Scotland, then Glasgow, as the venue for this conference. The credit for the eventual choice of Glasgow as the conference venue belongs, in large measure, to him. He lobbied extensively and negotiated successfully with the many interested parties. To have been part of the kilted delegation at the 2001 IFLA Conference in Boston which issued the formal invitation to delegates to hold the 2002 Conference in Glasgow must have given him great satisfaction. Those closest to him report that, being Robert Craig, he hid his satisfaction well.

Crowning national recognition of Robert's abilities and achievements came in 2000, when he was awarded the OBE for services to librarianship. Now a proud grandparent, Robert started to 'slow down'. In January 2001, in addition to his other duties, he was seconded as an advisor to the Minister for Enterprise and Lifelong Learning in the Scottish Executive.

With the help of an imaginary garden, a football team, a pipe and a pint of Guinness, let us draw back a curtain and look briefly into Robert's world beyond librarianship.

In the 1950s, in his spare time, Robert's father successfully cultivated a third of an acre of land, growing, under glass, tomatoes and fuchsias. Outdoors, he grew all kinds of vegetables, chrysanthemums and sweet peas. Robert was arguably the least unwilling of the sons dragooned into helping and over the years, encouraged by his father, he developed into a keen gardener. In the autumn of 2001, Robert and Ann moved house from Hamilton to Stonehouse. Their new home came with a large uncultivated back garden – a daunting prospect. However, like his father, Robert does not dwell on problems, only solutions. Standing in his back garden on a December evening, listening to his imaginative plans, you find yourself nodding in agreement and even throwing in the odd suggestion as he makes next year's garden take shape before your eyes. The fact that it is 9pm and you cannot see a thing is somehow irrelevant.

That *Bellshill Speaker* of 1970 described Robert as a football fan. More accurately, for most of his life, he has been an incurable supporter of Glasgow Rangers. He is one of those individuals who understands and agrees with Bill Shankly's comment that, 'Football is not a matter of life and death. It is more important than that'. The support for Rangers was and is a family thing with, for years, three generations of Craigs taking their seats at every home game. One of Robert's big regrets is that, unlike his brothers, he was

Andrew Miller and Loudon Craig

not in Barcelona to see his team lift the European Cup Winners trophy.

Anyone who has been in a bar with Robert knows that while the conversation will be great, it is essential to find a fairly large table. Three pipes, two tobacco pouches, a penknife, pipe cleaner and matches, are all carefully laid on the table – and all this before he sits down. What follows is that most arcane of rituals – the filling of his pipe. Meanwhile the Guinness is settling. He chooses a pipe, mixes the tobacco, fills the pipe, strikes a match, lights the tobacco. There is a deep, satisfied drawing in of breath. He reaches for the Guinness, sips and nods appreciatively, puts down the pint and the pipe and, only then, begins to talk. He has never said, but we are convinced that he has discovered that there is a direct correlation between the time it takes to fill his pipe and the creation of the perfect pint.

However, it is time to let this curtain close again, to respect his privacy and leave him with his pipe and pint, talking to his friends. It is time to ask a question.

Who speaks for Scottish libraries? Who can make the profession and the public listen, believe and commit to the ongoing adventure? In the fifties and sixties, it was people like W.B. Paton, Neil McCorkindale and Robert Walker. In the late sixties, seventies and early eighties, it was people like Peter Grant, Alan White and Alex Howson. In the late eighties, nineties and into the 21st century, it has been and is Robert Craig.

He presents a friendly, easy-going façade on the platform and in the committee room, yet, as with all who enjoy a successful, active and prominent career, he has steel in his soul, a talent for making the difficult seem easy, a skill for seeing the wood as well as the trees and an unsurpassed ability with people and situations. This, as well as being lucky, or perhaps, making his own luck. He can be sympathetic and ready with helpful advice when this is required. He inspires loyalty, radiates confidence and seems unflappable but, in fact, is a classic example of the principle, 'Fail to prepare; prepare to fail'.

It is because of people like him that, despite the 'slings and arrows' of multiple reorganisations, today's library profession is still strong, credible and evolving. We can only be grateful. Our closing words are Martin Luther's and they define exactly where the Robert Craigs of our profession have brought us:

> We are not yet what we shall be but we are growing toward it. The process is not yet finished but it is going on. This is not the end but it is the road.

Listen and believe.

Part Two

THE BOOK IN SCOTLAND

Libraries are a force for good because they provide opportunity to read, learn and so improve one's mind, lot and performance. This simple fact needs constant reiteration and endorsement. Libraries and what they offer are frequently promoted under new names; disguised, but also facilitated, by changing, temporarily fashionable, titles and initiatives – 'lifelong learning', 'people's network', 'content', 'learning information centres'.

Underpinning all such labels, however, are the basic skill of literacy, the wish to learn and, above all, ready access to works of imagination and information which are themselves the product of free, enquiring minds and which exhibit all shades of opinion. Undeniable technical advances notwithstanding, society has not yet developed a better delivery mechanism for this than the library, whatever it may be called from time to time.

To fulfil their role, libraries need a secure flow of material for their collections. They have a natural partnership with all the elements of the book world – author, publisher, bookseller, reader – and a vested interest in their vigour and well-being. They also need the informed support of individual users and wise, well-directed advocacy. Robert Craig has been Scottish libraries' advocate *par excellence* and has formed positive working relationships throughout the book world.

2

A reader's salute to libraries

Janey Buchan

Settling down to put together one's thoughts and experiences for a *Festschrift* to a librarian seems a good idea until you ask the first question – 'How?' My first reaction is to slide into a sort of romanticism-cum-sentimentality. The second is to get a grip and realise that my reaction to libraries is a bit like the roller-coaster – the machine in a fairground which sends you hurtling round and round and, at the same time, up and down. So here is my library roller-coaster.

Eschewing romanticism, it is still a sense of warmth and pleasure which suffuses me as I remember my first library ticket; I realised that I was in a world of 'the big girls' playground', being grown up, making a choice for myself. I got a 'reader's ticket' and today when I go into libraries of all sorts in all sorts of places and see them referred to as 'learning centres', serving 'users', I am swept with feelings of near-violence. Learning centres? What do they think libraries have always been? Now we're on to the roller-coaster with a vengeance.

For many of us, the public library, the art gallery and museum, public broadcasting in the shape of the BBC, were what we got in life. Luck played a huge part in it too: luck in having the parents or friends that we did; luck in where we lived – near a good library or gallery. Of course, we didn't go around realising how lucky we were, or acknowledging that fantastic world we were able to enter. Indeed, if anyone had come round telling us that we were part of things labelled 'socially inclusive', we'd have wondered – 'What kind of language was this?' Totally foreign to us, then and now.

I was first jolted into realising what we had when, during a spell of ironing one afternoon, I listened to a radio talk and discussion programme. The main contributor was the writer Marghanita Laski. She talked about how, when she was young, she and her friends blamed all the ills of their time on the Victorians. Narrow minded, repressive, patronising, keeping young people in their place. Until she said, 'I suddenly realised how marvellous they were in one respect. If it hadn't been for the Victorians and free public libraries, how could we have read as much as we did …?' She

Janey Buchan

continued, 'I thought that, if it hadn't been for them and the service they brought in and enthusiastically drove forward, we would now be in a sorry state. If we didn't have them, how could anyone invent them now?'

Down went the iron and I sat down to listen more intently to the discussion. For over 30 years I have used her thinking – always acknowledging the source – and it never fails to elicit, in committee or public meeting, a slightly stunned reaction. I know that a leading person in the field of social work in Scotland has told friends and acquaintances how grateful he was to be given this cast-iron defence of public spending in support of thinking, new ideas, innovation, etc. It is unanswerable.

One very happy occasion when this argument was used was at a fringe event during the television festival and conference which coincides with the annual Edinburgh Festival. My husband was adumbrating a scene where we could go before a committee and say, 'Look, I've got this great idea. We'll get hold of a really big building, line all the walls with shelves as well as having free-standing bookcases, have separate rooms where people could read newspapers or magazines. And it would all be free. All kinds of books – mountains of them – and the whole cost would be borne by the rates.' And pausing slightly, he continued, 'Since I see Andrew Neil (then of the *Sunday Times*) in the audience, I could ask – "How would today's *Sunday Times* treat such a programme?"' He didn't need to add another word – the audience got it all right, and they thundered their support. Their dislike of Andrew Neil and the paper was all too obvious. Yet trying to argue for a well funded public library service would, we all know, simply not be on anywhere in the UK, if we did not already have them.

When the library service began to lend LPs and, occasionally, pictures and prints, another step forward was taken. It really did seem to us that new services and openings were being forged, and we began to think of how we could argue for others.

Exactly when the difficulties of this present period began, I am not quite sure. Maybe it was when the awful cry of 'Cuts' was heard throughout the land. There surely is a good book waiting to be written on what cuts were made in past times and which were never reinstated. There is rarely a public outcry when libraries are cut back, closed or altered beyond recognition. It is not only in the public library service either that this is so. I really do find it painful to walk into a college or university and see students staring into a screen, moving a mouse, having that glassy-eyed look which mechanical means of information induces in each and every user. Never to leave your desk, wander around the shelves and take down a book which you think might be the right one for your present work, seems to me quite terrifying. I shall return to this.

Bookshops too are, in the words of the Scots song, 'sairly altered noo'. But one brave soul really stands out; the original owner of the great Strand

Bookshop in New York firmly stated in a magazine interview before his death (and his family are still tied to the sentiment), 'You'll never get a cup of coffee in this bookshop.' Amen to that – you can still browse in his and some other bookshops.

I get angry with the stereotyped attitude to book-lovers, but particularly librarians; the treatment of them in films and television is a real judder on my roller-coaster. We've all seen it – we still see it when we watch old B-movies on afternoon television (and there's another good book waiting to be written!). When we would settle down occasionally with a cup of coffee on an afternoon and start searching for something to watch and landed on one of these movies, my husband would yelp, 'God Almighty! Did we once pay good money to go and look at this?' And the answer is that we did. How the movie moguls must have loved us.

The heroine is a really dull woman – rarely a dull man for a hero – wearing unfashionable clothes, hair up in a bun, thick specs. The story moves on and suddenly she lets down the bun and beautiful flowing hair is there. Off come the specs (but no explanation as to why she doesn't trip over the nearest chair and break her leg!) and she is also in the most fashionable of clothes. Where did they come from? Oh, we've all 'been there, done that', all right.

Yet there is no 'Hang on a minute ...' from viewers. Why not? We would not sit back and allow other professions to be so maligned or misinterpreted. To see that it still goes on, you only need to read newspapers and, more particularly, columnists. In the late autumn of 2001, such an example of clapped-out stereotyping appeared in one of our better UK broadsheet newspapers. The only indignant letters rejecting it came from women librarians – not one reader, let alone a 'library user', in to-day's language, took it upon themselves to defend either the librarian or the service.

Why is this? If the world of libraries and books doesn't jolt us into action and we cannot remember just what they meant to us, how come that all and sundry are keen to be in these truly awful pages in the newspapers at Christmas or summer holiday times, giving out with what book people ought to be buying? In Scotland, we live in a small country and there isn't much going on that we don't somehow or other get to know about. Assistants in bookshops know who does and does not come in to buy or order up – even with that pleasurable activity being drafted in to yet another Internet affair. In these past weeks it has been a real lift to read angry letters in newspapers, pointing out that we can all see who is recommending what book – and that they are often from the same publishing house. If Anya is published by X, isn't it odd that she'll recommend books from the same stable? Since it had never occurred to me to look at this, I utter the good old Aussie phrase, 'Good on you, mate'. Perhaps these lines will goad people into action the next time a library is under threat of being partially closed,

Janey Buchan

altered beyond recognition, or re-named and given one of these niddy-noddy titles which so besmirch our lives.

That the Internet, the e-mail, the website are in all our lives to stay is not in dispute. What we must hope will be increasingly disputed is whether they should be the be-all and end-all of our lives – and particularly, of our reading, library lives. We cannot repeat often enough that you cannot curl up in your bed at night with the Internet, but you can with a good book. That these mechanical means are increasingly producing mechanical language and expression is, I am glad to see, beginning to deeply worry some people. In recent weeks, the Principal of a long-established university in Scotland almost exploded when, in a 'library' conversation, funding was being discussed – and deplored. 'If this government puts out more spin-doctoring about libraries being funded, drives towards combating the low levels of literacy and other projects, when they really mean another load of Internet points, I'll … I'll …' and then it tailed off as the man was almost lost for words. The Internet and all the technology that goes with it is important and can help many people. But only if we make sure that at least as much (if not more) time, money and effort go into the information, literature and culture carried on the Internet, as go into the hardware, computers and so on.

In recent months, there have been in some broadsheet newspapers (but not in any tabloid), photographs of stunning new libraries – Norwich and the London School of Economics spring to mind – and the architectural correspondents deal with them. Nowhere is there reference to what is in these new buildings and I have been sorely tempted to go and ask to be shown round; and then I could ask – 'What did you get for stock replenishment?' It is of no comfort at all to find, within weeks of the glowing words about the new building, another article, from staff and readers, pointing out the difficulties of working in the place and the paucity of books, periodicals and other materials.

Sir Richard Eyre, former Artistic Director of the National Theatre, writing recently in some despair about the state of the theatre in the UK, said, 'The theatre in the English speaking world is the greatest glory of our civilisation.' I don't think any thinking person would disagree, even if 'theatre' were not at the top of their personal priorities. How it got there is worth a thought, too. The book, the printed, spoken and sung word, also contributed; and the public library, the municipal gallery and museum service and, in its better days, public broadcasting were always working alongside other forms in the arts and in cultural life generally.

That the library is, throughout the world, the mainstay of hundreds of places – cities, universities, industrial bases (especially the mining industry) – never ceases to amaze and uplift me. In recent years, when getting the Centre for Political Song under way at Glasgow Caledonian University, I have simply walked into many libraries and I have been, without exception, warmly welcomed and time and interest have been shown to me and the project. A good example is the Free Library of Philadelphia, which was founded by Benjamin Franklin. I asked if they had a music collection or curator. Both. The woman who was then the Curator was full of interest and clearly was thinking on her feet as to how they could link into what we are getting off the ground at Glasgow Caledonian University. 'Do you have anything that could be looked on as "political song"?' I asked. 'We've got boxes of stuff upstairs', was the reply – 'campaign songs'. And the first thing to click onto is the fact that in American English, 'campaign' songs means Presidential campaigns and not, as in the UK, campaigns around issues from capital punishment to CND to apartheid to Liberal campaigns about 'land'(and the Liberals have always been singing!). Chicago was another gem to call in on – especially to find a young woman librarian in the Harold Washington Library who came from Dundee. She immediately fetched other members of staff and I got from them for the first time what I've subsequently heard everywhere else – 'We've never collected song, but song is everywhere in our collection.' That there is nowhere in the United States, or anywhere else that we've been able to check on, collections or centres for political song, is still amazing me.

Books have to be published and, although the world of publishing is now largely in the hands of conglomerates, university presses throughout the world operate and still manage to publish and open doors for us. *Singing for survival* is a title from the University of Illinois Press (published in 1992) and in my despairing days as a Socialist trying to survive in the ghastly world of 'New' Labour, I think that we'd better start getting this volume into every library. It is the work of Gila Flam, a woman ethnomusicologist whose parents survived the Lodz ghetto – and their singing survived with them. I am now a firm enthusiast for the University of Illinois Press. But finding out what they are publishing is difficult for those not on the Internet. Why?

When a leading writer, singer, book man superb said to me, 'There are too many books being published' I almost thumped him. I sense danger in such talk. We can all feel annoyed, concerned at how the world of the book is going nowadays, but we hold fast to its importance, its survival and flourishing – the alternative is too awful to contemplate. In our own country of Scotland, we have had some success in getting into print what is in our libraries. Tom Leonard's *Radical Renfrew* remains a most marvellous piece of effort, co-operation and downright love. Scotland should be more proud of it than it has been and when there are the usual exchanges of gifts at public events, this book ought to be among the first few items to be considered. Well done Renfrew. We should be compiling a list of what, had they but money enough and time, other libraries could do. It might shock

Janey Buchan

some of today's wannabes and smartasses into action. None of us would mind if they shared some of the glory – *shared*, not commandeered.

Why, in this roller-coaster world, haven't more similar works appeared? Be reassured that there are readers, librarians, councillors, desperate to get a similar show on the road, but thwarted at every turn. I have a great distaste for what a friend calls the Auntie Beenie Syndrome. 'That cannae be true; it's no' what happened to my Auntie Beenie' – and that, according to their lights, is that. I tend to use, 'A personal experience is very rarely a universal truth'. Neither of us has had much success in fighting Auntie Beenie off, if truth be told. Two personal experiences now, to give a taste of what might be possible, if the ordinary back-bench councillor, MP, MSP or MEP were listened to.

I served on a committee in Glasgow Corporation which had libraries, galleries and museums within its remit. My Freudian slip is clearly showing when I admit that I cannot remember the exact title of the committee. It was a period of my life when I was constantly at book auctions and in and out of bookshops of all kinds – and I could weep now to think of how many there were in Glasgow. I put up to the committee the proposal that we should look at the possibility of us having a Town and Gown paperback publishing house, with the core of its list being the rare books in The Mitchell Library and at Glasgow University.

I had been searching for the Child *Ballads* in any printed form and they never seemed to come up on any list or auction catalogue. I knew that in paperback reprint they would sell. I knew too that natural science fetched amazing sums when it came up at auction. I was given no help whatsoever, from either staff or elected members, and had to set off on my own. It was clear that the then City Librarian was determined that I wasn't coming anywhere near *his* books. I also approached a Professor in the English Literature Department at Glasgow University. Here, I was treated like something that should be put under a microscope in the Science Faculty. 'How odd. What a peculiar woman. Not a graduate, yet sitting here telling me ...'. At least I learned that his idea of what the University should be doing was to reprint Scottish Victorian novels. That I could have discussed that subject with him pretty well never crossed his mind. It never got anywhere and in later years I bought an entire set of the Child *Ballads*, in paperback reprint from a well known publishing house in the US, at a price which was a bit beyond what we could afford. They still sell and fetch over £100 at today's second hand prices. Town and Gown in Glasgow were never involved or mentioned.

My experience in the galleries and museums work of the committee, at a slightly later date, was equally disgraceful. By this time, I was Vice-Chairman but the Chairman was, like the City Librarian, an *expert*, and not even to be asked a question, let alone challenged in his rigidity. The day before a committee meeting, he approached me in the corridor and there followed this conversation: 'Do you think you could manage to take the committee tomorrow?' 'Oh, I think I could manage that.' 'I have to be somewhere and cannot get out of it.' In Glasgow-speak, I thought, 'Whit's up? He's no' leaving me to take the Chair without a good reason.'

I nipped down to the Town Clerk's office to ask what was on the agenda. He was a downy old bird and, pushing his specs down his nose, said, 'Mrs Buchan, are you being dropped in it?' I replied, 'Probably.' He then produced the agenda and told me I would have to take the committee through agreeing to buy a painting for £75,000 the following day. I said that was OK – what was the painting? It was the famous – even then – *Head of Alexander Reid* by Van Gogh. I could not believe it. £75,000? Ha'pennies.

I twigged immediately that this Chairman had been on the Corporation when Dali's *John the Baptist* was bought for £8,000 – and Glasgow had gone bananas. Well worth a dig in the archives now, to see what that time was like. This man thought that if there was this carry-on over £8,000 what, in God's name, would they do over £75,000; and he decided to clear off and drop me in it. Not a clue that life and attitudes had moved on, that Glasgow doesn't turn a hair usually when a theatre or hall is closed, but will really go their dinger if anyone touches an art gallery or its contents. I wish I knew why.

I therefore called up the BBC and STV, told them to get the cameras down to the City Chambers, and I did a piece for the evening news bulletins, saying that the committee had this wonderful opportunity … didn't think that the committee members would be anything other than delighted to be part of a body which would be on record as bringing this famous painting to Glasgow and at such a price … the generosity of the family of Alexander Reid …

It went sailing through committee. Within 24 hours a man I knew sent £40 on behalf of his four children for the years that each had enjoyed Glasgow's Galleries, at no cost of entry. A pub in Govan Road had a collecting box on the counter and sent the contents in – all of this despite there being no public appeal; I knew that I could not overstep the mark by saying on TV that the Corporation would welcome one. I also knew then that you only need a little thought to ensure that you can always take the public with you in any endeavour that is right-hearted.

I look back at a distance of nearly 40 years and cannot believe it. I was Vice-Chairman and did not know what the agenda was. No item was ever discussed between me and the Chairman. His 'Do you think you could manage …' still raises a laugh, as I have the reputation of being a more than competent chairman of any committee. Following the purchase of the painting and subsequent success of it being in our ownership, this man's vicious animosity to me knew no bounds. The woman who chaired the

Janey Buchan

committee when I proposed a Town and Gown publishing house had a similar attitude.

Since then, I have always warned people going into any area of elected office – and I do stress 'area', as we should not accept 'levels' as being anything other than a patronising misuse of language – that they ought to make sure that they have other people putting their heads above the parapet with them. Today's political climate – in *all* parties – makes it impossible for anyone, in or out of elected office, to have a good idea. Funding will clearly be one of the problems, but above all, there will also be this attitude that only 'stars' can think anything through properly. In the ranks of the Poor Bloody Infantry of Labour's army, we call it 'New' Labour and are always leery of them all.

So this has been my libraries roller-coaster. It moves on to remember, and salute, every single person in the huge world of libraries and librarians who have enriched the lives of me and my family and all our friends. And it rests at the end on my family. When the letters came in on the death of my husband, not least of the very touching ones came from the staff of the House of Commons Library. 'We loved him. He was always coming in with an interesting request. Never ever just looking for help with a speech …'. That our books went into the library of a new university – Glasgow Caledonian University – was my decision, but it was in keeping with our good life together. And the book and a love of it was one of the pillars of this life.

Our son too, when small, provided librarians with a good realisation of how valuable they were, and are, to all of us. We lived then beside Pollokshields Library. One day, the librarian on duty in the children's section heard this thumpety-thump noise and looked out to see where it was coming from. She couldn't see anything, went to investigate further and found this small boy with a toy barrow which he had been bumping up the flight of stairs and which had some half dozen books in it. 'Could you read me a story?' he asked. I've no idea how she coped in explaining to a three-year-old that that wasn't what librarians really did (though nowadays, story-telling is often a feature of the children's library – and a good thing, too). That his children now are equally thirled to books is a simple pleasure.

I am pleased beyond words to set down, however badly, this salute to the world of the book – from writer, to publisher, printer and binder, bookseller, and the library and the librarian. In today's language – I owe you; all of you. Alongside you, I also owe everyone who labours in the public interest and especially those in the sister arts. I've never been anything but lifted and steadied by this world.

Recently, I brought back to Glasgow from the bookstore of the Harold Washington Library in Chicago a number of T-shirts, sold in aid of AIDS Research and in support of people with AIDS. Across the front, it read: 'Practise safe sex – take a book to bed.'

I do salute you, but I also want to lift every voice in concern over where libraries are today, as compared to where they could be, and, in my other world of song, use the truly great American campaign song:

If I had a hammer,
I'd hammer in the morning,
I'd hammer in the evening,
All over this land.
I'd hammer out danger,
I'd hammer out a warning,
I'd hammer out
A love between my brother and my sister,
All over this land.

Sing on and we shall some day get the world of the book, the library and the librarian back to where it started with the Victorians.

Janey Buchan

3

Literature, nation

Jenny Brown

Work as if you were living in the early days of a better nation
Alasdair Gray, 1983

There are many who believe that literature is poised to assume centre-stage in the next decade
UK Cultural Sector, Policy Studies Institute, 2001

The vital contribution Scottish literature has made to the new sense of identity in Scotland was celebrated in the opening ceremony of the Scottish Parliament on 1 July 1999. The poetry of Robert Burns, Iain Crichton Smith and a young schoolgirl, Amy Linekar, was a prominent part of the ceremony, while the new MSPs quoted the likes of Scott, Sir David Lindsay and MacDiarmid. Many will agree with A.L. Kennedy's words: 'I think Scottish writing has contributed to the moves that set up a Scottish parliament, but it did that by being non-aligned and anarchic and critical and all the things it is and I hope will remain.'

It is still too early in the life of the Parliament to know exactly what kind of difference devolution will make to the arts, and to literature in particular. Many involved in literature keenly felt the lack of specific reference to writing and to writers in the Executive's first National Cultural Strategy[1], published in 2000. Two Ministers later, the first Annual Report[2] on the strategy made specific reference to ensuring that the 'fundamental importance of writing and writers' is recognised. The late Enric Miralles, Catalan architect of the new Parliament building, was clear about the central role of literature in the life of Scottish people, and he proposed that the artwork of the building should reflect this. Following Miralles' untimely death, and the sequence of events with the management of the building and its spiralling budget, it remains uncertain whether this vision will be part of the finished design.

While politicians struggle to come to terms with the best way to acknowledge literature, contemporary Scottish literature is buoyant and dynamic to a degree not seen since the days of Robert Burns and the vernacular revival in the 18th century, or Walter Scott and the flowering of the Scottish novel in the 19th century. The publication of Alasdair Gray's groundbreaking masterpiece *Lanark* in 1981 together with the linguistically radical narratives of James Kelman, who won the Booker Prize in 1994 for *How late it was, how late*, detonated an explosion of new fictional talent: Iain Banks, A.L. Kennedy, Gordon Legge, Candia McWilliam, Janice Galloway, Ali Smith, Duncan McLean, Alan Warner, and last but by no means least, Irvine Welsh, whose searing anatomy of drug culture and urban dysfunction *Trainspotting* in 1993 rapidly reached cult status. In recent years the huge popularity of crime writers Ian Rankin, Val MacDermid, Denise Mina and Christopher Brookmyre has turned Scotland into an epicentre of the detective fiction genre.

Scottish poetry, too, has reached new heights. The solid foundations of a multi-tongued tradition ensured by the late eminences Sorley MacLean, Norman MacCaig and Iain Crichton Smith and Scotland's greatest living poet, Edwin Morgan support a magnificent poetic edifice: Liz Lochhead, Douglas Dunn, Don Paterson, Kathleen Jamie, John Burnside, Robert Crawford, Donny O'Rourke and Kevin MacNeill are among the many voices increasingly recognised far beyond Scotland's boundaries. Writing for children, too, is enjoying a new revival, while the astonishing success of J.K. Rowling's *Harry Potter* series represents Scotland's greatest literary phenomenon since the publication of Walter Scott's *Waverley* novels.

In 2001 the film version of *Harry Potter and the philosopher's stone* – the first book by a writer who, five years earlier, had to rely on a Scottish Arts Council (SAC) bursary in order to complete its sequel – is breaking box-office records all over the globe. It is a compelling parable of the alchemy which can be effected by the timely investment in a writer's future potential, and a powerful argument for doing away with the concept of 'subsidising' literature. The Scottish Arts Council has played a major role in the nurturing of Scotland's writers, either by awarding grants to allow them time to write, or by supporting their first published books. Many leading writers acknowledge early support from SAC, including Bernard MacLaverty, Anne Fine, Janice Galloway, Alan Warner and Andrew Greig. Publication grants supported the first published fiction of James Kelman and Ian Rankin. Other writers have pointed to the support offered to them at critical stages of their development by the SAC-funded writing fellows. Many published writers in the Highlands have spoken of the support offered by the Writing Fellows at Ross and Cromarty, Aonghas MacNeacail and Brian McCabe. Des Dillon, in his two years at Castlemilk Library in Glasgow, proved to be a catalyst to local writers, whilst also developing his own writing, both for screen and publication. After joining his group at Castlemilk, one member, Mamie Laing, received an SAC bursary, and has become a script-editor for STV's *Take the high road*.

Jenny Brown

The Writers' Bursaries scheme remains extremely competitive – SAC receives four times as many applications as it is able to fund. Some 25 writers receive bursaries each year of varying amounts, with a current ceiling of £10,000. To meet demand from writers with little or no record of previous publication, a pilot scheme was introduced in 2001 offering ten bursaries of £2,000. Such was the quality and number of applications that the scheme is set to continue and expand.

More substantial awards to individual artists have been on offer since 1999 in the form of National Lottery funded Creative Scotland Awards. These awards were designed for artists based in Scotland who have already made an important contribution to their field, and the intention was that the awards would provide artists with a major opportunity to experiment, to refresh their skills and to realise imaginative ideas. Fourteen awards of £25,000 have been offered each year, and writers to have benefited include Janet Paisley, Alice Thomson, Kathleen Jamie, John Burnside and Angus Peter Campbell.

New writers are assisted less directly by other SAC-supported schemes. A range of literary magazines is supported to provide a platform for new writing. These include well-established titles with long pedigrees like *Chapman* and *Cencrastus*, and newer publications such as *Northwords*, *The Eildon Tree* and *Markings*, which provide a national-via-regional focus from the Highlands, the Borders, and Dumfries and Galloway respectively. Support is given to Moniack Mhor, the writers' centre situated near Inverness, which provides short, though intensive, residential courses to anyone interested in writing. The results of these courses are often spectacular.

One of the most successful initiatives undertaken within the publishing field is the Canongate Classics series. In 1987, then SAC Literature Director Walter Cairns invited publishers to come forward with proposals to establish an affordable, high quality paperback series which would bring back into print works of Scottish literature. Canongate was successful in securing funding, and the resulting series (now running to over 100 titles) has been instrumental in ensuring the study of Scottish literature in schools and universities and its enjoyment by the general reader. It is no coincidence, perhaps, that this milestone in Scottish publishing and in the nation's rediscovery of its literary traditions coincided with the first wave of exciting new literary talent. More recently, SAC developed the publication of *Shorts*, an annual volume of short stories by new writers in partnership with Polygon publishers and *Scotland on Sunday*. The first volume sold 5,000 copies and reached number two on the Scottish Bestseller List.

For a time it seemed the main scope for further development lay in funding from the National Lottery, distributed by SAC since 1997. Successes included support for a series of pocketbooks linking visual artists and writers in a 'generalist vision of Scottish culture', and an ambitious scheme by the

Scottish Library Association to place three copies each of 36 specially selected Scottish titles into every secondary school library. The biggest National Lottery grant made to a publisher was awarded to Neil Wilson Publishing in 1999 to establish a literary imprint entitled 11:9 – named after the date of the referendum on devolution - for new Scottish writers.

The most recent 11:9 title, *Glasgow kiss* (2001), is an anthology of the work of the many writers' groups from the Glasgow area, reflecting a national trend which has seen an explosion in collective literary activity across a wide range of social levels, involving not only aspirant writers, but newly-enthused readers too. Yet it is within recent memory that a readership initiative was a one-off literary event. One of the fundamental problems in the organisation of the first Edinburgh Book Festival in 1983 was the perception that literature is an individual art form, a private communion between writer and reader. In the early 1980s the first Waterstone's branch had yet to open, and there was no tradition of spending one's evenings with other interested readers, hearing an author talk or read.

Now much of this has changed, and literary events are very much part of everyday life, particularly in cities – at some points in the year in Edinburgh and Glasgow you could spend every weekday evening hearing different writers read at bookstores. The spectacular success of the 2001 Edinburgh International Book Festival testified that in a relatively short period, the frequently-sounded death-knell for reading – lamented as the victim of an accelerated leisure culture inimical to the written word – has been proved to be extremely premature. The book is back, if in fact it ever went away.

Readership initiatives have now evolved to become something distinct from these author events, shifting the focus away from the writer, and back towards the reader and his or her response to the writer's work, and rightly so. Books cannot exist without authors, but in a very real sense texts do not exist either until readers read and recreate them; the recent empowerment of the individual is a welcome move away from the writer as cult personality. The recent rise in popularity of reading groups which enable discussion of texts in the absence of their authors is evidence of a new, and healthy, equilibrium between reading as both a solitary and a social activity.

The Scottish Arts Council has long supported publishing and writing, but it is only relatively recently that it turned its attention to the reader as the essential third side of the triangle. Although the UK as a whole often seems awash with statistics about readership, samples of research carried out in Scotland are so small as to be thought inaccurate. In 1989 SAC produced its *Readership report*[3], a brave attempt to 'look at the state of readership at all ages, but with an emphasis on younger age groups, with a view to establishing if there was a decline and if so, whether there were any new steps SAC might take in an attempt to reverse the trend.' The report did find signs that the reading habit was being eroded. Its recommendations

Jenny Brown

make interesting reading today. Among them was a call for an annual promotion of Scottish literature in selected libraries in Scotland – this became the very successful Now Read On promotion. It recommended information about reading for young children be available in clinics and nursery schools – Book Trust Scotland took this on, and launched its Books for Babies promotion. The report further recommended a touring bookbus which would cater at different times for different ages of young readers – this became a reality during the Readiscovery campaign in 1995, and turned into a project which took to Scotland's roads for almost five years.

Today, support for readership occupies a significant part of the SAC literature budget. Three of the revenue-funded organisations vigorously promote reading – Scottish Book Trust, the Edinburgh International Book Festival and the Scottish Poetry Library, housed in its magnificent new building in Holyrood, providing a national resource for poetry. There is a literary projects scheme which supports a diverse range of literary events around Scotland, such as the recent successful literary festival in Aberdeen, Stanza, the poetry festival in St Andrews, or the Wigtown Book Town Festival. Through this budget annual initiatives such as National Poetry Day are supported.

The most important support for readership is the Writers in Scotland scheme, now administered on SAC's behalf by Scottish Book Trust, and regarded as the country's single most visible, effective and far-reaching scheme for literature. In seeding new readers in communities all over Scotland, and by making reading and literature come to life, the scheme is central to many areas of Council and government priority. The scheme encourages readership from the earliest age, stimulates creative writing, develops new audiences for literature, and supports individual writers. SAC's development work in the field of readership continues: in the last two years attention has been focused on literature for children and young people following consultation and research into future methods of support for literature for these groups.

One notable off-shoot was East Lothian Libraries' Book Now project, which received Lottery funding for a two-year pilot in East Lothian and also further afield. The first campaign, 'Working Title', took poetry to train commuters and supermarket shoppers in a genuinely innovative and successful fashion. Recipients of funding, however, do not necessarily have to be bibliophiles or literature professionals. One of the most imaginative yet simple projects funded came from a television production company, Lomond; this was *Storybook TV*, a video which presents the work of four Scottish authors reading their work to young children.

Effective though such projects are, they can tend towards the ephemeral or the hit-and-miss. What is still missing is a strategic, national approach to readership, and it is hoped that the appointment of a National Readership Development Co-ordinator will assist this in the future. Looking over the

Border, there are initiatives such as the Reading for Life conference organised by Arts Council of England in 2000, a seminal event which called for a new aesthetic in the approach to reading, the growth of Readers in Residence in English libraries, and the pioneering work carried out by the Opening the Book team.

The current Scottish Arts Council budget for literature is £1.4 million, or 4% of the organisation's total artform spend. This supports three main areas of activity: writing, publishing and reading. Revenue support is given to two Scots language organisations and eight literature organisations including the Scottish Storytelling Forum, the Gaelic Books Council and the Association for Scottish Literary Studies. Over the past few years, it has become an increasingly dexterous and demanding juggling act to distribute support for all this burgeoning activity from a low funding base. In common with other areas of SAC, there has been mounting concern about the effects of public funding restrictions and standstill or negative funding settlements on the Literature Department's ability to respond to the needs of its constituency. In 1999, with the support and encouragement of the organisations, a review of Scotland's literature organisations was commissioned. It had two aims: to identify improvements necessary in order to ensure that literature in Scotland could develop and thrive, and to assess the current situation of the organisations.

The report's findings were clear: literature in Scotland is severely underfunded. The organisations aspire to a national mission out of all proportion to their inadequate core funding, and struggle constantly to provide the level of services needed, and expected, due to inadequate staffing, facilities and resources. There was considerable potential identified for greater co-operation and co-ordination between the organisations. As a result, the Literature Forum for Scotland was established in 2001 with the aim of supporting and promoting literature in Scotland, at a national level. The report also recommended possible alternative models of support for literature in Scotland, including the possibility of a Literature Council for Scotland.

Another important finding underlined in the report on organisations was that most Scottish writers are unable to make anything approaching a comfortable living from their writing. This led the Literature Committee to undertake a detailed investigation of the economic situation of writers. The results were presented at a major gathering of writers on midsummer day, 2001. Over half the writers surveyed earned less than £5,000 a year from their writing, but a small number earned over £100,000. The majority of respondents felt confident about their future careers, whatever the level of income, and just over a third rated the current profile of literature in Scotland as high or very high. Over half were happy with SAC's current models of support for writers, but expressed a strong desire for government to improve conditions for writers by giving tax exemptions.

Jenny Brown

In autumn 2001, SAC drafted a plan for literature, based on its ongoing research and wide consultation with the Literature Forum, individual writers, publishers, librarians, literature organisations and with the general public. The plan, entitled *Literature, nation: developing literature in Scotland in the 21st century*[4] sets out a national approach to developing the artform in and furth of Scotland. It sets out a vision for the next five years:

> Literature is one of Scotland's principal national assets. Many of her writers, past and present, are renowned internationally. In the global world of the 21st century, where the knowledge and skills of a country's people will be crucial to success, literature will help to equip every Scot to live and work, and to reflect, communicate and engage, in this new and complex environment. Literature assists people to develop the essential skills of literacy, articulacy, independence of thought and enterprise; it enriches leisure and instils cultural self-confidence by promoting the nation's sense of identity and its diverse cultures. Literature is also the carrier of our different languages. Setting literature at the heart of all Scotland's communities through accessibility and lifelong learning will give Scots a greater understanding of their own country, its international links and its place in the world.

It is a vision which is not only attainable, but deeply necessary.

References

1. Scottish Executive. *Creating our future … minding our past: Scotland's national cultural strategy.* HMSO, 2000
2. Scottish Executive. *Creating our future … minding our past: Scotland's national cultural strategy. First annual report.* HMSO, 2001
3. Scottish Arts Council. *Readership report.* Scottish Arts Council, 1989
4. Scottish Arts Council. *Literature, nation: developing literature in Scotland in the 21st century.* Scottish Arts Council, 2001

4

Bookselling and publishing in Scotland

Lorraine Fannin

If a book is worth reading, it is worth buying
John Ruskin

Publishing and bookselling are the commercial aspects of two respected pursuits: the creative process of writing books and the cosy, thought-provoking act of reading them. The interface between these two is a matter of business. If books are not produced, marketed, sold, then literature does not flourish. Some two decades ago, publishing led the way and bookselling followed; they were partners in a trade run largely by those who believed passionately in the work they published and sold. Now bookselling dominates the relationship, and it is the business which matters.

The publishing of books has long been seen as the process of recording and defining the intellectual life of a country; so Scottish publishing carries this weight of expectation. Any publishing company, as interface between writer and reader, must provide, on one hand the creative force which can turn an average manuscript into a good and readable book, or coax an idea into a classic work; and, on the other, the financial wizardry to pay author, designer, printer and packer from the proceeds left after selling a modest quantity of the books to a hard-bargaining book selling chain, where books are 'product' and the retailer's cut is more than half of the cover price. The recent dilemmas of the Scottish publishing industry are the same ones which other industries face in a time of change from family-owned businesses to shareholder-funded companies, in which pension-fund investors with a need to make short term profits are a major driving force.

It is worth beginning this examination of the trade in books by looking at some current statistics. There has always been an assumption, comforting and pleasant to those of us whose work is with books, that people in Scotland are keen readers. It has its roots in the solid image of the autodidact, of widespread use of libraries, of long and cold winter nights spent reading by the fireside. Unfortunately this assumption does not carry over to the buying of books at the start of this new century. It is unfortunate for those who depend on the economic health of the book business in Scotland for a living.

Lorraine Fannin

In the first year of the new millennium, fewer Scots purchased books than people in any other region of the UK. Only 39.5% of the population of Scotland bought one book or more in the year 2000[1].

This is in contrast to the south of England where almost 54% of the population bought books. Further confirmation of the Scots' reluctance to buy books comes from the average sum spent per buyer: £77.83 per annum for buyers in Scotland, compared to £95.87 for Londoners. Two UK regions spend less per head: Tyne Tees and south-west England. Closer analysis of these statistics only compounds the gloom. One hundred people in London will spend each year around £4,870 on books, which is 58% more than the £3,074, which the same number of Scots will spend. In Wales, the hundred people will spend 30% more than the Scots; indeed Tyne Tees is the only UK area where the spend per hundred people is less than in Scotland.

It is instructive also to look at who is buying these books, UK-wide. In our youth-orientated culture, this may surprise us: some 56% of all books are bought by the over-45s. The heaviest spend per book buyer is in the 55 to 65 age group, at £114 per annum. This includes the section of our population known as the 'baby-boomers', those born just after the Second World War, numerically a large group, whose disposable income is now at an all-time high. But even the over-65s, brought up on austerity and thrift, spend on mail-order books almost double the amount which is spent by the under 45s.

There are clearly some key questions to be answered. Who writes and who publishes the books on offer – and why do they do so? How do these 39.5% of Scots buy reading material? How fast is the process changing? Has today's book business changed out of all recognition from that which existed a century ago? What or how might we read in the future? What help may be available in Scotland? And within the context of this volume, there is the important question: will the commercial and the library market for books diverge?

In Scotland the book market is dominated on both sides by large companies, most of which are managed from southern England and owned in London, New York, Paris or Germany. For decades, this conglomeration of book publishing businesses happened with mergers and acquisitions in the UK trade. In more recent years, the process has run through bookselling too, and the Scottish bookselling scene is now dominated by the large empires of W.H. Smith, of HMV through its ownership of Waterstone's, of Borders which established its base in the UK market through the acquisition of Book Etc, and of Ottakars who have rushed to fill smaller niches in every town where the large chains have left a gap.

The majority of books sold in Scotland are published from London. A Whitaker BookTrack report[1], states that around 80% of UK publishing comes from eight large publishing groups. The remaining 20% comes from up to

10,000 other publishers. None of the eight large groups has more than 12% of the total market, though the amalgamation of Random House and Transworld into the ownership of German media group Bertelsmann creates a greater market share for the combined unit. Only the university presses (Oxford and Cambridge), Pearson and Hodder Headline (owned by W.H. Smith) are UK-owned. In terms of turnover, the highest ranked Scottish-owned company is D.C. Thomson at number 33 on the list, with Mainstream Publishing at number 48. From the 110,000 new books published annually in the UK, fiction is the largest category. Scottish-published books do enjoy substantial sales, even if, as we shall see later, the sales are hard-won.

It is assumed that Scottish publishing describes the output of publishing companies based in Scotland. However many commentators disregard, wrongly it could be said, the output of companies which do not publish books of 'Scottish' interest (those who publish legal, medical or reference work). They also tend to omit books published by companies whose ownership is outside Scotland (HarperCollins, for example), although within Scotland their turnover may be high and the company may be a significant employer of publishing professionals. This tendency diminishes Scottish publishing in the media and perpetuates the 'tartan and whisky' image, to the general disservice of the industry.

Publishing output from Scotland today covers almost the whole book spectrum: fiction and poetry, biography, academic, children's, photography, maps and guides, business and self-help, art and music, history and reference, medical. Dominated by the aforesaid HarperCollins, whose distribution, administration and reference publishing activities are all based in Glasgow, it also includes divisions of other large groups: Harcourt Health Sciences, once known as Churchill Livingstone, Chambers Harrap, and Butterworth. There are also many institutions, academic, cultural and social, who publish significant lists of books in Scotland and contribute to the overall business.

One publishing strand, however, now sadly lacking in the Scottish publishing industry is educational material. This was originally the mainstay of companies such as Chambers, Blackie and Oliver & Boyd, but the investment needed to develop material for the new curriculum rendered the Scottish market unprofitable for many of the companies. There is still a need for published material which meets this need and the publishers who provide some of it in Scotland are usually small and under-resourced. This is a major gap.

The main trade publishers, however, are small-to-medium sized independent firms which have grown up in the last twenty years, a time hailed as the second flowering of publishing in Scotland, and it is within this group that most of the recent growth in the industry has come. They are all owned in Scotland at present. Most of them are managed by strong individuals with special interests, drive and a focus on building their company.

Lorraine Fannin

There have been mergers within Scottish publishing, but on a small scale. Canongate took in Rebel Inc. as an imprint. Polygon is publishing the dictionaries of the Scottish National Dictionaries Association; Birlinn bought John Donald Publishing and Mercat Press took on the list of Aberdeen University Press and the trade titles of The Stationery Office Scotland. There may in future be further sales or mergers. However there is little incentive for Scottish publishers to attempt to create a joint structure of a size which would rival the conglomerates. History shows that any such company created would be unlikely to remain in Scotland and could not easily bear the stamp of the current publishing directors, which would inevitably cause a loss of focus.

But the fact still remains that, however strong the Scottish publishing sector may be, it faces enormous challenges in selling its books to the large chain stores who prefer to trade with giants like themselves. Unparalleled expansion in Scotland by the bookshop chains mentioned earlier has brought a homogeneous and sophisticated veneer to the market, but it has also been damaging to local business. Recently we have seen the oldest established bookshop in Scotland, John Smith of Glasgow, succumb to pressure and withdraw from the retail trade, selling its assets to a large library supply company. Indigenous Scottish bookselling companies struggle to compete with the massive buying power of the huge chains with apparently limitless marketing budgets. Since the demise of the Net Book Agreement allowed those chains to offer deeper and deeper discounts to buyers, the perception has grown that only they can offer value for money. Recent research has shown that author, title and availability all rank higher than price for the individual consumer. Add to this the fact that only some 50 titles are discounted in most stores at any one time, a tiny fraction of the books available, and it becomes apparent that there is clever marketing at work.

In Scotland, people in the main cities have a choice of large Waterstone's bookshops which started out as a book-lover's paradise. Now owned by HMV Media, this chain is now primarily driven by profit rather than a need to enhance its reputation, and will hold in stock only those titles on which the publisher is willing and able to offer very high discounts, long credit and an open invitation to return anything unsold. Buying is stringent, and a London head office makes marketing decisions, contrary to the early philosophy of the chain.

Ottakars came some years ago, a smaller chain occupying large but not enormous sites in both major and minor cities and towns and showing some of the book-loving characteristics of the early Waterstone's shops. Next to arrive was Borders, an American giant with a great line in cut-price books, a wide range of magazines, music, videos and good coffee. They, too, like to control their stock centrally and every book on their shelves is filtered through a warehouse in southern England. The purchase of the John Menzies retail chain by W.H. Smith was carefully monitored and once again many of the worst fears were realised. Buying through the chain's headquarters in London was focused on a UK-wide offering of mainly mass-market titles. Their buying systems could cope with 'local books' in individual shops, but could not deal with the cultural differences of Scotland as a country.

There remains the major indigenous chain, James Thin, which has expanded into England but continues to be a significant supporter of Scottish publishers. There are also many independent bookshops outside the main cities, but most are small and many claim to struggle as ever more purchases are made in vast shopping malls from chain stores. [Editors' note: Shortly after this article was written, James Thin went into administration. Part of the company has been sold to Ottakars.]

Bookselling on the Internet is a significant and challenging development. The rise of Amazon is well documented and that company continues to develop market share, though the bulk of its sales comes from a relatively narrow band of bestsellers and computer/Internet titles and it struggles to be profitable. Retailers of all kinds are now offering on-line sales and publishers are establishing their own websites selling books direct. It is difficult for small companies to establish a web profile and co-operative efforts can be useful. In 2000 the Scottish Publishers Association set up Scottish Book Direct, a mail order and Internet direct sales project, for this purpose[2].

Sales to libraries were once a staple and bedrock of the small to medium-sized publisher in Scotland. These sales often made possible the publication of a culturally significant work. Now library sales are of little commercial importance. Despite statements of intent to ensure that Scottish material is purchased for public libraries, there has been a widespread failure by local authorities to set up systems which will allow this to happen in a significant way. Library supply, now also driven by the discounts on offer, has contracted to a small number of suppliers, most of whom are in England, and who may not present Scottish material adequately.

There are, obviously, enormous problems to be faced in achieving sales by independent publishers outside London. Therefore authors suffer and many, who make a promising beginning thanks to the gargantuan efforts of their small publisher, feel nonetheless short-changed by the system, and depart for a large London house at the earliest opportunity. Later they often look back with regret at the personal links they had with their first small press. It is a joy for Scotland but a huge dilemma for the future of its publishing that Scottish writers are enjoying an almost unprecedented popularity world-wide, as the talents of Alasdair Gray, James Kelman, Janice Galloway and Ian Rankin are celebrated. Many were first published, their reputations made, with small Scottish publishers. Polygon and Canongate both have a high reputation for finding and nurturing new talent. But many

Lorraine Fannin

of these authors are now published in London and the rewards of their popularity are reaped by London companies. It is hard to earn profits from an unknown writer; harder still to lose the writer to London just when the name is established. Money to invest is scarce but vital.

What happens, therefore, when the Scottish publisher can no longer afford to take these risks with new writing or the London taste moves on to a new fashion? Scottish writers may then have fewer and fewer opportunities for publication. What if no Scottish publisher existed to take that first risk on James Kelman or Alasdair Gray? And should Scotland rely on having its writers published elsewhere?

A number of small presses are disproportionately dependent on public funding support for the development of their list; this may inhibit their success in the marketplace but without this strong support a great deal of publishing activity could not take place. It is not easy to define how publishing rests within government or public support structures. Publishing may be seen as a strong commercial industry, providing information and cultural resources. Within an arts funding framework, it may receive support for its contribution to national culture and for its role in bringing the work of writers to the public; in a business environment, the industry may appear uncompetitive in attracting investment and rewarding the shareholder quickly. At the same time, publishing remains a necessary strand in the development of literature in Scotland. It is this role as the interface between writer and reader which brings it within the remit of the Scottish Arts Council (SAC).

The SAC's support for publishing has always been directed to 'literature'. The definition and emphasis has not remained constant. A decade ago, a key objective of this SAC funding was to bring back into print a number of classic Scottish texts and children's books. There was also support for significant non-fiction work. Now the support is directed primarily to new writing, fiction and poetry. Prioritising fiction, poetry and new writing as 'literature' for the purposes of public support needs wider debate; many publishers feel that other forms of writing should also be validated. Publishing does support information provision on other art forms such as music or visual arts.

Publishers of 'literature' need an efficient infrastructure to sell the work in today's book market. In a UK context, large companies have their own competitive infrastructure; they are, however, notoriously risk-averse and prefer to publish known or established writers, with the result that new writers often appear first within smaller presses and magazines. These smaller companies also need a commercial, usually non-fiction, strand within their lists, in order to generate enough profit to remain in business. It has been recognised that there are too many works of fiction published for them all to receive the attention both publisher and author believe they deserve.

When public funding support for fiction writing is requested or offered, a dilemma arises. If the work is highly commercial, it may not receive support. If the work is not commercial but of high merit, it may qualify for funding support, but that support is unlikely to make the work into a commercial success; it will merely allow it to appear in print, possibly for a minority readership. This may not be what the writer or the funding body expects. So an infrastructure to provide sales, marketing and distribution channels is vital for Scottish publishing.

There is an overwhelming need for Scotland's publishing concerns to thrive as businesses. In recent decades, the very welcome support from the Scottish Arts Council has encouraged many publishers to embark on significant new list developments, and some schemes are offering alternative but useful means of support. The basis of the funding support, to help publish work of quality, but which is likely to be highly commercial, is acceptable within a cultural framework; a more constructive view may be to use the public funding support as development money to fund infrastructure development, which can help all publishing companies and types of list, including literary publishing.

Comparisons are made with countries like Denmark, Iceland or Sweden, whose boundaries define their language. In those countries, indigenous publishing flourishes, even though they have relatively small populations, because it delivers foreign literature and educational resources as well as work from their own writers. In similarly-sized English-language territories, which border a larger neighbour, such as Scotland, Ireland, Wales or even Canada, there is a danger that indigenous publishing is squeezed out by the more powerful US and UK companies. A mix of publishing, both literary and commercial, is needed within peripheral English-language regions to ensure the survival of regional or 'small-nation' publishing.

It has been noted that the advent of the Scottish Parliament has brought a heightened expectation that Scotland's publishing industry will fulfil the cultural and political aspirations of its writers and its political commentators. At the same time, the publishing and bookselling businesses of the English-speaking world are becoming more centrally driven, monolithic and ever blander in the offering they make to their customers. Internet retailers add to this trend. Unfortunately, within Scotland there is a tendency to lay blame for this worldwide situation on the existing publishers in Scotland, without whose enterprise and willingness to take risks there would be no indigenous industry.

What publishers in Scotland have shown, however, is an unusual and highly beneficial willingness to work together. A major part of this effort is co-ordinated through the Scottish Publishers Association (SPA), with other strands strengthening the outcome. SPA activities include export sales assistance, direct mail sales, trade information provision, marketing initiatives,

Lorraine Fannin

book fair attendance, training and distribution. In the present climate of change, the detail and manner in which these initiatives are set up may alter, but the basic outlines remain necessary to allow Scottish publishing to participate in the wider world publishing marketplace. For example, it had long been seen as important to set up a joint book distribution centre in Scotland and in 1995 Scottish Book Source was set up and has developed with help from the SAC National Lottery Fund. The distribution business, now referred to as part of the 'book supply chain', continues to innovate and Scottish Book Source must invest to remain efficient and competitive.

So what of the future? Will there be a Doomsday scenario, in which books are no longer read, reading is restricted to the seeking of information, and publishing is controlled either centrally by one or two world players or by individual writers? Or will publishing become a streamlined partnership between new technologies and new media, exploiting 'content' in every possible form in the new 'Information Age'? All grand predictions need to be viewed carefully, but it is already clear that large companies will grow even larger, and that only a relatively small number of books will make much money for author and publisher. The role of the library within the publishing industry has changed and the book buying habits of the library services have altered the economics of certain kinds of publishing.

For everyone there will be pressure on time spent reading; competition from other leisure pursuits is great, especially for children. The Harry Potter phenomenon, however, shows that it only takes a really good story to beat off the competition. Readers, with limited time available, will be highly selective. They will not buy extensive reference volumes to find a small amount of information, but will rely on the Web to sort and sift information instead. Web 'content' providers will need conventional publishers' skills to provide what is sought. Academic and reference publishing will offer more work on-line. The profitability of this trend needs very careful examination, as there is still an expectation that information on the Web is free, with the consequent threat to copyright law.

People with less time to browse are already directed by marketing strategy towards choosing books by interest or social status. The trend to publish for a specific readership may increase - eg young urban women (City girl), gritty youth culture (Irvine Welsh), suburban life (Joanna Trollope), and historical sagas for older readers (Catherine Cookson). This is not a new trend but the more specialised splitting up of the targeted readership is interesting.

There is also a belief that we are currently entering a period in which new technology will transform the shape of every activity, cultural, creative or business. In fact, the changes in the publishing industry have happened in waves over the last 30 years as technology development altered print methods, television transformed our leisure habits and the cinema devoured stories. The main prediction of the last decade – that the Web will kill off the printed word – is no longer so strongly supported. The obvious reasons are now acknowledged: the difficulty in reading large amounts of text on screen; the questionable portability of devices used to access material in new media; changing technology which can render formats obsolete very quickly; and the narrow appeal of books published only on-line. It does, however, remain a major benefit in selling books to busy consumers, and it also allows new authors to be tested.

Commentators have concentrated on the changes likely to be made by publishing directly on the Web, but in fact more profound changes in publishing are coming through the use of new technology to offer a wider range of production methods, costs and processes. Already digitisation of images and transfer of text and pictures by e-mail, ISDN or other means has brought huge advantages in print production. Short-run print technology has allowed minority-interest work to be produced economically, and digital technology is increasingly able to offer a wide range of print-on-demand facilities that may revolutionise the publishing supply chain.

Journal publishing is now largely on-line; the economics and procedures involved are well suited to exploit the advantages of new technology. Publishers are willing to license their material for digital exploitation, but tend to offer it on a short term, non-exclusive basis. Lasting partnerships have not yet been formed and few companies have had significant financial returns from new media development.

Publishers in Scotland have been eager to embrace new technology developments, and with a great deal of the production process remaining in-house, costs can be cut and shorter print-runs become more viable, helping new writers appear in print for the first time. Many Scottish publishers are considering further development in the area of digital print. Increasing use of digital technology by libraries and the adoption of such technology by publishers may help to bring some of the missing Scottish material into libraries. A brighter future based on technological development, however, is not the hope we should hold. That which is crucial is a belief by Scotland's people and cultural institutions in the value and importance of what is written, published and created within the country.

References

1. *Book sales yearbook, 2001*. Bookseller Publications, 2001
2. www.scottishbooksdirect.com

Lorraine Fannin

Part Three

INFORMATION POLICY, TECHNOLOGY & PRACTICE

I n information technology terms, Robert Craig's career stretches from the catalogue-and issue-focused automated library systems of the 1970s to the current widespread availability of computers in the workplace and the home, electronic collections, the World Wide Web and networks like JANET and NHSNet. Information technology has spread from its first homes in academic, business and research organisations to affect, serve and be used by everyone.

Robert Craig is not a natural 'techie'. It used to be said that the best way to conceal something from Robert was to send him an e-mail about it. At one time, that story may not have been apocryphal. Yet he has led the Scottish Library Association and the Scottish Library and Information Council to the heart of technological development and has convinced politicians and managers that libraries should play a critical role in ensuring the beneficial use of information technology in society.

The essays in this part of the book review recent developments and future prospects for information technology, national co-ordination and delivery of information, and implications for the work patterns and skills required of librarians. The availability of content has at last begun to match that of hardware. That is, the number and range of electronic texts have reached a sufficient critical mass to make true electronic libraries viable.

Moreover, material suited to the mainstream collections of public and school libraries is now available electronically; formerly, electronic publication targeted primarily academic and special libraries, mainly in science, technology and medicine. The realisation of a true national (ie, nationally available) electronic library is in sight, re-awakening the ideals of librarians of the late 19th century, and encouraging long-standing ambitions for universal bibliographic control. Content development and provision have at last achieved their proper priority.

5

National information policy: realities and prospects

Ian R.M. Mowat

The first question which the author of this essay posed to the editor when approached for a contribution was – 'Which nation do you have in mind?' While the context was clearly Scotland, issues of nationality have become more complex in recent years than for many decades past. It would be quite sensible to talk about a UK national information policy. Post-devolution, it might be even more appropriate to talk about a Scottish national information policy. Although this writer has only ever seen the concepts of Europe and nation linked by Eurosceptics in a virulently negative rejection of the idea, it might even be possible to talk of a European 'national' information policy - at least for those who think 'they' are out to get you. Over-riding all of these, of course, is the idea of a global information policy. The International Federation of Library Associations and Institutions (IFLA) has been pursuing such a policy for many years with such objectives as Universal Bibliographic Control[1], while the arrival of the virtual library makes physical boundaries less important in the delivery of information.

Are national policies irrelevant in the era of globalisation? Does the development of the virtual environment make physical constraints redundant? Alternatively, as Clifford Lynch has argued[2], does the Internet make possible a virtual nationality, allowing small ethnic groups isolated in larger alien environments to preserve their national identity through accessing the literature of the motherland? National policies (especially linked to ethnicity and language), stretching out to the diaspora, may actually be more important than they were before.

Since one of the objectives of this paper is to provide a vision, the vision which is offered is of a Scottish national information policy as a node in the global information strategy, aimed at both the civic nation in Scotland and the vast legion of those around the world with significant Scottish affiliation. Since even the Scottish National Party claims to be a party of civic nationalism, rather than one of ethnicity, it seems unlikely that there is any substantive case for an ethnically based policy. Linguistically the challenge is more interesting, since the policy ought to have something to

Ian R.M. Mowat

say about both Gaelic and Scots as well as English. But it would be foolish indeed to devote significantly disproportionate effort to two languages which are spoken only by a tiny minority of the population, unless it is seen as part of a global effort to preserve the rich diversity of multi-lingualism against the galloping encroachment of the world's three or four leading languages. In that context, the role of a Scottish national information policy in preserving the output of, for example, Cape Breton Gaelic[3] or Ulster Scots[4] may be as significant as any efforts by the Canadians or Irish.

Should there be a national information policy? For those who have struggled for such a policy for many years the question is hardly worth asking. Librarians like order and discipline and national information policies have a Ranganthan-type attraction of every book in its place for every reader[5].

Dominating such prosaic practical considerations, however, are wider issues. Underlying a belief in an information policy is the belief that information is valuable for society and this writer has no doubt that, in the eternal struggle for a democratic and prosperous society, information is a vital commodity. An informed society is better able to judge between the options presented to it and to penetrate the hypocrisies and lies peddled by those intent on swaying public opinion to sectional or personal advantage. Whether it be in judging between the rival claims of political parties or the competing advertisements of manufacturers, access to appropriate information can make an enormous difference.

For those who truly believe in the capacity of information to improve our quality of life, it may be that the national dimension could be considered restrictive. This writer has heard it stated that any country with less than 20 million population is almost inevitably doomed to corruption because of the close interconnectivity which small societies enjoy – the crony politics of recent discussion. While countries like Denmark may be held up as refutations of the universality of such a theory, the disadvantages of small societies in the 21st century do not seem far to seek: limited markets for quality products; a tendency to insularity; even, in the case of a successful country such as Denmark, a restricted ability for critical self-examination.

Yet, even for small countries, the argument for a national information policy is strong. The case of Sir Walter Scott is an interesting illustration of the way in which a small country's input to the global information bank is affected by presentation. Some twenty years ago, this author undertook a survey of European bibliographic centres, prior to the establishment of the *Bibliography of Scotland*[6]. One of the more interesting findings of that survey was that, whereas the *Deutsche Bibliographie* appeared to have no difficulty in distinguishing Scott as a Scottish author, the *British National Bibliography* thought it proper to lump him in with others under English literature. Since the impact of Scott on Romanticism both in the United Kingdom and in Europe was critical and since that impact has coloured the European view of Scotland for two centuries up to the present day, some clarity in the way in which information about him is presented can be seen to be of some importance.

More prosaically, actions, in the main, follow funding. If effective information policies are to be implemented and followed, they will be dependent upon a sensible use of limited resource and the Scottish government and community are best placed, in a Scottish context, to ensure that the necessary input of resource is delivered to achieve such a result.

If an information policy is desirable, what should be in it and who should be responsible for its creation and implementation? For several centuries, Scots have grown accustomed to a multi-dimensional approach to national issues and it would be in keeping with this tradition to develop an information policy which takes advantage of the existing and developing strands of information control elsewhere in the world. In this scenario, Scottish effort would be concentrated on adding value to existing products to ensure that the community served got maximum benefit.

A comparison might be made with present attitudes to international air transportation. Twenty years ago government policy might well have been to attempt the creation of a Scottish national carrier. In the light of the recent failures of companies such as Sabena and Swissair, the existing policy of encouraging a diversity of carriers providing the maximum range of service seems to make most sense.

Even in a United Kingdom context, consideration of when to go it alone and when to work with a larger community is complex and confused. Britain is very open to outside influence (with the role of English as a global language, for the present at least[7], being both a source of strength for internally created information and of weakness in terms of the ability of foreign produced English-language products to infiltrate the home market with ease). It also occupies a dangerous middle ground – one of the largest economies in the world, with an imperial history that still colours decision making, and so tempted to go it alone, but not quite large enough to do so sensibly in every case.

Discussion on the creation of a British national union catalogue, for example, has been a recurrent topic for many years. The nearest that the UK has come to such a catalogue so far has been the creation of COPAC, the union catalogue of the Consortium of University Research Libraries (CURL). CURL has recently expanded to include the British Library and the National Libraries of Scotland and Wales, but exploration of an expansion of COPAC to include the catalogues of those libraries (especially the British Library) will be made more difficult by existing agreements between CURL and the Research Libraries Group (RLG) and OCLC – two US groupings with global pretensions.

Mention of the National Library of Scotland highlights the complexity of the Scottish context. The National Library faced a crisis in 2001 with its decision to close the Scottish Science Reference Library – a decision which has been increasingly fudged in the face of strong criticism. Yet it can be argued that the initial decision was a sensible one – acknowledging that the National Library of Scotland is not the body best placed to provide scientific information to the Scottish community in a virtual environment. The National Library is both a potentially key player in a national information strategy and an institution whose future may well be determined by the creation of such a strategy.

In the age of the printed book, Scotland has been extraordinarily fortunate to have in Edinburgh a resource which, through legal deposit, includes the published output not only of all the United Kingdom and Ireland but also (because of the global nature of publishing) a significant element of the serious publications of the United States. It has been a truly international resource. Although the British Library has been legislatively recognised as the national library for the United Kingdom in the British Library Act of 1972, the National Library of Scotland has fulfilled a number of national functions in relation to Scotland, such as the provision of a national inter-library loans service and the creation of a national bibliography (and related specialist bibliographies). In addition, it has provided leadership in the creation of co-operative bodies in the Scottish information scene – with both the Scottish Library and Information Council (SLIC) and the Scottish Confederation of University and Research Libraries (SCURL) amongst the significant creations for which it can share some of the credit[8]. Devolution has left the situation of the respective roles of the two national libraries a little uncertain and if the National Library of Scotland is to take a leadership role in the formation of a Scottish national information policy, both a pre-requisite and a useful outcome will be clarification of this uncertainty.

On the one hand, it can be argued that the National Library should be no more than a collection of material relating to Scotland, aimed primarily at the humanities. On the other, it is equally valid to claim that the National Library should be *a*, if not *the* focal point of a national information policy. Certainly, its print and manuscript collections represent a world view of Scottish interest[9] and it is reasonable to argue that this should continue in the electronic era.

However, it is far from certain that the leadership of a single institution (whether it be the British Library or the National Library of Scotland) is an appropriate way to meet national information policy requirements in the 21st century. Esko Hakli made an interesting and powerful case for the leadership role of a national library at the Information Scotland meeting in Edinburgh in 2001 and it is certainly true that, under his strong leadership, Helsinki University Library[10] has developed a national information policy for Finland which probably stands comparison with most other countries in the world. As ever, the view from outside is rather different to that of those on the ground. Despite the admiration of many foreign librarians for the Finnish achievement, many Finnish librarians and academics remain more critical of both what has been achieved and the methods which have been used.

A national information policy should reflect the priorities of the country it is intended to serve – otherwise there is little point in having one. When the new Scottish Parliament was set up in Edinburgh, there was much talk of a new form of politics, eschewing the confrontation of Westminster and building consensus. There is much current scepticism as to how far this has happened, but it is true that both the political partnership of Labour and Liberal Democrats and the structural processes of parliamentary committees may reflect, however weakly, a long-running vein of communitarian thinking in the Scottish psyche.

Although this author believes that, under appropriate leadership, the National Library of Scotland could perform at least as creditably as Helsinki University Library (despite the many differences between the two institutions and the two countries), there is at least a danger that directoral leadership will run counter to the medium term trend and generate unproductive conflict. A vacation spent catching up on the latest publications on medieval Scottish history has heightened awareness of the Scottish propensity to quarrel!

There is, too, a concern that if the National Library takes a leadership role, there will be a danger that the more traditional aspects of information will be emphasised. There is never sufficient resource to do all that is desirable. A national information policy has to be guided by general national priorities and must set its own priorities within its sphere of influence. As a representative of traditional librarianship, the present author would argue strongly in favour of the inclusion of, for example, considerations of preservation in a national information policy. But if we are to believe in the importance which government accords to social inclusion and better education, surely the development of the electronic future has to be a top priority.

With that in mind, it is less obvious that the National Library should be the driving force behind policy development. Indeed it might be argued that, since part of a national policy would be to determine the future role of the National Library, it should definitely not lead.

There is, in fact, no obvious single contender for leadership because of the various players who need to be involved. In addition to the library community, it is surely obvious in a Scottish context that the museums and galleries should have a say, more especially through the Scottish Cultural Resources Access Network (SCRAN)[11]. Similarly, the archives community, which has already pioneered a successful network of its own – the Scottish

Ian R.M. Mowat

Archives Network (SCAN) – has much to contribute[12]. But beyond these obvious players[13], there is a real need to involve not only the computer network specialists, currently engaged in developing Digital Scotland, but also the legislators (either directly or through their civil service agents), in order to ensure that governmental priorities are properly considered.

Whether or not publishers and booksellers should be drawn in is a debatable point. On the one hand, there is a useful model in the smaller countries of north-west Europe, of the various partners in the book industry working fruitfully, if not always harmoniously, together. On the other, Scottish publishing is no longer the force that it was a century ago and it is doubtful if the total impact of publishing houses based in Scotland would have a significant effect on information policy. Both publishers and booksellers might be considered, in the context of a forward-looking information policy, to represent the past, and there are many more creators of Scottish-based Web pages whose views might, with at least equal merit, be considered.

Since it is probably better to build on existing structures than to start out on a completely new road (pragmatically it saves time and philosophically it can be argued that new structures merely hide old prejudices rather than get rid of them), there seems no better a body than SLIC to begin the process (or rather, to continue it, since many of the building blocks are either in place or under construction). SLIC by itself, however, would be insufficient to represent the views of even libraries throughout Scotland. Certainly if inclusion, rather than direction, is to shape the development of policy, a mechanism would need to be developed to give ownership to a wide constituency.

In order to be successful, a national information policy would need to take account of the competing directions in which so many of the key players face. Amongst the leading universities, for example, there is a real potential conflict of approach between the cross-sectorality which a national information policy might encourage and the attractions of working together with like-minded universities south of the border and elsewhere in specialist organisations such as CURL and RLG. The existence of OCLC demonstrates that cross-sectorality can work on a global scale, but to make it work would require a significant departure in approach from the petty-minded, backbiting insularity which afflicts policy makers in so many Scottish institutions – including those who pride themselves on their depth of vision and broad international perspective. If the flaws in the Scottish psyche are to be overcome with the minimum of difficulty, as much attention needs to be paid to the process by which the policy is determined, as to the contents of the policy itself.

And what should the contents of that policy include? It would be presumptuous indeed to list authoritatively the key elements of an information policy when it has just been argued that process is a vital part of the activity. However, this author would be disappointed if the policy did not include the following issues:

The distributed national electronic resource (DNER)

This has already been claimed as the first priority. The phraseology of the Joint Information Services Committee of the Higher Education Funding Councils of England, Scotland and Wales and the Department of Education for Northern Ireland (JISC) has been used deliberately. If much of the rest of the world looks with admiration at JISC's achievements[14], it would be small-minded indeed for Scotland to do otherwise. Taking the identified components of the DNER – discover, locate, request, deliver – it would be necessary to determine how far the UK model is already delivering acceptable solutions and how far local departure is required.

An example might be the conclusion of licensing agreements with publishers for electronic content. A cross-sectoral approach might place greater emphasis on the need for wider access than JISC currently entertains. The financial inducements, legal framework and organisational structure would need to be considered. Although a separate licensing agenda might be desirable, it might be found just as effective to empower an agency such as JISC to operate on behalf of the whole Scottish community.

Similarly, with respect to the development of particular elements of the DNER, care would be needed to ensure that Scottish effort dovetailed into broader coverage. The Co-operative Academic Information Retrieval Network for Scotland (CAIRNS) project[15] has been a trail blazer for the United Kingdom as a whole in creating a virtual union catalogue. But its success demonstrates both the strength and weakness of the existing Scottish effort. Undertaken on a shoestring budget, with research rather than service as a priority, CAIRNS is not currently capable of delivering the search and retrieval support which is required, especially if non-bibliographic information elements are considered. Any sensible policy surely needs to address how service delivery is going to be made in our brave new world. At the same time, even if CAIRNS is satisfactorily developed in a Scottish context, it will not be a satisfactory search and retrieval tool unless it has effective links to the wider world.

The distributed national collection (DNC)

Again, UK-wide terminology (derived, in this instance, from the work of the Higher Education / British Library Task Force to the Research Support Libraries Group[16]) has been adopted to identify the important issues relating to the surviving collections, whether in print or some other medium. Issues

Ian R.M. Mowat

such as procurement (is it sensible that various consortia within Scotland negotiate separate deals for the purchase of books and journals? It may be, but it certainly needs investigation.), holding, access, preservation and storage need to be addressed. Investigation of the role of the National Library of Scotland will be important, but it will also be crucial to remember global efforts in these areas. When it is faster and no more expensive for Edinburgh University Library to obtain an inter-library loan from the National Library of Australia than from the British Library at Boston Spa, a broad outlook is imperative. We may not wish to move all at once to a global strategy, for perfectly practical reasons, but any sensible policy will look to building strategic alliances with partners elsewhere.

Regulation

Although the regulatory framework is implicit in both of the above sections, it is possibly here that something can be done to make Scotland a better place than if it had remained merely North Britain. Many of the issues which constrain or bound information activity are the result of British or European Union legislation or are affected by world agreements on trade. In the areas of licensing, freedom of information, data protection and censorship, however, those developing policy should be aware of what can be done locally.

Postscript: Robert Craig

In a *Festschrift* dedicated to Robert Craig it is legitimate to ask – 'What has he to do with national information policy, the topic of this essay?' It is a question no sooner asked than answered, since none can doubt the contribution which Robert has made to the formulation of specific policies and to efforts to bring these specifics into a useful whole. His political skills can, of course, be infuriating if used in a cause to which one is opposed, but none can doubt those skills and few would argue that they have not been put to effective use on behalf, not just of the library community in Scotland but, more importantly, for the benefit of the whole realm. As ever with those who do their work effectively, he is likely to be even more missed in his absence than he was appreciated in his presence.

References and notes

1.   The IFLA position on Universal Bibliographic Control can be found at www.bubl.ac.uk/journals/lis/fj/icabc/v25n0196.htm
2.   Lynch, Clifford. *Libraries and worldwide access to information* - a

paper given at the OCLC Users' Council meeting, Dublin, Ohio, 25 May 2000

3. Cape Breton Gaelic is reported on in the website www.ceolas.co.uk

4. Ulster Scots is explained on the website www.thenisite.com/politics/ulsterscots.htm

5. Ranganathan's laws are outlined in the website www.epcc.ed.ac.uk/epcc-tec/seminars/seminar-Jun99-material/sld037.htm

6. Mowat, Ian R.M. *A study of some European national bibliographies.* (British Library Research and Development Report, no.5468) British Library, 1979

7. Whether or not it is accurate, an advertisement seen in Chicago airport in 2001 forecasting that, by 2003, Chinese will be the most common language on the Internet gives food for thought on the longer-term dominance of English.

8. The National Library of Scotland website is www.nls.uk

9. This is reflected both in its historic collections which, for example, contain manuscript material relating to the prominent part which Scots played in the development of empire; books and manuscripts, too numerous to mention, which relate to the impact which Scots have had elsewhere in the world; similar holdings, such as the globally important collections of Lutheran pamphlets, which reflect subject themes of interest to Scots; and in the modern holdings which, as noted above, receive legal deposit material linked to many countries.

10. Helskinki University Library has served as both the national library and the main library in the humanities of the University of Helsinki. Moves are afoot to weaken the latter link because it is felt that there is too great a conflict of interests for both functions to be performed with equal success. *See* Geleijnse, Hans, Gellerstam, Goran, Mowat, Ian R.M. *and* Kyllikki Ruokonen, Kyllikki. *Helsinki University libraries: report of an assessment panel.* University of Helsinki, 2000

11. The SCRAN website is www.scran.ac.uk

12. The SCAN website is www.scan.org.uk

13. If we are all in danger of seeing easy solutions elsewhere, we are equally at risk of overlooking our own successes. At a conference in Warsaw in November 2001, the author was struck by the high opinion in which both SCAN and SCRAN were held by Polish information specialists.

14. The JISC website is www.jisc.ac.uk

Ian R.M. Mowat

15. Information about CAIRNS can be found at
    http://cairns.lib.gla.ac.uk

16. Higher Education/British Library Task Force papers are listed in
    www.bl.uk/concord/pdf_files/blhe-overview.pdf

6

Developments in information technology, networks and services

Derek Law

While there is some common consent that we are moving to an information society which will be based on a knowledge economy, some of the macrotrends to be seen in Scotland are worrying. New demographic projections show the Scottish population in decline and set to drop below five million, while month on month figures at the end of 2001 show Internet usage in the UK dropping for the first time. The former represents not only a declining birth-rate but the traditional Scottish problem of exporting its most talented individuals, now those best equipped to deal with the emerging information society. The latter may reflect a growing disenchantment with the Internet. One cause at least may be failure to deliver high speed connectivity to the home. Whatever the cause, it would be difficult to base a knowledge economy on declining Internet usage if the trend persists.

However, within Scotland itself there is a vibrant information science sector. Although only two universities (Robert Gordon and Strathclyde) have long-established departments of information science of the traditional sort, with the function of training librarians, at least four more have departments or groups working on elements of the information sector. In addition, the National Library of Scotland, the Scottish Consortium of University Research Libraries and the Scottish Library and Information Council have been keen proponents of digital libraries and related research. There is a wide recognition that, in a small country, moves towards significant resource sharing will be essential. That recognition does not however extend to the Scottish Parliament's Enterprise and Lifelong Learning Committee which noted that 'It does not appear, on present trends, that the main universities will become powerful drivers of the knowledge economy'[1], although it is unclear whether this says more about the Committee's lack of perception, or the universities' lack of marketing. Against that may be set the experience of small nations from Finland to Singapore[2], which have shown that national planning and government support can deliver fundamental change.

Derek Law

These larger trends may be taken to suggest that the move towards an information society is not a 'given' in which the only issue is the pace of change. However, the vibrancy of the public information sector, the access which we have to government and policy makers in a small country, and Scotland's long tradition of social and public service give grounds for believing that we can take advantage of government support to deliver the developing vision of Digital Scotland[3]. This initiative aims to 'achieve universal access to the Web, bridge the digital divide and help people achieve real benefits from the Web in their day-to day lives ... [and] to make Scotland a world class digital nation'.

Technological, economic, sociological and governmental factors

The development of the infrastructure to support an information society is a seriously complicated endeavour much closer to rocket science than to plug and play. The skills associated with that development lie largely in higher education, where the Scottish Higher Education Funding Council's (SHEFC) early decision to invest in Metropolitan Area Networks – urban based broadband networks aimed at the research community – has given Scotland a significant cadre of experts in networking. Technology has, however, proved a never-ending treadmill, with a dizzying pace of change. Insofar as any trends can be detected, perhaps the most important are ubiquitous computing and the convergence of hand-held technologies.

Ubiquitous computing revolves around mobile computing devices. Although these have comparatively slow data transfer speeds compared with desktop devices on high speed networks, this is increasing rapidly and is in any case more than adequate for almost all normal and educational purposes. Coupled with operational Bluetooth enabled equipment, this wireless technology allows computers to be used anytime, anyhow, anywhere.

Although most laptops remain too heavy for easy casual use, a blizzard of new converged devices is emerging into the market place, from small sub-laptops, to Web-enabled mobile phones with MP3 players and hand-held personal digital assistants (PDAs) with e-mail capabilities. This technology clearly has a long way to go, but we may expect soon to see acceptably sized devices which can cover all document and communication needs. This comes very close to the concept of wearable computing – a dream of mad scientists only three years ago!

However, technology is a necessary, but not sufficient, condition for the development of a knowledge economy. There is little value in placing technology on top of existing dysfunctional institutions. We need to build an Internet civil society which develops people rather than machines and which can understand that e-mail is more important than the Web, and that content production is more important than content consumption for a knowledge society. In fairness, investments in projects such as the Scottish Cultural Resources Access Network (SCRAN) and the New Opportunities Fund (NOF) funding for content creation suggest that this message is at least partly understood.

Much of the hope for the development of a knowledge economy must come from the development of an education system which itself recognises the use of technology in education. At present, we have in most cases what is known as 'The Vesalius Conundrum'. Were Vesalius to return to a university teaching hospital, he might enter a ward and would watch helpless and uncomprehending as surgeons carried out keyhole surgery on the heart. However, he could then enter the medical school and quite happily give a lecture to anatomy students on the circulation of the blood. This trend is changing, with the wish to move from 'sage on the stage to guide on the side'. Coupled with this conundrum is a growing failure to value information skills. This stems from the growth of the group described by Plutchak[4] as 'the satisfied inept'; those who, because they can use the Internet for searching, assume that this is all that is required; those who confuse ease of use with ease of understanding.

At a UK level, all governments for the last thirty years have failed to understand that machinery does not fix social problems and institutions. A whole string of initiatives revolving around the concept of technology in the classroom have assumed that the placing of technology in educational settings will produce technologically gifted students. Uniformly, they have failed to provide adequate training, support or content, failing to grasp that the real costs and skills are associated with technology ownership, not technology acquisition, and that social issues and social organisation will determine the adoption of technology.

The Scottish Executive may be showing more prudence. Its Digital Scotland initiative does have a focus on technological infrastructure, but the appointment of programme advisers from the education and information sectors gives hope that there will be a real understanding of such issues. It must certainly rank as some form of achievement to have had a government minister solemnly declare the importance of metadata! The government agenda for a digital Scotland has two key features. The first revolves around social inclusion and remedying the democratic deficit. Technology has huge potential here, whether interactive broadband to the home, or wireless computing to personal devices. The digital divide is a pat phrase, covering many ills but describing a societal problem of great import and magnitude. Early attempts to tackle this can only be welcomed, provided that it is recognised that, ultimately, what will deal with these issues is not the technology itself, but content, training and support. The second key feature is open education and lifelong learning. Although Scotland has commendably high participation rates in tertiary education, there remains a significant

Derek Law

need for lifelong learning, continuing professional development and re-skilling – issues which a variety of initiatives, such as Glasgow's 'Real – the Learning City', are attempting to address.

A final challenge for government is not just to offer appropriate skills to its population, but to persuade them to remain in Scotland and help develop the Scottish knowledge economy.

The development of IT and networks

The Bangemann Report[5] for the European Council infamously proposed that the creation of a network infrastructure was the responsibility of the market and not of the state. This conclusion was perhaps weakened by the author's subsequent employment by a private sector telecommunications provider. Almost by definition, such networks will not stretch to non-profitable areas of the community and it must be the responsibility of the state, whether by direct provision or by contractual requirement, to ensure equal access for all.

Oddly, this has been recognised even in a UK driven by market theory. The Joint Academic Network (JANET) was created at the height of the Thatcher era and has been followed in turn by NHSNet and the People's Network. Each of these networks has recognised the desirability of connecting its entire community, to the benefit of all. The People's Network is the latest recognition of this. This triumph of the Library and Information Commission is currently being rolled out and, although the funding is being bid for at local authority level, the clear intention is to build a distributed, rather than an incoherent, system.

Thus far, and most regrettably, there has been precious little interaction between these network sectors, despite meetings, seminars, projects and research. The philosophies of JANET (open network) and NHSNet (closed network), but both centrally organised, differ from that of the public library network, which is open, but locally managed. It is otiose to attempt to ascribe blame in all of this. JANET began first, simply because higher education had a greater and earlier need for high bandwidth than other sectors. The fact that this need stemmed from research possibly gave higher education rather superior notions of who they might talk to, but this has long gone and there is now a general desire for co-operation which only 'the system' and departmental budgeting prevents.

Robert Craig famously described this in a Scottish context, noting that we now face the prospect of building three tramways from Edinburgh to Glasgow rather than a single, fast Intercity service. There are some small signs of hope, in that JANET now extends into further education and some schools; local authority connections into schools can hardly ignore this. NHSNet looks much more difficult to link, but again one must hope that a small country will find it easier to rationalise and organise the management of scarce resources and be less patient of turf wars.

National initiatives

The arrival of the electronic library in the UK could be dated from 1990, when the Computer Board of the then University Grants Committee and the Research Councils decided to – or at least was persuaded to - invest in a national site licence for *Science citation index* for higher education. This developed as the BIDS service at the University of Bath[6]. This ultimately led to the Follett report and the major post-Follett series of projects and new services, all of which ensured that the information revolution remained high on the agenda of all universities for the following decade. A whole plethora of initiatives followed, initially mainly for higher education, but culminating in the People's Network and a £50 million programme for content creation from the New Opportunities Fund.

Tentative steps towards cross-sectoral co-operation were mounted by the Research Support Libraries Programme. These have really only borne fruit in Glasgow, where the Glasgow Digital Library has been set up as a cross-sectoral project embracing university, college and public libraries within the city and creating collections of digital resources of common interest on topics such as Red Clydeside. Even there, progress has been made in a rather slow and limited way.

More encouragingly, the British Library took possession of its magnificent new St Pancras building and was able to turn from a period of introspection to a more outgoing approach to partnership. This has led to the British Library's Co-operation and Partnership Programme[7] the main strand of which, the Full Disclosure project, aims to make available all of the nation's resources through a programme of retrospective catalogue conversion. Although this involves relatively small sums, the new leadership in this area suggests a welcome desire to break down sectoral boundaries.

Within Scotland, a consistent attempt has been made to develop a national strategy and national systems for the sharing of library resources. Much of this has been based on work commissioned from the Centre for Digital Library Research at the University of Strathclyde[8].

But perhaps the best example of cross-sectoral and cross-domain activity has been the aforementioned SCRAN[9]. This rich resource has proved an excellent example of nationally planned sharing of distributed resources. It has been much admired internationally and is a tribute to what vision and leadership can produce.

Derek Law

The creation, purchase and distribution of information

Singapore has, quite properly, had much praise for its vision of the intelligent island. Behind that lies a vision of the trading future of that country as an information entrepôt for South Asia. From this would seem to flow the concept of information arbitrage. This has a number of dimensions, as yet largely unexplored, although all would seem to stem naturally from a reformulation of Ranganathan as 'the right information to the right user at the right time'. Naturally and firstly comes the identification of the right product.

As information becomes a global commodity, so it can begin to be traded on that basis. *Medline* and *ERIC* can already be acquired on various bases, ranging from free to expensive, depending on how much added value the supplier provides. A next obvious step is time-shift purchase. It would make sense for UK libraries to purchase night-time only access to Australian-based data (ie, day-time access in the UK), in order to smooth loads. Despite the rueful and widespread remark that WWW stands for World Wide Wait, little if any thought has thus far been given to database topology and how it can be bought and sold in relation to time. More generally, this can be seen as using professional skills to optimise value for money. Although initial interest has focused on content, there is a growing understanding that there are possibilities for new ways of offering services. Particular initial interest has been shown again in using time-shift to provide round the clock reference services in partnership with libraries in Australia. This would take advantage of the swiftness of Instant Messaging to use a fully staffed day-time library in Australia to deal with the minimal level of overnight inquiries in Scotland and *vice versa*. For the sake of some initial cost, but then marginal activity, it appears that an undreamt-of degree of comprehensiveness can be offered. We may expect that this initial thinking will lead to a flowering of distributed services whose costs can be borne jointly where they could not be supported individually.

Identifying websites is also a more complicated issue than at first appears. Initially, we have concentrated on the simple issues associated with quality. Which site is the most comprehensive and most accurate? At the same time, we note ruefully how inaccessible some sites are and that the average life of a URL compares favourably with that of butterflies, but little else. As yet, there has been almost no interest in developing an equation balancing accessibility with quality. Is a site which is 100% comprehensive, but effectively available only six hours a day, superior to a site which is, say, 75% comprehensive, but effectively available 24 hours a day? In other words, might the Pareto principle – the 80/20 rule – apply to information?

However, even if these new roles are developed and explored, the key role of the librarian remains the same as ever: to be independent, authoritative and right, through the selection and provision of access to reliable resources which meet the needs of the client group.

Implications for providers, libraries and users

Four major areas of activity pose challenges. The first challenge is content. Content selection is not in principle different from the work of a traditional acquisitions department. However, a range of options is beginning to open up which will make this a more complicated process. There is a growing interest in consortial licensing for regional groupings. The best deals seem to come with cross-sectoral agreements, where the whole educational system can be brought together and schools and colleges given access to research materials, effectively at marginal cost. However, there is also a need to consider the cost of mirroring information, as opposed to providing bandwidth to access it. At present this is a fairly tortuous process. There are no standard agreements for mirroring data and even at national level between government agencies, these can prove tortuous to provide. Famously, and after two years of negotiation, the National Institutes of Health's (NIH) *Visible human* database was only mirrored in the UK by placing it at Glasgow University. The NIH were worried about the potential longevity of the host and arrangements in case of failure. These worries only disappeared when it became clear that Glasgow University pre-dated Columbus's voyages to the Americas.

Much (too much?) energy has been expended on exploring purchasing models, considering subscription, leasing, purchase, pay-per-view and so forth. This has effectively been a debate conducted in the science-technology-medicine (STM) arena, focusing on expensive, big science journals. While expense is of course important, science nevertheless remains a minority activity in most institutions and there is a grave danger that we are developing models aimed at a minor sector of the market. Whether such models will be apt for small learned societies in the humanities is rarely considered. It is also at least arguable that we shall generate more 'free' and non-commercial material in an electronic environment and should therefore concentrate on developing models which look at the economic issues of data ownership, rather than at considering purchasing models which preserve the rights of global corporations. If such ideas as the Open Archives Initiative take off, the developing STM model will be seen as a temporary aberration rather than a path to the future.

A further important aspect of content is its creation. This is first manifested in the identification of content for creation. Commercial providers tend to digitise text-rich and therefore less expensive material which is heavily used. Libraries tend to choose image-rich but relatively little used special collection and copyright free material, creating resources

Derek Law

closer to exhibitions than publications. As both groups gingerly get to grips with the impact of digital material, the two approaches are understandable and usefully complementary. A variation of this comes with born digital material. In truth, most published material is born digital these days and then converted to paper, but more dramatically, a whole range of new database resources has opened up, ranging from the images created by digital cameras, to satellite data, weather maps, genome databases, speech recognition, census data and so on.

In passing, one might note that much time and effort has been devoted to issues of intellectual property rights in content. No satisfactory agreed position has yet emerged between, at one extreme the proponents of open systems, such as Ginsparg[10] and Harnad[11], who believe in the free exchange of ideas, and leisure corporations, such as Disney, who see education as an extension of the entertainment industry. Some see this as a great barrier to digital developments, although another view is that the charging of VAT on electronic content is at least as big a barrier to its growth. While librarians have debated this with publishers in a rather isolated way, it has been enormously cheering in the last year to see the petition signed by 30,000 scientists from over 170 countries[12] calling for changes in the basis of journal publication. For the first time, it appears that scientists may be beginning to debate the future of scholarly communication. It may then be hoped that a new consensus will emerge eventually within the academy.

This leads to the second great challenge, which is in metadata. With some complacency, librarians are prone to amused commentary on the stumbling efforts of computer scientists to address metadata issues and to discover that the organisation of knowledge is indeed a difficult topic. However, our own profession's response of simply adding another field to the machine readable catalogue (MARC) record does not inspire huge confidence that we have undertaken a fundamental reappraisal of information in electronic formats. It is at first sight difficult to understand how systems designed for the description of unchanging physical objects placed in a single physical location are necessarily ideal for the description of changing and dynamic electronic content replicated in different forms at different places at different times. Nevertheless, metadata is our own area of professional competence and much time, effort and research are being expended on addressing these issues.

The third grand challenge is preservation. Preservation has been a major stumbling block to an enthusiastic switch to electronic collections. Much loved scary tales of changing technologies, of the real life-span of new storage technologies, of the problems of embedded software, have all contributed to an environment where it seems more prudent to retain the paper copy. Nor is it clear who 'owns' the preservation problem – publishers, national libraries or authors. In practice, significant research expenditure is beginning to bear fruit and projects such as the Consortium of University Research Libraries (CURL) Exemplars in Digital Archives (CEDARS)[13] at Leeds University and the Networked European Deposit Library (NEDLIB)[14] at the Royal Library in The Hague are beginning to show potential solutions.

The fourth and final challenge may loosely be described as user support. Law's Law[15] decrees that 'User friendly systems aren't'. One of the expanding roles of librarians will be that of providing the initial training and ongoing support which will allow users to gain the most from systems. This author finds it no coincidence that the drive for single authentication and logon, as embodied in the Athens[16] system for higher education, was developed through the former NISS service at the University of Bath in response to user need, rather than through commercial pressure. Commercial systems, it may be noted, chose to develop Digital Object Identifiers, a system of potential benefit to commercial suppliers, but of no real use or value to users.

Quality management

Older heads will remember the Youth Opportunities Scheme of the 1970s. Although primarily designed to curtail unemployment, it supported large numbers of projects in libraries. These varied from catalogue retro-conversion to major indexing projects, notably of local newspapers. These created a huge and rich resource which has largely been allowed to disappear through neglect. A recent attempt by this writer to discover the fate of one project revealed that the data were not simply created on now unplayable media, but that in any case the originals had been lost. This fate seems to have been replicated. While the waste of several million pounds in this way might seem comprehensible in the context of what was really a job creation scheme, the same fate seems to be approaching for the £50 million of data and metadata created via the Non-Formula Funding for Humanities programme. The website for the programme is now very difficult to find and when it is found, the data is progressively surrendering to entropy as links are broken and websites moved. It is to be hoped that the same fate does not befall the NOF funded projects, but, sadly there seems little effort thus far to learn the lessons of the past and to ensure that a preservation strategy is in place before the data are created.

A key issue in the failure to preserve data may be the absence of any recognised standards for data centres and, by extension, the absence of any authorised data repositories to manage and preserve both digitised and born digital material. Quite apart from the technical issues of media changes, technological obsolescence and media life-spans mentioned above, there is a range of issues such as version control, refresh rates and authoritativeness which have so far not been addressed. The imprint says a great deal about a

Derek Law

book and its probable authority and we have expectations of the standard and quality of a work from, say, Edinburgh University Press. On the other hand the electronic address ed.ac.uk can (and does!) imply anything from material by a Nobel prize-winner to illegal or simply wrong information from a hijacked address. Some form of kite-marking of repositories will have to be brought into place to ensure trust and authority.

Although electronic legal deposit has been much bandied about and is a necessary and desirable step, it is less obvious that national libraries are the natural and normal repositories for these electronic data. To be sure, they must have a role in organising the deposit of electronic data, but, rather than recreating vast new structures, the standards and models to be followed may be better found in existing national data centres, such as Edinburgh Data and Information Access (EDINA) at Edinburgh University.

Cross-sectoral activity and problems of sectoral boundaries

Cross-sectoral working was an issue high on the agenda of and much addressed by the Library and Information Commission, which believed passionately in it and which used its authority and its small pot of research funds to drive forward co-operative activity and to develop the People's Network initiative. Sadly its successor, Resource has shown little interest in continuing this much admired work at a UK level and has even removed the pot of funding previously dedicated to library research. Fortunately, at a Scottish level, the Scottish Library and Information Council has provided a vehicle for ensuring that there is good library co-operation in Scotland, while the National Library of Scotland has also provided useful fora and partnerships for co-operation.

Despite the Scottish claim for a tradition of working together, much work has tended to be sectorally based. We can already see barriers and firewalls being erected between different communities and it is important that these are broken down and a climate of trust created. For the first time in recent memory, the availability of money is not the first and over-riding concern. Much more important is the need to build trust so that local government can work with higher education, the health service with industry, even Glasgow with Edinburgh. Since devolution, Scotland has found a new sense both of community and purpose and there can rarely have been a better time to foster and improve community relationships. The Scottish Executive has a major role to play in facilitating these interactions.

The goal for all small countries must be a distributed national resource. The recent financial problems which have beset the National Library of Scotland[17], forcing it to close the Scottish Science Library, have been a useful reminder of the need to maximise and share the range of resources in a situation where there are few, if any, comprehensive collections.

Conclusion

Robert Craig has worked tirelessly for the goals of sharing and co-operation across all sectors and for the role libraries and librarians should play in the transformation of Scotland to a knowledge based economy. Another Craig, Craig Brown, the former Scotland soccer manager, shares his sentiments on how that will be done. He remarked at the start of the Euro '96 campaign that 'Bagpipes and claymores won't win us games.'[18] Only skill and competence win games. Both Craigs are determined to see a future Scotland with skills and competence in abundance.

References

1. Scottish Parliament Enterprise and Lifelong Learning Committee. 2001

2. Moore, Nick. The international framework of information policies *in* Elkin, J. *Managing Information*. Open University, 2000

3. The Digital Scotland website is http://www.scotland.gov.uk/digitalscotland/default.htm

4. Plutchak, T.S. On the satisfied and inept end user. *Medical Reference Services Quarterly*, 8, 1, Spring 1989, p45-48

5. Bangemann, Martin *Recommendations to the European Council: Europe and the global information society*. 1994 http://www.ispo.cec.be/infosoc/backg/bangeman.html

6. Law, Derek. The development of a national policy for dataset provision in the UK: a historical perspective. *Journal of Information Networking*, 1, 1995, p103-116

7. The Library Co-operation website, hosted by the British Library, is http://minos.bl.uk/concord/index1.html

8. Nicholson, Dennis. Digital Scotland, the relevance of library research and the Glasgow Digital Library. *Program*, 35, 2001, p1-14

9. The SCRAN website is http://www.scran.ac.uk/homepage

10. A brief summary of Ginsparg's work may be found at http://www.news.cornell.edu/releases/July01/ginsparg.archive.ws.html

11. Harnad describes his views at http://www.ariadne.ac.uk/issue8/harnad

12. The scientists' open letter is at http://www.publiclibraryofscience.org

13. Information on CEDARS is at http://www.leeds.ac.uk/cedars

Derek Law

14. Information on NEDLIB can be found at http://www.kb.nl/coop/nedlib

15. Law's Law is the present author's despairing attempt to find immortality

16. The website for the Athens access management system is http://www.athens.ac.uk

17. The National Library of Scotland published more information on its website at http://www.nls.uk/news/index.html

18. Macdonald, Kenny. *Scottish football quotations*. Mainstream, 1999

7

Boxes and wires: IT, SLIC and information delivery

Elaine Fulton

The explosion of information and communications technology (ICT)-related initiatives in the latter years of the 20th century and the early 21st century is fundamentally changing the way in which organisations and individuals work. This change is affecting not just traditional information specialists but the whole community.

For the first time in many years the development of ICT initiatives is being driven by central government, who see access to ICT services and information on the Internet as a major weapon in the fight against social exclusion. Encouraging active citizenship by reducing the digital divide will widen educational opportunity and develop the ICT-skilled workforce so crucial to economic stability and development. Information is also being recognised as an enabling force, with the potential to empower and enhance the skills of individuals.

It is against this background that libraries and information services are now required to re-shape themselves to deliver relevant information services to their users and the wider public. Major initiatives like the National Grid for Learning (NGfL), the People's Network, the New Opportunities Fund (NOF) digitisation programme, the Scottish University for Industry (SUfI) and the Modernising Government agenda are having and will continue to have a major impact on the development of library and information services. They have provided the sector with an opportunity to raise its profile, which in the recent past has been diminished to some extent by the development of information and communications technology. It has become evident that technical solutions are only tools and that the skills and knowledge of the library and information sector are even more crucial as the world of electronic content envisaged through NGfL, People's Network, SUfI, etc develops.

The Scottish Library and Information Council (SLIC) was established in 1991 and has consistently encouraged innovation and development of services through a variety of mechanisms, many of which have been underpinned by information technology. The culmination of the Council's development of this strategy came in March 1999, with the publication of

Elaine Fulton

Enabling seamless access: making the case for a national information strategy for Scotland[1]. It is against this background that this essay intends to map the history of developments and attempts to measure the relative success of library and information services in developing strategies for information management in the 21st century.

Libraries and ICT development – a background

Libraries world-wide have embraced ICT for many years and library automated systems have developed from basic library catalogues to sophisticated integrated software solutions supporting not only catalogues, but circulation, acquisitions, serials and community information.

Administrative pressures and the need to provide additional functionality and services to users within ever-reducing budgets often drove the use and development of ICT in libraries. The library profession, which perhaps like no other has a strong spirit of co-operation and collaboration, has worked together for over thirty years to develop international standards such as machine readable cataloguing (MARC), Anglo-American Cataloguing Rules (AACR) and more recently z39.50. This spirit of co-operation has extended to working with library system suppliers world-wide to develop management software to sustain and support information delivery.

Such standards, used properly, initially enabled the sharing and exchange of bibliographic resources. This has not been without problems. Some early attempts at co-operation in Scotland failed, not least the Scottish Libraries Co-operative Automation Project (SCOLCAP), a project instigated with the best of intentions, but in hindsight perhaps launched before its time. Current standards were not used across the board and the ICT infrastructure and software had not developed sufficiently to sustain the project long term. Attempts were made by the National Library of Scotland, through related development of the Inter-Lending Service, and to some extent by the higher education sector through various projects, to pick up some of the issues raised by this project. However, the void left by its failure did not really begin to be addressed until the advent of the Internet and z39.50 in the 1990s.

Gradually, the ability to offer user services beyond electronic access to the library catalogue has developed to such an extent that many libraries are now offering self-reservations, self-issue and renewal as a matter of course. The Internet became one of the most important social and cultural stimuli of the later 20th century. Through this medium, library and information services now have the opportunity to provide 24-hour access not just to catalogues, but also to a range of electronic resources and services. It is in the management of and the content creation for these resources and services that the future challenge lies. Libraries have moved into a new age, where information is not confined by library walls and expands at a rate faster than any printing press could ever publish. The profession of librarianship, information and knowledge management is exposed to a global audience and how well it addresses this new challenge can perhaps only be measured by the status of and numbers in the profession in ten years time.

Education, education, education

The mantra of Tony Blair in the General Election campaign in 1997 gave an indication of the intention of the Labour Party should it succeed in winning the election after 17 years of Conservative government; behind this was an intention to widen educational opportunity beyond schools and academic institutions. This had been foreshadowed in the previous year:

> The information superhighway should not just benefit the affluent or the metropolitan. Just as in the past books were a chance for ordinary people to better themselves, in the future online education will be a route to better prospects. But just as books are available from public libraries, the benefits of the superhighway must be there for everyone.[2]

Labour's landslide victory in 1997 launched a swathe of initiatives related to lifelong learning. A number of key reports, some of which had been commissioned by the previous government but were seized on by the new administration, provided direction for the Labour government's commitment to fund and set targets for the delivery of lifelong learning. In hindsight, some targets were unrealistic in the current economic climate, particularly for those tasked with delivery in local government.

National Grid for Learning

The National Grid for Learning is a structure to source educationally valuable content and post it on the Internet. The Grid will also develop a programme to enable access to that content in schools, libraries, colleges, universities, workplaces, homes and elsewhere. It will be a key pillar to deliver education and lifelong learning using advanced technology[3].

Scottish University for Industry

SUfI declared its intentions as follows:

> SUfI will be a broker, connecting people, businesses, public and voluntary organisations who want to improve their skills with the

Elaine Fulton

people who can offer them the learning they need, delivered how, where and when most convenient to them. It will aim to stimulate interest in learning and improve access. It will take learning to non-traditional locations, like the high street, business parks, libraries, shopping centres and even football clubs. It will connect people and businesses who want to learn, with the people who can offer them the learning they need.[4]

New Library: the People's Network

This project will link all public libraries to the Internet by 2002[5]. Over 600 libraries in Scotland will be equipped with ICT facilities and trained staff, and will support lifelong learning in its widest sense whilst enabling wider access to other initiatives such as the Scottish University for Industry and the National Grid for Learning.

In a Scottish context, devolution and the establishment of the first Scottish Parliament in 300 years was on the agenda. This and the developing lifelong learning agenda would be powerful influences in the establishment of policies for a new era in Scottish politics and culture and would have their impact on information services and libraries. Generic United Kingdom policies, in particular in the area of learning, began to reflect the quest for policies that better reflected a separate Scottish identity. The National Grid for Learning and the University for Industry developed their own brands for Scotland, offering slightly different delivery models than elsewhere in the United Kingdom.

From 1997 to the establishment of the Scottish Parliament on 6 May 1999, these policy issues developed apace and new themes began to appear:

- the quest for the United Kingdom to be a socially inclusive society and, in particular, the desire to minimise the digital divide;
- the call for joined up working amongst appropriate projects, partners and sectors, in the interest of best value;
- Modernising Government agenda: the government set a target of making all government services available on-line by 2005.

SLIC set up a small working group to develop a national information policy. It was perceived that those countries that were best equipped to compete in global markets with a flexible workforce had policies which recognised the value of information in the economy as a shared resource. The European Parliament tasked member states with developing national information policies.

Following the establishment of the new Scottish Parliament, as new policies emerged and more detail was available on the specifics of projects such as SUfI, the People's Network and NGfL, it became clear to the SLIC working group that there were synergies across many of the programmes. It was clear that better value could be achieved by a coherent approach to the development of a national information policy, which not only addressed the issues of the technical infrastructure, but also co-ordinated an approach across all initiatives and projects to enable seamless access to information. It also became clear that the development of ICT for library and information services had lessons that could inform the development of ICT for wider public use. Many of the e-services envisaged by government were already under way in library services of all kinds; the extension of this would be the key to securing the future of information and library services. The publication of the working group's report[1] in March 1999 could not have been more timely. Crucially, the report was not about libraries; it was about the delivery of information and its role in underpinning economic regeneration. It argued that high quality, easy-to-access information would have an impact on economic competitiveness, learning, governance, health and culture, and it highlighted the role library and information services could play. It met with agreement across the sectors, industry and political parties of all sides.

This document was the key to getting libraries and information services into the political arena. This, of course, had been one of the objectives behind the formation of SLIC, although the degree to which this has now been achieved would perhaps surprise even those involved in the foundation of the Council. The work of Robert Craig in achieving this cannot be underestimated. In his time with the Scottish Library Association (SLA) and the Scottish Library and Information Council, he has established a valuable network of institutional contacts. This network has been further extended through the good offices of successive chairpersons of SLIC, including politicians such as Peter Peacock, formerly of The Highland Council and now a Scottish Executive Minister, and Rosemary McKenna MP, Chair of SLIC, 1998-2002. Access to persons of influence in this way has been crucial in persuading an audience beyond libraries of the importance of an information policy and strategy. The report encouraged the newly-established Scottish Parliament to create the Digital Scotland Task Group, charged with researching and developing a strategy to ensure Scotland was amongst the leaders in the information society.

But what of libraries?

SLIC has since its inception tried to encourage innovation and development of services, through its grant-aid programme, the development of standards and strategy and more recently through Challenge Fund projects.

Elaine Fulton

It has tried to encourage library services to initiate ICT and lifelong learning related pilot projects which could test ideas and provide practical experience to assist others. Some of the areas which could impact on the future development of information and library services are highlighted below. The main thrust of innovation has centred on the People's Network, lifelong learning, Digital Scotland and the creation of electronic content.

People's Network and lifelong learning

The publication of *New Library: the People's Network*[6] saw the establishment of a template which would take public libraries into the new millennium. The report envisaged that the New Library would:

- enable people to prosper in the information society;
- be an integrated component of the education system;
- be open and accessible to all;
- be the information gatekeeper;
- offer opportunity to all citizens to be involved in the democratic process.

The report caught the imagination of the new government to such an extent that it provided ring-fenced funding via the New Opportunities Fund for the connection of all libraries in the United Kingdom to the Internet by December 2002 and, crucially, to provide training for all staff in basic ICT competencies to enable them to assist users in using basic software packages, the Internet and e-mail. A further report entitled *Building the network*[7] outlined in more detail how this would be achieved.

The New Opportunities Fund provided £11.5m for technical infrastructure and £2.7m for staff training in Scotland. In addition, Scottish organisations would have the opportunity to create electronic digital content via a £50m UK fund offered by NOF. The themes of this project are:

- education - lifelong learning;
- citizens' information - participation in society;
- business and the economy - training and employment;
- establishment of training and learning centres.

The scale of this one-off investment is unprecedented in public libraries; not since the time of Andrew Carnegie had libraries received such an injection of cash and support and significantly it came for the first time via central government. The question asked at the time was – 'Why libraries?' This was answered in the New Library report itself:

- there are 4,759 libraries in the UK;
- 58% of the population hold library membership;
- 10 million people use libraries on a regular basis;
- using libraries is the fifth most popular pastime in the UK.

These statistics were received with amazement by the profession, but also by the government, impressed by the number of people who could be effectively reached through an existing network.

Announcing the funding, the then Minister for Culture, Media and Sport, Chris Smith, spoke of the 'defining moment for public library services'. Hidden within these words lies the threat that future development and funding of the public library service is dependent on the success or failure of the People's Network.

The Library and Information Commission and its successor, Resource: the Council for Museums, Archives and Libraries, had, at all stages, involved SLIC with the development of the programme. However some of SLIC's own programmes have also helped to inform developments.

In 1997-98, the then Scottish Office Education and Industry Department allocated some £300,000 to be distributed through SLIC for innovative ICT projects in public libraries in Scotland. Six projects received funding. However two, in particular, paved the way for the development of lifelong learning and creation of electronic content. These are discussed below.

Dumfries and Galloway Council received funding to create a Cybercentre in the Ewart Library in Dumfries as a discrete unit within the Library offering Internet access and a series of basic ICT courses for the public to develop their core skills. The new facility meant the children's library in the Ewart was integrated with lending services, while the vacated area was refurbished and transformed with up to date PCs, printers, scanners and video conferencing facilities. It signalled a transformation for public library services. Its impact on colleagues, the public and, most crucially, politicians was immense as now they could see the implications and benefits of the implementation of the New Library concept. In the first few months, over 40% of the users of the new facilities had not previously used the library service. Libraries now had the ability to expand their user base and reach parts of the community they had been targeting without success for years. It also emerged that over 10% of these new users also began to use the traditional library services as a result of their visits to the Cybercentre. Although, at the time of writing, evidence of this nature is still limited, this

Elaine Fulton

trend of increasing user numbers seems sure to continue as other library services develop ICT and lifelong learning facilities.

Dumfries and Galloway continued to develop their services. From the experience of the Cybercentre they identified a need for dedicated staff to support this work. Users required mediation and help and as they began to roll out ICT facilities across the region staff were required to trouble-shoot and assist remote users. They secured two year funding from SLIC to employ an ICT Field Officer to undertake these duties. This pump priming of services by SLIC enabled the library service to integrate the post into core services and to demonstrate a secure framework for delivering the People's Network. Dumfries and Galloway was one of six authorities to gain exemplar status for their application to the New Opportunities Fund for People's Network infrastructure funding. In 2001 they achieved SUfI learndirect Scotland status.

SLIC was able to develop the concept of lifelong learning in libraries through another, albeit smaller, amount of funding from the Scottish Executive and the fledgling Scottish University for Industry, which was seeking to establish a network of learning centres and learning opportunities in a range of environments. The existing public library network gave SUfI the opportunity to work with partners other than traditional learning providers and to assess the possible quality of learning that could be made available.

One of the key criteria for success in accessing some £102,000 of funding was evidence of working with a range of community partners to deliver the programme. Once again six local authorities were successful, delivering a range of small to medium sized learning centres serving the needs of individual communities. Significantly, the authorities awarded a grant were different from those successful in the first round of challenge funding, thus beginning to spread the lifelong learning experience into a significant proportion of Scotland's public libraries in preparation for the development of their People's Network applications.

Moray Council was one of the grant recipients, one of the first public library authorities to secure its People's Network allocation and one of the first to achieve SUfI accreditation. East Renfrewshire opened four learning centres through this funding; they too have achieved SUfI learndirect status and opened Scotland's first People's Network library in Giffnock in the autumn of 2001.

Through additional Scottish Executive funding, SLIC was able to appoint, on a temporary basis, an additional member of staff to support all 32 public library authorities in their preparation of applications to NOF for staff training and infrastructure funding. The process to secure this funding was rigorous and rightly so. The combination of this staff support and the experience gained in the preparation of previous funding applications is seen in many quarters to be the reason for Scotland's success in obtaining six exemplar plans and only two failures in the first round of bids for infrastructure funding. By the end of 2001, all Scottish authorities had secured their allocations and had started working to implement their plans to ensure that all 608 public libraries are connected to the Internet by December 2002.

It is disappointing, however, that not all libraries in Scotland, or indeed in the United Kingdom, were able to meet the minimum bandwidth requirement of 2Mb. A combination of factors have contributed to this situation, including: rural location; the high cost of on-going revenue rentals; insufficient funding for local government to cover higher bandwidth costs; the fact that the telecommunications companies did not make available this bandwidth to local authorities at a reasonable cost; and British Telecom's failure to 'un-bundle' the local loop to the expectations of other telecommunications companies.

Hopefully, this is an issue on which Digital Scotland pathfinder projects will improve.

Digital Scotland

The Scottish Parliament swiftly picked up on the arguments outlined in the *Enabling seamless access*[1] report and set up the Digital Scotland Task Force to consider how best to secure Scotland's position as an international centre in the democratic use of advanced information and communications technology. A series of working groups was established to report to ministers. A great many issues were addressed, perhaps too many, as it seemed that there was too much to do and issues were too complex to resolve easily. This, as well as the natural fear of making mistakes, has perhaps slowed progress. The Task Force remit included e-business, e-education and learning, e-public services, e-inclusion and e-communities, communications infrastructure, skills and organising information. The recommendations were aimed at four main priority areas:

- encouraging universal access;
- providing information and services relative to need;
- increasing take-up of online services;
- developing leadership and co-operation.

SLIC participated in this process via its Director, Robert Craig. The Council's specific interests were in the development of a robust and affordable infrastructure which would offer sustainability to the People's Network, the National Grid for Learning, higher and further education and

Elaine Fulton

the Scottish University for Industry. However, one of the main areas in which information agencies and library services in Scotland could offer knowledge and experience was in the organisation of information and a working group was formed to look at the development of the standards to enable seamless access to a range of information sources.

SLIC had been active in this area for some time, having established an Advisory Group on Interoperability and Access. Through the Joint Academic Network (JANET), libraries in higher education had, until this point, the most experience in developing communications infrastructure and services. In Scotland, there was also considerable knowledge and experience which would help inform the developing standards on interoperability and access. Although dependent on the experience of the higher education sector, membership of the working group also included representatives from SUfI, the Scottish Cultural Resources Access Network (SCRAN), Learning and Teaching Scotland, the Glasgow Telecolleges Network and archive services. The aim was to reach a consensus across the sectors and domains on developing a safe path for interoperability. The working group report recognised current and developing standards, including MARC, AACR2, the e-Government Interoperability Framework (e-GIF) and the Learning Object Metadata/International Metadata Standard (LOM/IMS) – developed by the Institute of Electrical Engineers. It recommended that organisations be encouraged to adopt these in the creation of metadata for information and learning. Importantly the work of this group was then able to feed in to the Digital Scotland Task Group on Organising Information.

The Scottish Library and Information Council and the Scottish Library Association had already been developing their own electronic resources on their shared website SLAINTE, which followed these standards. With the Centre for Digital Library Research at the University of Strathclyde and Napier University, both SLIC and SLA were attempting to develop mechanisms to support the sector in the adoption of these standards.

The Centre for Digital Library Research ran several important research projects supported by the Scottish Confederation of University and Research Libraries (SCURL) and the Joint Information Systems Committee (JISC). In SLIC's view these projects had an important role to play in achieving seamless access. Particularly important is the Co-operative Academic Information Retrieval Network for Scotland (CAIRNS) initiative. CAIRNS allows simultaneous, one-stop searching of multiple collections of print and electronic resources held by Scottish libraries and information services. SLAINTE is part of this network. CAIRNS allows the creation of regional or special interest groupings through the adoption of international metadata standards and the use of z39.50 software.

SLIC was able to support the development of this valuable research project in two ways: firstly, through research funding to the Scottish Portals

Initiative, which sought to achieve the participation of non higher education services in the CAIRNS service; and secondly, by supporting the Confederation of Scottish Mini-Clumps (COSMIC). COSMIC is a cross-sectoral and cross-domain focus group aimed at encouraging and supporting co-operation and developing a research and development programme to enable seamless access to resources.

This activity has been on-going since 1999. While there is a small measure of success for the sector, in recognising that standards should be followed and that quality information is crucial to develop 24/7 access to information resources, the Digital Scotland initiative has not provided funding to develop this strategy further; nor did it publish the *Organising information*[8] report submitted to the Scottish Executive in February 2001. Nevertheless, SLIC itself published an amended version of the report in the autumn of 2001 to enable organisations to develop their strategies to achieve these goals.

In the winter of 2001, a considerable breakthrough was achieved. Arising out of the *National cultural strategy*[9], the Scottish Library and Information Council was asked by the Scottish Executive to develop a cultural portal on its behalf to support and promote cultural activity in Scotland. The portal would be developed using the standards outlined in *Organising information* and it is hoped that this activity will stimulate the adoption of standards in content creation in other organisations.

The development of Scotland as a digitally skilled nation depends on the availability of quality electronic content and services and a robust telecommunications infrastructure. The Scottish Executive established a Ministerial Advisory Group in 2001 to investigate how best to secure reasonable cost high bandwidth for the public sector to ensure that its major policy initiatives are achieved. Without fast, efficient and robust access, the National Grid for Learning, the People's Network, the Scottish University for Industry and the Modernising Government agenda are not achievable, and much investment rests on such an infrastructure being in place.

Whilst there is lots of 'dark fibre' underground, there appears to be little incentive for the telecommunication companies to light up the fibre and make it available at reasonable cost to a range of public and private sector organisations. In September 2001, Wendy Alexander, Minister for Enterprise and Lifelong Learning launched *Connecting Scotland*[10] – the Scottish Executive's broadband strategy. The strategy advocated the importance of pervasive and affordable broadband connections for all parts of Scotland. This will be encouraged by the aggregation of public sector demand and two pathfinder projects have been established in the Highlands and the South of Scotland to test the arguments put in the strategy.

A complementary strategy, *Connecting Scotland's people*[11], was launched in late September 2001. This outlined the Scottish Executive's strategy for

Elaine Fulton

digital inclusion and identified a number of steps to address the digital divide. It also detailed progress on initiatives such as the People's Network, adult literacy, Training for Work and the appointment of Digital Champions.

Of the future?

The twin forces of these initiatives give library and information services the opportunity to play a pivotal role in the development of Digital Scotland.

The Scottish Library and Information Council and the Scottish Library Association have tried to ensure that both their memberships are prepared and equipped to deal with the challenges of information management in the 21st century. Only time will tell ...

References

1. Scottish Library and Information Council. *Enabling seamless access: making the case for a national information strategy for Scotland*. SLIC, 1999

2. Blair, Tony. *New Britain: my vision of a young country*. Fourth Estate, 1996

3. The National Grid for Learning in Scotland website is http://www.ngflscotland.gov.uk/

4. The Scottish University for Industry website is http://www.scottishufi.co.uk/index.shtm

5. The People's Network website is http://www.slainte.org.uk/Peopnetw/Penehome.htm

6. Library and Information Commission. *New Library: the People's Network*. Library and Information Commission, 1997

7. Library and Information Commission. *Building the New Library network: a report to government*. Library and Information Commission, 1998

8. Scottish Library and Information Council. *Organising information: implementing standards for interoperability and access*. SLIC, 2001

9. Scottish Executive. *Creating our future....minding our past: Scotland's national cultural strategy*. HMSO, 2000

10. Scottish Executive. *Connecting Scotland: our broadband strategy*. HMSO, 2001

11. Scottish Executive. *Connecting Scotland's people: digital inclusion*. HMSO, 2001

8

Future librarians: professionals for an information society

Judith Elkin

The agenda set by the government over the last few years has provided a golden opportunity for a new role for library and information services in the new millennium. Two key documents underpinned early government policies: *Our information age: the government's vision*[1] and *The learning age: a renaissance for a new Britain*[2]. They set out the government's intention to enable people to take advantage of the new information age, concentrating on five key areas: transforming education; widening access; promoting competition and competitiveness; fostering equality; modernising government.

Whilst there has been some re-thinking, these priorities remain high on the government's agenda and provide an opportunity for libraries and librarians to play a significant role in the new culture of learning, in countering social exclusion, in contributing to the knowledge economy and in economic regeneration.

But what are the particular skills that librarians and information professionals possess and how might these need to change as we look to the future? In an age of increasing complexity with regard to the range and quantity of information available, the role of the information professional as: handler and manager of information; trainer of others to use information effectively and efficiently; evaluator of quality information and information provision; carer for user needs, becomes ever more critical. This is the traditional role, but it needs to adapt and change to cope with the demands of modern society, so in addition it needs flexible, adaptable individuals who can manage change innovatively, imaginatively and proactively, recognising new opportunities and grasping new challenges.

The diversity of the information profession

Library and information work has changed rapidly in recent years. The strategic and operational value of good information provision is recognised by a wide range of employers. Information handling and information management in all their various guises are increasingly seen as crucial for survival in a burgeoning diversity of markets: health; financial and legal information; software development; publishing; multimedia; research; information brokering; information consultancy; knowledge management. In addition, the traditional areas of the academic, public, government and special library sectors have widened in terms of their definition of service delivery, with information specialists taking on enhanced roles as mediators, educators, consultants and learner support.

As we increasingly become part of the information and learning society, can we identify what the core skills of the information professional are? Are they different from the core skills of the traditional librarian, or are they essentially the same, but now required in a new guise, or across a range of media and technologies? Thus:

- information-handling skills: cataloguing; indexing; general management and organisation of information; organisation of knowledge;
- training and facilitating skills: helping people of any age, background, specialism or need to use libraries and information resources; user support; user education and instruction;
- evaluation skills: selection; critical evaluation and review; quality assurance of information; ensuring fitness for purpose;
- concern for the customer: carer for user needs.

These are largely skills which other professionals do not possess, or rather, are not combined in the people-oriented, socially aware, end-user aware sense in which librarians have traditionally operated. However, they are also skills that other professionals are adopting, as they try to make sense of the increasingly digital environment.

Role of libraries in society

The now defunct Library and Information Commission (replaced in April 2000 by Resource: the Council for Museums, Libraries and Archives) had a good stab at demonstrating the critical role of library and information services in the 21st century and the future and on-going need for skilled librarians. The Commission's approach was cross-sectoral, recognising that many of the strengths of library and information services pervaded all sectors, whether academic, public, government, commercial or special. An early policy statement, *2020 Vision*[3], laid out the vision for library and information services in the 21st century. It focused on: content – providing universal access to the products of the human mind; connectivity – creating a digital library of the UK's intellectual heritage of culture and innovation; and competences – equipping individuals and organisations to play their full role in a learning and information society.

A subsequent policy document, *Libraries: the lifeforce of learning*[4] highlighted the role of libraries and information services of all kinds as 'catalysts for learning', offering quality learning places in their many different environments. Specifically, they would provide: gateways – via connectivity and access to information, advice, guidance and quality assurance; opportunity – via content and its availability, sustainability, fitness for purpose, quality and range; and capacity – via personal support, championing learners in developing individual competence.

For many people in society, library and information services are the 'learning places of choice', the 'places where knowledge occurs'. Library and information services place the 'learner at the centre' within their traditional role of underpinning learning. They are inclusive and familiar, offering an accessible, neutral learning space. Increasingly important in today's learning society, library and information services are networked to other learning centres and work with other agencies at local, national and regional levels.

Whilst this advocacy approach to promoting the value of library and information services in fulfilling parts of the government's policy agenda has rather disappeared from Resource's agenda, the fundamental statements of where libraries are vital in society, both today and in the future, remain pertinent and are helpful in assessing the changing skills that librarians need to operate effectively in future scenarios.

Changing skills of librarians: higher education

The Fielden Report on human resource management in academic libraries[5], though now some eight years old, highlighted four key areas where the competences of existing staff would be most challenged in future and where new sets of skills would be required. It predicted that subject librarians would need an understanding of teaching and learning skills and, almost universally, library staff would need to know how to access and navigate in electronic databases. It identified the need for much improved customer care and service attitudes in the academic library sector, with a greater focus on providing a system more responsive to the needs of customers and thus a more sensitive delivery of services. The report suggested that new forms of team-working would be needed to help build commitment to the basic goals of each library and information service.

The report predicted, correctly, that there would inevitably be a demand for a significant improvement in staff training and development, in particular to cover updating of information technology (IT) skills and competence;

Judith Elkin

customer service skills; management skills, especially financial; team-working skills; leadership; strategic thinking skills. These still hold true today, despite subsequent dramatic changes in the higher education environment: a significant increase in overall student numbers, with the introduction of student fees bringing more accountability, more student debt and a decline in mature student numbers. Inevitably, academics have looked to new teaching methods and strategies to cope with increased numbers and a more diverse student body, with a greater concentration on distance, flexible and innovative learning strategies, but accompanied by limited investment. An increase in network access and networked electronic information has put a new focus on the library as both resource provider, in print and electronic forms, and as guide and tutor to students and academics, stimulating more effective use of resources and network use.

A recent report from the Association of University Teachers[6] reinforces much of this, predicting librarians and other academic-related staff working with academic colleagues in teaching and training students and providing a wide range of learning support; all this against a backdrop of huge increases in student numbers, doubling staff/student ratios and widespread use of information and communications technology (ICT) in teaching and research. Increased information technology skills will allow more involvement in preparing teaching materials and integrating learning technology into course teaching to create 'managed learning environments'. Librarians in higher education will increasingly become specialists who complement academics, as is already happening in some of the more forward-looking academic libraries, with the move from hybrid to electronic libraries entailing far greater user education, of both students and academics, by library staff.

Changing skills of librarians: public libraries

Public libraries, too, have undergone huge change in recent years. From a point of considerable decline just a few years ago, there has been tremendous burgeoning of new initiatives, alongside the huge opportunities afforded by the People's Network[7]. The concentration in children's libraries on Bookstart-type initiatives, family reading and learning groups and homework clubs have given a much higher profile to the potential of libraries in the child's development. This has been paralleled for adults by a re-focusing on reader development and new forms of support for business and economic regeneration.

The five new roles identified for public librarians in the New Opportunities Fund training for the Public Library Network[8]: net navigator; information technology gatekeeper; information consultant; information manager; educator mirror closely the changing demands being made on academic librarians.

In a recent interview, Baroness Tessa Blackstone, Minister of State for the Arts, praised public libraries and their potential for grasping new technologies and contributing to the delivery of e-government services:

> Libraries have been amongst the first public services to recognise the scope that new technologies offer for extending the range of information and services ... The library community also understands the role it can play in bridging the digital divide ... In general, I welcome the sector's far-sightedness in developing information services of all types – which, by supporting and empowering citizens, are vital to the modernising agenda.[9]

Changing skills of librarians: business and special libraries

Within the business community in particular, the advent of the Internet and wide use of e-mail has seen businesses as well as individuals suffering from information overload. Reuters Business Information undertook a number of independent, international surveys which emphasised the problems of information overload. Their first survey, of some 1,300 managers in Britain, America, Australia, Hong Kong and Singapore, *Dying for information*[10] was followed by *Glued to the screen*[11]. These surveys show an 'excess of information is strangling business and causing personnel to suffer mental anguish and physical illness' and use terms like 'information junkie' and 'data-holic'. The consequences of this information glut included time-wasting, delaying important business decisions, distraction from job responsibilities, stress, job dissatisfaction, illness and breakdown of personal relationships.

Later still, *Out of the abyss*[12] showed that information overload was still a major issue on the personal and business level, but people were starting to understand the problem and learning how to cope with it. What appeared to be happening around the world was:

> Individuals and businesses are rejecting multiple sources of information in preference to a single source that they believe will actually give them all the information they need ... Those who learn quickly how to harness the power of information for competitive advantage will set a standard for information management that others will follow. Those who don't risk falling into the abyss of stress, confusion and poor productivity.

But does this mean that information is being used efficiently or effectively? If ever there was a case for information professionals, this is it!

Judith Elkin

This has partly accounted for the parallel, and growing, interest in knowledge management, particularly within the business and special library sectors. A research project in 1999 looked at the development of knowledge management within the business field and the skills required of library and information specialists to compete in this new market. Some of the key differentiators identified in the report, *Skills for knowledge management*[13], were:

- business knowledge, nous and partnership;
- information management and knowledge management skills;
- IT capability;
- leadership;
- process and project management;
- communication and negotiation skills;
- benefit and value management.

Changing skills: digital environment

Thus, in all sectors, we find a steady move towards a digital or hybrid environment dominating thinking about future developments. Reviewing the future of the profession, Lynn Brindley, the Director of the British Library, states clearly:

> The future of libraries is not, and should not be directly linked to the future of physical libraries. Possibly the most skilled librarians will preside only over a virtual library … Skills in collection building should be transferable and valuable in assessing, validating and selecting for access digital resources; linking digital and non-digital in a hybrid environment is important; creating pathways for different kinds of users in different subject domains is a critical (if messy) role; making some sense of the Web jungle serves users well.[14]

This is reinforced by Professor Tom Wilson, recently retired Head of the Department of Information Science at the University of Sheffield, in an interview looking back over his long career in professional education:

> ICT is now so ubiquitous that the idea of an 'information profession' is fast disappearing, as everyone discovers a need for information skills. That need will grow and coming generations will be better prepared to satisfy that need. The 'information professional' will

look, I suspect, a lot like the librarian of the immediate post-war period, but operating in an electronic environment – the organiser of resources, indexer of sites, 'reference librarian' and so on.[15]

Changing skills: information literacy

Some of this thinking has stimulated a re-definition of information literacy, as people grapple with the demands of the digital environment. An early definition of information literacy, albeit largely assuming a print-based environment, sets the scene:

> To be information literate, a person must be able to recognize when information is needed and have the ability to locate, evaluate and use effectively the needed information ... Ultimately, information literate people are those who have learned how to learn. They know how to learn because they know how knowledge is organized, how to find information and how to use information in such a way that others can learn from them. They are people prepared for lifelong learning, because they can always find the information needed for any task or decision at hand.[16]

A rather better definition comes from the American Library Association's Association of College and Research Libraries:

Information literacy is:

- a set of abilities requiring individuals to recognize when information is needed and have the ability to locate, evaluate and use effectively the needed information;
- increasingly important in the contemporary environment of rapid technological change and proliferating information resources;
- related to information technology skills, but has broader implications for the individual, the educational system and for society.

Information technology skills:

- enable an individual to use computers, software applications, databases and other technologies to achieve a wide variety of academic, work-related and personal goals.[17]

Judith Elkin

A report commissioned in 2000-01 by the Information Services National Training Organisation (isNTO) to ascertain the skills requirements of the information services workforce in the knowledge economy, echoes the need for a re-thinking of skills:

> Information experience and specialist skills aligned to organisational goals will undoubtedly be high in demand. The key skills required by the information workforce will include the ability to understand and identify with organisational business objectives, communication, team working and negotiation ... Knowledge and information literacy will be crucial to the success of all organisations ... information literacy must be recognised as a core organisational competence.[18]

Changing skills: summary

Within the contexts outlined above, information professionals should have a crucial role to play in the future development and implementation of the global information infrastructure. To participate fully, the information professional of the future will need:

- high level information-handling and information literacy skills;
- high level ICT skills;
- high level management and leadership skills;
- transferable skills, perhaps moving between sectors;
- to be good communicators;
- to be flexible and adaptable;
- to be innovative and imaginative;
- the ability to be proactive;
- the ability to help and educate others.

Sandra Ward, in a paper celebrating forty years of the Institute of Information Scientists[19] and comparing the skills required by information scientists in 1959 with those required in 1998, highlighted the following behaviours as critical today:

- self-belief;
- vision and creativity;
- opportunistic;
- confidence and willingness to take risks;

- focused service ethic;
- team playing and partnership;
- ambition.

In other words, traditional skills need enhancing by IT, management and leadership skills, allied to significant personal skills. High flyers in the profession may always have exhibited these skills; what is now needed is for such skills to be much more pervasive amongst professionals at all levels.

Are the skills available?

But are the skills available and are they really necessary? The Director of the British Library, predicting the team of professionals she needs to run a major national library[14], questions this:

> Our profession has the relevant skills to move from being reference librarians to information analysts and knowledge interpreters in a variety of contexts and again some of our best professionals are engaged in this work but not enough ... Those librarians who undertake these major tasks well are invaluable. Those who hide behind the professional guise but cling to process and procedures do not add value to any library or indeed to the profession. In as far as librarians do adapt their skills and approaches there will be significant roles for them in the future digital world.

and goes on to add:

> Arguably, I need excellent librarians together with Web designers, lawyers, rights managers, technologists, leading computer scientists; people with publishing experience, pedagogic experts, project managers ... I need people, including librarians, with higher level skills and specialisms, and who are individuals willing to take risks, work in teams, be entrepreneurial, outgoing, manage projects, work quickly and approximately, and live in the messy world of the digital, where structured processes and procedures are often irrelevant. I see these skills sometimes in the best of my IT colleagues, although I have to concede that both the IT and library professions contain large numbers of individuals who do not fit this description.

Echoing the concern about the quality of the workforce, a recent public library workforce research report[20] asks how we find the leaders of tomorrow:

Judith Elkin

... a time bomb is slowly ticking away under public libraries ... For the first time in nearly two decades, the public library service has been given the opportunity to position itself as a key component in the lives of people, to become 'the people's network' and an integral part of the information age. However, this research has indicated that there is some way to go before it has the staff and leadership that will help turn that rhetoric into reality.

Professional accreditation and quality assurance

This is potentially very serious for the future of the profession. Where do the professional bodies fit into the above scenario, in terms of workforce planning and development? Certainly, through rigorous course accreditation, paralleled with formal quality assurance. But is this too narrow a responsibility for the future direction of the profession and too inflexible to respond rapidly to both the changing environment and societal needs?

Professional courses in the United Kingdom are currently offered by 16 university schools and departments of library and information science. Courses vary considerably; some are largely postgraduate; others have a mixture of undergraduate, postgraduate and research students. There are also numerous courses on information systems, information management, knowledge management, business information technology, etc which cover in more depth the technology but, on the whole, still miss out on the people skills, social awareness and in-depth information handling and user concerns.

The majority of the mainstream courses seek accreditation from the professional body representing both the Library Association and the Institute of Information Scientists (unified and formally designated as CILIP: the Chartered Institute of Library and Information Professionals from April 2002). In assessing courses for accreditation, the professional bodies are primarily concerned with 'relevance to current and developing practice in librarianship and information science,' ie 'the principles and management of the production, organisation, analysis and provision of information and information services; the study of information from its generation to its exploitation, and its transmission in a variety of forms through a variety of channels.'[21]

The course accreditation checklist does not 'stipulate the precise requirements for course content' but expects courses submitted for accreditation to 'provide students with appropriate knowledge and skills to enable them to enter the profession'. Currently, course content is divided into five main categories: Information Generation; Communication and Utilisation; Information Management and Organisational Context; Information Systems and Information and Communication Technologies;

Information Environment and Policy; Management and Transferable Skills. The criteria and ensuing course content are 'modified from time to time to reflect the professional bodies' appreciation of changes of emphasis or the widening scope of the subject'.

In addition, all university academic departments in the UK are subject to quality assurance subject reviews by the Quality Assurance Agency (QAA). The recently published QAA subject benchmark statement for librarianship and information management[22] defines the discipline as follows:

> Librarianship and Information Management encompasses the study of information, from its generation to its exploitation, so as to enable the recording, accumulation, storage, organisation, retrieval and transmission of information, ideas and works of imagination. Historically identified with the organisation of recorded knowledge, articulated through the medium of librarianship, information science, archives administration and records management, the subject area has expanded to cover the theory and practice of librarianship and information management in a broad range of environments. A process of continuous evolution has brought the discipline into proximity with other cognate subject areas such as knowledge management, publishing and communications.

It identifies general transferable skills as:

- knowledge acquisition and understanding;
- autonomy and ability to learn;
- management skills;
- communication skills;
- information and communications technology.

What appears to be missing here is the concentration (and importance) of people skills mentioned earlier.

Continuing professional education

Within this quality assurance framework, the 'library schools' are turning out highly educated, computer literate, people-orientated, highly employable individuals, the majority of whom get employment very quickly in a wide variety of information, research, business and media environments. However, the very diversity of demands on higher education, and the broadening

Judith Elkin

markets into which information students move, mean that initial professional education is broad-based and cross-sectoral. It cannot easily cater for the needs of specific markets. Much of the specific needs of particular employers must be done through post-qualification training and development. Initial professional education is only a starting point, with all professionals needing to continue to develop their personal, social and professional skills throughout their lives.

But how is this catered for? Badly, I suspect. There is still a yawning gap in post-experience training. The professional bodies and other training providers offer impressive menus of one-off, one-day, non-accredited training programmes and most of the special interest sub-groups of the professional bodies run annual conferences, or workshops, or seminars. But there is very little beyond that. There is very little sustained, developmental continuing professional development (CPD) and there is no requirement for such from the professional bodies. These are areas ripe for development by the new professional body, CILIP, but, I would suggest, working much more closely and constructively than to date with the academic departments and training providers. Compulsory continuing professional education and re-accreditation throughout life should be the natural (and timely) concomitant of this: another challenge for CILIP!

Summary

The framework and the political climate have changed in the last five years. The emerging information and communication technologies are the new literacy and the successful communities of tomorrow will be those who, given access, are informed and educated in the use of these technologies. The emerging information and learning society will depend on a skilled and literate workforce. There is a need to equip people with information-handling skills that will make them more effective as citizens and more productive as individuals. Librarians have a range of traditional and newly emerging skills which are appropriate in both the traditional and the new, electronic and networked environment. Information professionals are at the gateway of this new society, as mediators, interpreters, guides, navigators, intermediaries and educators to more diverse media, technologies and resources.

Will the library-information profession grasp these opportunities, or let other professionals pave the way for a future managed information environment? I am confident that Robert Craig would wish for the former; he has striven throughout his working life to ensure a strong, active and changing profession.

References

1. Central Office of Information. *Our information age: the government's vision.* Central Office of Information, 1998
   http://www-0.number.10.gov.uk

2. Department for Education and Employment. *The learning age; a renaissance for a new Britain.* The Stationery Office, 1998

3. Library and Information Commission. *2020 Vision.* Library and Information Commission, 1996

4. Library and Information Commission. *Libraries: the lifeforce for learning.* Library and Information Commission, 1997

5. Higher Education Funding Council England. *Supporting expansion: a report on human resource management in academic libraries, for the Joint Funding Councils' Libraries Review Group.* (Fielden Report). HEFCE, 1993

6. Association of University Teachers. *Building the academic team.* AUT, 2001 http://www.aut.org.uk

7. Library and Information Commission. *New Library: the People's Network.* Library and Information Commission, 1997

8. Library and Information Commission. *Building the New Library network: a report to government.* Library and Information Commission, 1998

9. Quoted in *Library Association Record*, *103*, 9, September 2001, p534

10. Reuters Business Information. *Dying for information: an investigation into the effects of information overload in the UK and worldwide.* Reuters, 1996

11. Reuters Business Information. *Glued to the screen: an investigation into information addiction worldwide.* Reuters, 1997

12. Reuters Business Information. *Out of the abyss: surviving the information age.* Reuters, 1998

13. TFPL. *Skills for knowledge management: building a knowledge economy.* Library and Information Commission, 1999

14. Brindley, L. What use are librarians (working in libraries)? *Relay: the journal of the University College and Research Group*, 51, 2001, p5-6

15. Wilson, T. D., quoted in Hyams, E. As much fun as possible. *Library Association Record*, *103*, 7, July 2001, p427-428

16. American Library Association. *American Library Association Presidential Committee on Information Literacy. Final report.* American Library Association, 1989
    http://www.ala.org/acrl/nili/ilit1st.html

Judith Elkin

17. Association of College and Research Libraries. *Information literacy competency standards for higher education.* American Library Association, nd http://www.ala.org/acrl/ilintro.html

18. TFPL/ isNTO. *Developing skills for the information services workforce in the knowledge economy.* TFPL, 2001

19. Ward, S. *Forty years of the IIS: presidential paper given at IIS AGM,* September 1998.

20. Usherwood, R. *and* Proctor, R. *Recruit, retain & lead: the public library workforce study.* Department of Information Science, University of Sheffield, 2001

21. Library Association *and* Institute of Information Scientists. *Joint accreditation instrument: procedures for the accreditation of courses.* The Association and the Institute, 1999

22. Quality Assurance Agency for Higher Education. *Librarianship and information management: QAA subject benchmarks.* QAA, 2000

Part Four

POLICY, ADVOCACY AND PROFESSIONAL BODIES

Robert Craig has radically overhauled and extended the professional advisory structure for libraries in Scotland and has created mechanisms that support librarians throughout Scotland, in all sectors. Believing that professional bodies have a responsibility for advocacy, he has enhanced both the capacity of the Scottish Library Association (SLA) - now CILIPS, the Chartered Institute of Library and Information Professionals in Scotland - and the Scottish Library and Information Council (SLIC) to pursue that role and their credibility in performing it.

He has been both the ardent, effective advocate and the honest broker. Formulating ideas and policies; making these attractive to the people who may influence the future of libraries; convincing these people of libraries' potential; and then harnessing their support in libraries' service. In doing so, he has won for libraries a position of trust and influence with policy makers and decision takers.

Therefore, this section examines the role of professional bodies in the formulation and promotion of policy and development plans. It deals with policy promotion and emphasises the need for practical achievements. It addresses the domestic and the international context, analysing the work of the SLA, SLIC and the Library Association (now, of course, the Chartered Institute of Library and Information Professionals), as well as that of the International Federation of Library Associations and Institutions.

9

A wider role for professional bodies

George Cunningham

The development of professional bodies in Britain has taken a different route from that in most other countries. A lot of that difference is attributable, I suggest, to the strongly entrenched tradition of voluntary activity in this country. We have, of course, exported some of that habit to other countries of the Commonwealth especially to those, like Canada, Australia and New Zealand, whose governmental institutions were established when 'voluntaryism' was at its height 100 years ago. Even so, surprise is still expressed by visitors from those countries when, for example, they find that a great part of our judicial business is initially handled by voluntary lay magistrates who are not lawyers and are not paid a penny for their work. Our professional bodies grew up in and grew out of that tradition, with first steps taken without governmental input or recognition and some degree of oversight by the state following only afterwards.

Within this pattern, there has been, over the last century, a considerable similarity in the development of professional bodies. They have tended to start as purely private institutions formed by people who felt a need to exchange knowledge with colleagues in the same field. They have then moved on to provide training for aspirants to the profession and the award of certificates of qualification which gradually came to be recognised and later sometimes insisted upon by employers. Official recognition was conferred at some point along the route in the form of chartered status. There are now hosts of professional bodies which share this history of development.

A further shift has taken place over the last 50 years as the academic institutions, universities and, until recently, polytechnics, took over from the professional bodies the provision of basic education in the various disciplines, leaving the professional bodies to concentrate on the award of the professional or vocational qualification afterwards. Professions which were at first filled by non-graduates have become graduate entry professions, as is illustrated by the library and information profession, nursing and many others.

George Cunningham

As these developments took place, there was often more than one body seeking to represent a particular profession and there were other situations where bodies overlapped in their coverage. The outcome, as it exists today, is a vast number of different professional bodies, varying in status and in the extent of their activity, in their staffing and in their wealth. The accountants have their Institutes of Chartered Accountants (separate for England and Scotland), the Chartered Institute of Management Accountants, the Association of Chartered Certified Accountants and the Chartered Institute of Public Finance and Accountancy. For decades the library profession had the Library Association (LA) and its two estranged daughters, Aslib (originally the Association of Special Libraries and Information Bureaux) and the Institute of Information Scientists, the last two claiming to represent interests which they thought were inadequately covered by the LA. Despite repeated efforts in the accountancy field, there has been no success in amalgamating the different bodies, one at least feeling that its members face more strenuous tests than the others. As Julius Nyerere said about Britain's efforts to form a Federation of East Africa: once each state has its separate identity, its flag, its anthem and its airline, it is almost impossible to get its leaders to sink that identity into a wider union. All the more reason to welcome the success of the Library Association and the Institute of Information Scientists in succeeding, not at the first attempt, in uniting to create the new Chartered Institute of Library and Information Professionals. It is an unfortunate fact of life that the names of unified bodies are longer and less elegant than those they replace.

Although government normally prefers to keep its distance from the doings of professional bodies, there is strong evidence that it is not only willing, but increasingly keen, to intervene in some sectors. The House of Lords Select Committee on Science and Technology produced a major report in November 2000 on *Complementary and alternative medicine*, urging that steps should be taken to bring together professional and quasi-professional bodies active in fields stretching from osteopathy through traditional Chinese medicine to kinesiology. The report was warmly welcomed by government and measures are in hand to induce such bodies to come together and get them to adopt codes of conduct and to regulate training and practice. Similar pressure is being applied in other sectors with the formation of sector 'lead bodies'.

The scores of organisations operating in this forest undertake advocacy in the political field to widely varying degrees. Those like the Magistrates Association or General Medical Council are long accustomed to making representations to government in order to influence legislation and administrative action. Others have been more reluctant to get into that business. Indeed, some have entertained doubts as to whether it is proper for them to do so. In 1984 the Library Association was bogged down in an internal dispute on just this point. Some argued that for the LA to start lobbying politicians would put its Royal Charter in jeopardy; this despite the fact that even the original Charter of 1898 specifically authorised the Association to 'watch any legislation affecting public libraries, and to assist in the promotion of such further legislation as may be considered necessary for the regulation and management or extension of public libraries'. Further fears arose from the fact that the LA, unusually among professional bodies, was a registered charity. That too, it was thought, might be put in jeopardy by political lobbying. I think my first useful work as Chief Executive of the Association was to allay those fears. I warned the Association that it, and all its constituent branches and special interest groups, must stay right away from the ballot box. We could stoutly condemn actions and inactions by central or local government but must never, ever go on to advise people how to vote in the light of these views. The Charter gave us a firm base for taking to do with parliamentary activities and, as for charitable status, the charity commissioners had often indicated that they would only be aroused if an organisation made political lobbying something more than a marginal and ancillary part of its activities. On that understanding, the Association has robustly pressed its views in the UK and Scottish administrations and legislatures and, of course, in the European Union, whose activities are increasingly impinging on the affairs of the profession.

The business of political lobbying is not an easy one. A large number of profit-making companies – well over 50 of them in London alone – now exist, making a great deal of money out of helping to get their clients what they want. It has to be said that not all of these firms are better informed and more skilful than their clients when it comes to walking the corridors of Whitehall or the Palace of Westminster.

Along with the burgeoning of these lobbying firms, there has been a huge increase in the number of people retained in-house by professional bodies, either to do the job of lobbying themselves, or to be the link between policy staff in the professional bodies and an outside firm of lobbyists.

Until the 'sleaze' scandals of the eighties and early nineties, it was common practice for professional bodies as well as commercial firms to retain one or more Members of Parliament to speak for them in the House and with government ministries. Not infrequently, these 'spokesmen', or 'parliamentary advisers' as they were sometimes called, were paid a fee for their trouble. In that period there were Members who seemed to be more interested in earning a fat fee for this kind of service than in representing their constituents, as they were more modestly paid to do. But the practice of paying a fee to MPs has fallen victim to the sleaze exposures and few professional bodies now do so. It is the view of this former MP that no professional body with a good case should need to pay a Member for such help. They may well have to pay a lobbying firm if they do not have in-

George Cunningham

house staff with appropriate knowledge and experience, but they would do better to steer completely clear of paying Members or Peers.

A major problem for all those seeking to affect legislation or government action is knowing early enough what is being proposed. The British government is notoriously secretive. Very well-established bodies like the Law Society, representing solicitors, or the General Medical Council, representing the medical profession, might be on an inside track, consulted by government at an early stage. But most professional bodies will first hear about a proposal when it is already at an advanced stage, in the case of legislation, when it is drafted and ready for presentation to Parliament. This secretive tradition is now breaking up. It is now not uncommon for Parliament and outside bodies to see proposed legislation in draft form. This allows amendments to be suggested without government losing face by a defeat in committee and also allows changes which government itself acknowledges as improvements. To some extent, this greater openness derives not just from pressure in the House but from the habits of European Union institutions which, with all their faults, have always been more ready to put proposals out for consultation while minds are still open to persuasion. There is a real move afoot to give to the subject committees of the House of Commons an explicit responsibility for looking at draft legislation within their fields before a Bill is presented.

There are a few simple rules governing behaviour for professional bodies wishing to influence government and parliamentary action. First, ongoing contact with the relevant bits of government should be maintained so that distant early warning is obtained of things to come. Second, a realistic assessment should be made of the chances of success. It is an awful waste of time and therefore of money if you are putting yourself up against what is clearly a brick wall. Third, within the total field in play, identify those objectives that matter most to your organisation and concentrate your limited bargaining power on those objectives. These rules and the risks attending this sort of work can be illustrated by a series of cases that the Library Association in London and, in one case, the Scottish Library Association, have mounted over the last 20 years.

In 1984 the Chancellor of the Exchequer, Nigel Lawson, thought that a bit more revenue could be got by imposing VAT on books and perhaps newspapers. Till then it had been agreed that books and newspapers should not be taxed, partly because of the old battles about 'taxes on knowledge'. This proposal prompted a joint campaign by the Booksellers Association, the Publishers Association, the Library Association and the Society of Authors, with the newspaper organisations sympathetically in support. At a modest fee, a firm of lobbyists was engaged to prepare and send briefing materials to MPs and officials. At an early stage a choice presented itself which well illustrates the complications of lobbying. Advised by civil servants, some thought that we should keep a low profile and rely on well argued briefs presented to officials and ministers. 'Don't irritate the people you are trying to influence by a high profile public campaign', they said. But some of us knew better. We said that in this case, the only way to get our way was to get across to MPs that they would have a lot of their constituents against them if they agreed to the tax. We concentrated on Members of the governing Conservative party and on those in marginal seats. We created a stink, with the motto 'Don't tax reading'. The outcome was that Lawson finally declared that there would be no VAT on books, and he added that he had never intended that there should be. We knew better and we had won. One moral from that incident is that, where a number of bodies share a common interest, they should co-operate to improve their clout, and reduce their costs; and if that means co-operation between staid professional bodies and more pugnacious trade associations, all the better.

By contrast, a few years later, the Library Association and a number of different organisations co-operated in opposing the government's intention to take Britain out of UNESCO, the United Nations Educational, Scientific and Cultural Organisation. We had success in getting a Select Committee of the House on our side. Unfortunately, as we well knew, Mrs Thatcher, the Prime Minister, was minded to take Britain out. We therefore did not on this occasion go high profile. We kept low in the hope that the more sensible views of lower ministers would prevail without intervention by Number 10. Alas, Mrs Thatcher had her way. The case illustrates two things: that you must adapt your tactics to the situation; and that, however wise your moves, you cannot guarantee success.

Another example of semi-effective action is a case in which Robert Craig, in whose honour this collection of essays is published, played an active part. In 1994 the Conservative government put forward a Bill to change completely the pattern of local government in Scotland. Today, of course, this would be a matter for the Scottish Parliament, but in those days there was no such thing and it fell to the Westminster Parliament to consider the proposals. The Bill was naturally one that suited the Conservative government although the Conservatives held only eleven of the 72 seats in Scotland. The Bill would abolish the two-tier pattern of district authorities and nine regional authorities and introduce a single-tier pattern of unitary authorities. Since there were to be 32 mainland and island authorities, each was naturally much smaller than the old regions, a few smaller even than some former districts within the regions. There were mixed feelings about this plan in Scotland. The large regional authorities, especially Strathclyde, accounting for half the population of Scotland, had not been wholly popular with district authorities. However, the abolition of the regions presented major problems for those services which could be sensibly organised only on the basis of geographical units bigger than the proposed new unitary

George Cunningham

authorities. Amongst the services so affected were school library services. Education, which included school library services, had been a regional responsibility. Would each unitary authority be able and willing to maintain them? Would it make sense for the smallest of these authorities to do so?

The Scottish Library Association decided it must lobby the Standing Committee to get changes in the Bill on this point and, failing that, to get some assurances from government on the subject. As retired Chief Executive of the LA, living in London and with knowledge of MPs and parliamentary procedure, I was recruited to work in tandem with Robert Craig to this end. Of course there were plenty of opposition party Members of the Committee prepared to argue our case. But it is a cardinal error in these circumstances to think that the opposition Members, even all of them united, can get what you want. The governing party always has a majority of votes in these committees and concerted pressure from opposition Members may only unite them against you. We were therefore careful to enlist Conservative Members as well as opposition Members. Amendments were drafted and briefs were prepared; and we made sure that the briefs earned their title by being as short as possible – MPs do not appreciate being asked to read a ten page document. The outcome was an amendment supported by all four parties represented on the Standing Committee: Conservative, Labour, Liberal Democrat and Scottish National Party. We got a Conservative, Bill Walker, to move the amendment as proof that this was a genuinely all-party initiative. Tam Dalyell, Archy Kirkwood and Andrew Welsh spoke in support for the Labour, Liberal Democrat and Scottish National parties. Phil Gallie was another Conservative supporter. Robert Craig and I had already held a meeting with the minister, Lord James Douglas-Hamilton, and extracted from him, not acceptance of the amendment, but support for the purpose behind it. When the amendment came up for debate, Robert Craig and I, though sorry that there was insufficient will on the Conservative side to vote it into the Bill, were pleased that assurances were given that went beyond those we had had from Lord James. Unitary authorities were to be encouraged to pool their work on school library services and not to let them suffer as a result of the re-organisation.

We had other fish to fry in the Standing Committee: in support of the value of library services in providing information within the new structures and other matters. We secured assurances on these too. The Scottish Library Association was not the only outside body to lobby Parliament on this Bill but it was certainly the most active and competent, as was recognised by members of the Standing Committee.

These examples illustrate the part that professional bodies can play in support of the interests of their members and of the services in which they work. It is a natural and proper part of their activity. Indeed, they should feel an obligation to seek to influence the laws and structures within which they operate and to acquire the expertise to do so effectively, while recognising that failure or partial success is as common as outright victory.

There is another field in which some professional associations have experimented: the organising of consultancy services using the expertise of their members. Local authorities, companies and other organisations often feel the need for advice from professionals who have long experience of issues with which the client body may be unfamiliar. Such requests for consultancy services can come from organisations both in this country and abroad. Certainly there have been many opportunities for experienced members of the library and information profession to assist in this way the operators of services world-wide. Some American academic institutions have combined to solicit such work for their people, with greater success than similar institutions in the UK. This too is a perfectly proper activity for professional associations and one which can be remunerative for their members.

Professional bodies have come a long way since their 19th century beginnings. They are an established and essential part of our broader constitutional structure. Their role in promoting and improving professional standards is well known, but they can and should contribute even more to society, by participating in policy formulation within their fields of activity and by ensuring that the wealth of expertise within their membership is made available outside the ranks of their members' current employers.

George Cunningham

10

The SLA and SLIC:
change, achievement and opportunity

Gavin Drummond

Throughout its existence, the Scottish Library Association (SLA) has been an effective professional body in the inward looking sense, caring for its members' technical-professional interests. It can be argued, however, that it is only in the last 20 years that the SLA has shown real awareness of the need to look outward also, and to influence senior decision makers, both politicians and managers. The change from an introverted, discipline-focused body to its present status – recognised and respected for its active advisory and policy-making work – is a significant achievement and is due to a variety of circumstances and personalities.

Four significant events helped to change the status and the influence of the library profession in Scotland:

- the failure of the SLA's attempts to achieve library legislation for Scotland;
- the establishment of a working relationship between SLA and the Convention of Scottish Local Authorities (COSLA);
- the appointment of a full-time Executive Secretary to the SLA;
- the establishment of the Scottish Library and Information Council.

The legislation debacle

Following the passing of the 1964 Public Libraries Act for England, many Scottish librarians felt rather like second-class citizens. The public library system in Scotland had no such statutory backing and there was no body to advise about libraries in Scotland which had the standing of the Library Advisory Council for England, established by the 1964 Act. Over the years, there was much muttering and moaning about the situation and many in the profession felt that the appropriate thing to do was to try to get Scotland included in an amendment to the English legislation. Fortunately the SLA Council decided to avoid such subservience and, instead, sought to take account of Scotland's unique legislative position by having the Scottish public library service covered by a separate Scottish Act.

Negotiations for the necessary preparatory work to be funded were entered into with the Library Association and, thanks to the sterling work of Alan White, then the SLA's representative on the Library Association Council, agreement was reached. SLA Council was advised at its meeting in May 1980 that a parliamentary draftsman would be appointed to prepare a draft Bill which it was hoped (expected!) would eventually be presented to Parliament, if the government would find the necessary time for it in its legislative programme.

The draft Bill was prepared and SLA members sat back, assuming this would be a panacea for the ills of the public library service, at least. Considerable surprise resulted when it emerged that there was no political support for the draft Bill! This might have been expected by the politically astute but, at that time, the organised profession in Scotland had not acquired that quality. It is fair to say that it was assumed the draft Bill was good, that the government would happily enact the legislation and that local authorities, which would have to meet the additional costs, would also happily accept the additional burdens. How wrong we all were!

The then Honorary President of the SLA, Richard Buchanan, Labour MP for Glasgow Springburn, arranged for a delegation to meet the Secretary of State for Scotland to argue the case for the draft Bill, although he considered the chances of success to be slight. George Younger, the then Secretary of State, was absolutely charming and listened to the delegation with sympathetic interest. The subsequent reply from his Private Secretary put the matter in perspective!

- the Secretary of State welcomed the Association's presentation of the case for legislation;
- he considered that existing legislation was adequate for the protection and regulation of the library service;
- he did not consider that time could be found for the Bill in the government's legislative programme;
- he was not prepared to take on responsibility for oversight of the library service, as that would be contrary to government policy of leaving local authorities to run their services in the way they considered most appropriate.

(It is amazing how often that phrase is used, by governments of all hues!)

Gavin Drummond

The Convention of Scottish Local Authorities link

The draft Bill was going nowhere at that stage, so the SLA decided to try to get support from the Convention of Scottish Local Authorities. For some years, the Association had been trying to appoint an Officer Advisor to the Convention's Arts and Recreation Committee, which dealt with the local authority library service. It is fair to say that its approaches had been rejected, thanks largely to the opposition of another professional body – the Directors of Leisure and Recreation – who considered that they could speak for the library service. Eventually however, after a long process of lobbying, and the support of several councillors on the Committee, a Library Advisor was indeed appointed. As that Advisor, the present author attended his first meeting in March 1982, when the SLA's request for COSLA to support the draft Bill was submitted. Alan White was also called in to the meeting to present it on behalf of the Association. He was given a very rough ride by the Committee, whose members were incensed that a group of professionals had produced a draft Bill which they saw as merely strengthening the hand of the professionals against the Convention and its local authority members. In short, they were not having it, and the comment that was repeated was - 'Who do these people think they are – trying to tell us what to do?!'

It was a seminal learning experience for the library profession in Scotland. The SLA became aware that it could not work on its own; in promoting any area of librarianship, it had to work in co-operation with senior decision-makers – managers and politicians – if any improvement was to be made in the quality of services provided. So often, out of disaster comes triumph or, at least, progress. And while triumph would be too strong a word for what has happened since then, that low point ultimately had a very positive outcome, whereby COSLA became supportive and helpful towards the library profession and local government library services. The COSLA view was that, generally, local government did not want to be told by central government what it should or should not do. However, it subsequently agreed that it would find a set of public library standards helpful, so that individual local authorities could use them as benchmarks against which they could measure their own services.

This led to the first of many co-operative exercises involving professional library organisations and COSLA on library projects – the first set of public library standards[1]. These were produced by a working party chaired by Brian Wilson, Chief Executive of Inverness District Council (which was not a library authority, therefore impartial). In addition to librarians, the working party's membership included a Director of Finance and a Director of Education, so it could not be accused of purely professional input or bias. The same partnership approach was used when standards were produced for further education college libraries[2]; a college Principal chaired the working group, which had college lecturers and a member of Her Majesty's Inspectorate in membership, as well as librarians. The resultant documents produced some significant improvements to services in public and college libraries around Scotland.

Subsequently, COSLA-sponsored working groups with librarians, educationists and managers in membership have produced standards for the school library service[3] and have revised and up-dated the public library standards[4]. COSLA's influence may have waned somewhat since the establishment of the Scottish Parliament, but for almost 20 years it was a strong, effective supporter of the library service. The library profession has been fortunate to have had the input of such officials as Ian Murray, Bill Livingstone, David Ferguson (whose untimely death was a blow to libraries, as well as to his family, friends and colleagues) and David Henderson, all of whom have been positive in their guidance and advice. Through them, too, it has been possible to maintain effective contact with the equivalent English local authority bodies. This has been an important benefit, as it was often difficult to achieve any systematic approach to national co-ordination through the representative library bodies established from time to time by central government.

There is no doubt that the COSLA-SLA partnership was highly effective for the local authority sector of the library profession and, in its time, has produced better results than might have been achieved had a Scottish public libraries Act been enacted. The concern now is that, with the establishment of the Scottish Parliament and the consequent change in the balance of power between central and local government, the time may again have come when the lack of an Act of Parliament could be detrimental to local authority services. Publicly funded services will be subject to continuing reductions and those services which do not have strong backing in legislation are likely to suffer. Currently, local authorities are required to provide an 'adequate' library service, but who can interpret exactly what such a vague statement means? This may be a major challenge for the professional library organisations in Scotland to take up in the 21st century.

The appointment of a Scottish Executive Secretary

Perhaps the most significant development in allowing the library profession in Scotland to make its presence felt with decision-makers was the appointment of a full-time officer for the Scottish Library Association. For most of its existence, the Association had operated thanks to the efforts of its Honorary Officers, many of whom put in a vast number of late night hours to ensure its effective working. A first breakthrough was the appointment of a part-time clerical assistant to deal with the servicing of SLA Council and its committees; Mary Barr did a sterling job, working at

Gavin Drummond

home from her dining-room table. Despite this, the demands on the Honorary Officers grew to such an extent that the SLA decided to ask the Library Association to appoint a full-time officer in Scotland, one who would be sensitive to Scottish issues generally and to Scottish legislative and administrative structures in particular.

Once again, thanks to the determined efforts of Alan White, the SLA approach was successful and the Library Association agreed to appoint a full-time Executive Secretary. Alan was quoted in *SLA News*[5] as saying:

> The LA Council accepted that the pressure on the part-time re-
> sources of the SLA had reached a stage where it was becoming
> impossible to represent adequately the interests of members in
> Scotland and that ever-widening relationships with other bodies
> required to be developed on a more permanent basis. This is one very
> successful outcome in a long campaign by the SLA for extra re-
> sources for Scotland.

The well-sharpened pencil of the then editor of *SLA News*, Alan Taylor, wrote[6]:

> This journal has, in the past, and with good reason, criticised the
> actions of the Library Association but the decision to appoint a full-
> time officer for Scotland deserves our praise. This appointment ...
> marks ... a recognition ... that the different government, education
> and legal infrastructure north of the border required a unique ap-
> proach. ... There is a limit to what can be achieved by Honorary
> Officers, no matter how much they try.

So, in 1984, the post of Executive Secretary was advertised and in due course, at the SLA Council meeting held in Aberdeen in May of that year, the announcement was made that Robert Craig was to be the first holder of the post. Robert had been Honorary Secretary of SLA since 1982 and had been actively involved in the affairs of the Association for many years.

Few, if any, in Scotland will disagree with the statement that the appointment of Robert Craig marked a watershed in the affairs of librarianship in Scotland. For the first time, there was a respected senior representative who could knock on doors, who could go out to influence decision makers, who would ensure that appropriate consultations took place before decisions which might affect the library service were taken. Strong working relationships were created with the Scottish Office, COSLA, higher and further education bodies and, outwith libraries, with the Scottish Arts Council, the Scottish Community Education Council, the trades unions; in fact, with anyone who might influence or effect the improvement of library services. For some years, the Association was represented at the Scottish Trades Union Conference and the COSLA annual conference. Many of the links that were created resulted in councillors, trade unionists and other decision makers becoming more aware of the role of their library service, its potential contribution to their lives and those of their constituents, and its consequent need for resources. Perhaps more importantly, the library profession was able to discover what were the key issues affecting these bodies and it could focus on how best to support them.

While many SLA members contributed to this change of focus for the Association, it must be stressed that much of the success was due to the efforts of Robert Craig. He brought to the post clarity of vision, determination (some would say bloody-mindedness!) and contagious enthusiasm which helped establish and enhance the credibility of the profession among all decision makers – politicians, advisors and senior managers.

The Association was moving into a phase of its existence where the normal 'internal' activities of a professional association had to be carried out, but must be pursued alongside a rapidly developing representational, advisory and occasionally adversarial role.

This development can be seen clearly in the subtle change made to the content of the Association's annual conferences. In the 1980s and earlier, these were mainly concerned with internal library matters, topics which were relevant to the professional interests and work of many attending, but which had little influence on the decision-makers, or on the social, cultural and economic environment in which libraries operated. Librarians talked to and listened to other librarians. That position had to change and over the last decade or more, the SLA Conference has been addressed by a range of MPs, representatives from higher education, local authority councillors, senior academics, business people and others. In the process, librarians have learned from these 'outside speakers', but also, and equally importantly, these influential people have been exposed to the role, contribution and needs of the library service in all sectors. As an aside, the Association can claim that, in the last ten years, its Conference has been addressed by all of Scotland's first three First Ministers!

The Conference has also provided a point of contact with representatives from library services in other countries and over the years this had led to links being created with, amongst others, Scandinavia, the USA and France. The establishment of the SLA Executive Secretary (now SLA Director) post has allowed the Association to develop international links together with the Library Association, but also independently, as opportunity has arisen.

Gavin Drummond

The establishment of the Scottish Library and Information Council

The SLA's influence and effectiveness had improved enormously, but there was a strong feeling that it had to carry out a wider representative role in Scotland than did the Library Association in England, where it shared the lobbying and influencing role with the statutory Library and Information Services Council (England). In Scotland, there had been many efforts to have a similar body appointed by the Secretary of State, but each approach had been refused. The sop for Scotland was the formation of the Library and Information Services Committee (Scotland) (LISC(S)), which was established as a sub-committee of the Board of Trustees of the National Library of Scotland. It had no full-time staff, very little funding and, initially at least, no formal capacity to advise beyond the Board of Trustees itself.

The establishment of LISC(S) by the National Library of Scotland was a helpful move, but the fact that it was a sub-committee with only a small financial input from the Scottish Office meant that it depended on the input of staff from the National Library who were already heavily committed to other (and their principal) duties. It compared badly with the position of the equivalent English body, the Library and Information Services Council. This latter body was serviced by the government department responsible for library services and employed full-time library advisors to carry out its administrative and research work.

In its years of existence, 1982 to 1991, LISC(S) carried out its duties reasonably effectively, but it was seen by the profession as something of a lame duck in terms of promoting libraries to government. While it was eventually given status as the Secretary of State for Scotland's advisory body on libraries, this was not backed up with any positive, tangible support, as is recorded in the report of LISC(S)[7] for the period 1982-84, which states:

> The servicing of the Committee by the National Library has naturally placed considerable strains on the Library's hard pressed resources and attempts have been made to persuade Ministers to accord the Committee the status of the Councils [ie, in England] by providing independent secretarial and research support ... [the present financial allocation] is comparatively modest and is sufficient to cover only administrative costs.

Over a number of years there were many discussions about how this situation could be improved and it is to the credit of LISC(S) that it was itself a leading member of the group trying to find a solution, given that any solution would result in its own demise. Following protracted discussions between COSLA, the Scottish Education Department, LISC(S), the National Library of Scotland and the SLA, a plan was drawn up to establish a Scottish Library and Information Council (SLIC). This body was not to be a replica of the English Council but was to be a Scottish solution to a Scottish problem. Existing Scottish organisations, such as the Scottish Community Education Council, were used as role models. The organisation design involved a partnership between government, the professional bodies and representatives from local authorities and other organisations responsible for and/or maintaining library services.

So SLIC was born, as a partnership organisation, with funding from the Scottish Office and from its members – organisations which provided library services, be they local authorities, colleges, universities, health boards and trusts, or commercial companies. It was established as a company limited by guarantee, with a Management Committee drawn from its members and funding bodies, thus including the Scottish Office, the National Library, representatives from all the library sectors (not necessarily librarians) clearly and from COSLA. Its articles and memorandum of association listed its objects, which included:

- to act as a focus for library and information services in Scotland;
- to review, monitor, evaluate and update standards for all sectors;
- to report to and advise the Secretary of State for Scotland on library and information matters, and to make recommendations.

The establishment of SLIC was a major achievement. SLIC met most of the representational and advisory objectives discussed by the library profession over many years. It provided Scotland with a body which was essentially independent of government, but still had the role of advisor to government; this was seen as being crucial. SLIC was a body which brought all sectors of the library service together alongside decision makers and politicians. It now had to prove that it was worthy of retaining the support which all library sectors had promised at an extensive series of consultation meetings held around Scotland in the period leading up to SLIC's formal establishment.

A major problem SLIC faced in its gestation period was securing the appointment of a Director of standing who would be able to 'hit the ground running'. Part of the difficulty was SLIC's inability to forecast income securely for even one year ahead. Initially, a very high proportion of SLIC's income derived from members' subscriptions and these (overwhelmingly public sector) members were themselves unable to provide advance guarantees of ability (as distinct from willingness) to pay. SLIC's Management Committee, conscious of the body's limited company status, was

Gavin Drummond

understandably reluctant to make a permanent appointment which it might be unable to honour. After two abortive attempts to appoint a Director, discussions were held with the SLA about the practicality of Robert Craig acting as Director of SLIC on a consultancy basis, working about two days a week. Negotiations were protracted, as Robert was already heavily committed to the work of the SLA, but, as one of the bodies which had fought for the establishment of such a Council, the Association believed it should be supportive and agreed the arrangement, on a trial basis in the first instance.

That arrangement persists to this day. To say that it has worked is something of an understatement, as from its early days the Council has been supported by nearly all of Scotland's library services, in all sectors. Almost without exception, local authorities, universities and further education colleges enrolled in SLIC when it was established and have remained in membership.

The fact that the SLA and SLIC, the two principal bodies representing the library and information service in Scotland, have shared the same Director has ensured co-ordination and avoided duplication of effort. In the early days, when the two bodies had separate offices, the SLIC work depended greatly on the staff based in its Glasgow offices as first Keith Webster, then Joyce Wallace helped to establish SLIC and its role. Initially, there may have been some confusion as to the different roles of the two bodies, but it rapidly became clear that the SLA was the professional body representing, primarily, librarians as individuals, while SLIC with its corporate-based membership represented libraries and library services and the organisations operating them. In many ways, given the shared Director, what mattered most was that one of the bodies took lead responsibility for any specific project. So, in effect, a Scottish solution had established a system where there was a co-ordinated approach to issues of concern to all sectors. Over the years that this arrangement has been in force, there have been many joint SLA-SLIC projects. These have succeeded because they are not seen merely as an initiative of a special interest group (librarians), but as necessary and sensible developments, enjoying the support of councillors and staff in local authorities, academe, healthcare and other disciplines.

The standing of SLIC is such that it has been able to attract chairpersons of position and influence from outwith the library profession who have given considerable time and commitment to the work and development of the Council. The founding Chair was Peter Peacock, then Vice-Chair of Highland Regional Council, now a Deputy Minister in the Scottish Executive. Professor Alistair MacFarlane (now Sir Alistair), then Principal of Heriot-Watt University succeeded him; the current holder of the office is Rosemary McKenna, MP.

Throughout, the support of the Scottish Office and the Scottish Executive has been critical to the success and effectiveness of the Council. It has provided increased funding over the years in response to SLIC's level of activity and its record of performance, but more significantly, it has consistently used the Council as an advisory body, thus enhancing its reputation and influence. The Council has also been used by government to disburse library challenge funding. SLIC's success in managing that work has enhanced its status, while at the same time, approving projects which have delivered significant improvements to library services throughout Scotland. It is fair to say that SLIC is now seen as an established and credible representative for the library and information service in Scotland. It serves its membership, it advises government, it focuses on issues of concern, it represents Scottish interests to UK government bodies and internationally. In short, it provides the representational facility, supported by political awareness, that the library profession had been seeking throughout the 1980s and 1990s.

And the future

The library profession must ensure that it has a representative and advisory structure which can provide the necessary advocacy for a service which, in all sectors, is likely to face severe financial restraints at the same time as it is being asked to do more work to meet government initiatives and pressure of demand from library users.

At the time of writing (January 2002), the announcement has recently been made that the National Library of Scotland must close its Scottish Science Library, largely due to lack of funding. This can only be bad news, both for the people that library served and for the profession itself. As a result of the People's Network development, public libraries are being allocated money for training staff in information technology skills, for the creation of learning centres in libraries and for the digitisation of certain special materials. It can be argued that this development merely takes libraries back to their roots as the lifelong learning facility for all in the community, but it is being done without adequate consideration of the existing pressures on staff and the need to upgrade equipment at regular intervals. There is a view that this could create a millstone round the neck of library services unless proper provision is made for the future financing of such developments.

This is a huge dilemma that faces the profession and there will have to be a concerted effort at all levels to resolve what could become an intractable problem. *Scottish Libraries* interviewed Robert Craig about libraries' contribution to the People's Network and quoted him as saying[8], 'Libraries are now on the Government agenda ... This is an opportunity for public

Gavin Drummond

libraries to move forward'. But he warned that the profession will fail to rise to the challenge at its peril and stressed that, '… it's up to us to carry it through'.

If libraries are to remain the central focus of learning opportunities for everyone in the community, then their needs have to be appreciated by funding bodies, at all levels and in all sectors. At a time when there are stringent pressures on public funding, it has to be argued that there is a financial cost in maintaining developments, as well as instituting them. New services require some new and continuing funding.

Dean Rusk, former US Secretary of State, is quoted as saying, 'the pace of events is moving so fast that unless we can find some way of keeping our sights on tomorrow we cannot expect to be in touch with today'. That seems to be the challenge affecting the profession at this time. We have a respected and organised professional structure, with SLIC and the SLA representing the views of the profession at national level and the former, in particular, being used by government as an advisory body which can take the lead on specific initiatives. This is remarkably close to the situation that the profession was trying to achieve twenty and more years ago.

At that time, chief librarians generally had a status and an organisational standing which assisted them to promote the needs of their services to their ruling bodies, though it must be confessed that they did not always do so with success. Nevertheless, they were in a position where they had a voice. In public libraries at least, that position has changed greatly and in the new, streamlined, management-led structures that exist in local authorities today, chief librarians are usually placed well down the management hierarchy. Yet at the same time, the role of the library service is being moved to the centre, driven by central government policy, technology and society's thirst for information. The conflict between role and organisational position presents a major problem to the promotion of the needs of the library service. In spite of the development of the profession at national level, this conflict must ultimately be addressed by librarians at local level. While other professionals have accepted the need to become involved in the corporate departments and to participate and even take the lead in managerial development and manoeuvring, few public librarians have done so. In the university sector, however, there are some interesting examples to follow.

In such situations, Dean Rusk's words become particularly relevant. Librarians will have to develop their managerial and political (small 'p') abilities and become more effective in arguing the case for their services in their organisation. Only by doing so will they ensure that both in the present day and in years to come, libraries remain at the heart of lifelong learning and of information provision to communities and organisations.

Over the last twenty years the Scottish library profession has discovered how to work in partnership with users and decision makers in promoting the value and the role of the services it provides. At a time when 'social inclusion' is a keynote of government policy, there is an urgent need for the profession to build on that achievement and, in the 21st century, to develop further an advocacy role which will ensure that libraries remain at the heart of their communities.

References

1. Convention of Scottish Local Authorities. *Standards for the public library service in Scotland: report by a working party appointed by the Arts and Recreation Committee of the Convention of Scottish Local Authorities.* COSLA, 1986

2. Scottish Library and Information Council *and* the Scottish Library Association. *Libraries in Scottish further education colleges: standards for performance and resourcing.* SLIC, 1997

3. Convention of Scottish Local Authorities. *Standards for school library resource services in Scotland: a framework for developing services. Report by a task group appointed by the Education and Cultural Services Forum of COSLA.* COSLA, 1999

4. Convention of Scottish Local Authorities. *Standards for the public library service in Scotland: report by a working group appointed by the Arts and Recreation Committee of COSLA.* COSLA, 1995

5. Full-time Executive. *SLA News,* 179 (January-February 1984), p3

6. Editorial. *SLA News,* 180 (March-April 1984), p1

7. Library and Information Services Committee (Scotland). *Report 1982-1984.* LISC(S), 1985

8. Dawn of a new era. *Scottish Libraries, 11,* 6 (Issue 66, November-December 1997), p11

Gavin Drummond

11

The Library Association and the Scottish Library Association:
a professional partnership

Bob McKee

E very year the Library Association (LA) Council toasts 'the harmony and progress of the Library Association'. Yet, the history of the Association has been marked as much by dissonance and division as by harmony and progress.

E.A. Savage, Chief at Edinburgh and Scottish Library Association (SLA) President at the time of the union between the LA and the SLA puts it vividly: 'Whether other professions have a disjunctive urge I do not know but certainly librarianship favours tabernacular sectionalism, an absorbing passion for one's own creed, and almost a hatred of others' creeds'[1]. The 'disjunctive urge' was in-built from the start. Although the LA was founded as the 'Library Association of the United Kingdom' it is significant that *Notes and Queries* commented on the great impetus that the new Association would give to libraries and librarians in 'England'[2]. This dissonance – between a UK-wide body and an Anglo-centric approach – continues today.

By the time this essay is published, the Library Association and the Institute of Information Scientists (IIS) will have united to form the new Chartered Institute of Library and Information Professionals – a union caused, or rather, made necessary, by the 'disjunctive urge', which saw commercial librarians and then information scientists form their own societies in 1926 (Aslib, originally the Association of Special Libraries and Information Bureaux) and 1958 (the IIS).

But unification has not simply been a preoccupation of the Library Association in modern times; it has been a recurring theme. The story of the LA is one of recurrent tension between the 'disjunctive urge' and the desire for 'harmony and progress' in a unified profession.

From its foundation in 1877, the LA had three characteristics: a bias towards London; a focus on the concerns of chief librarians; and tension between the scholarly bibliographers who had dominated the early years and the increasing numbers of 'town librarians' who emerged as municipal authorities came to adopt public library legislation. The result was the creation of a number of bodies outwith the LA. The Bibliographical Society was founded in 1891; and in 1895 a Society of Public Librarians was formed. A separate Library Assistants' Association was formed in 1895, later (in 1922) to become the Association of Assistant Librarians.

Disjunction in terms of particular interests – of bibliographers, of public librarians, of assistant librarians, and later, of commercial librarians and of information scientists – was paralleled by geographic separation. The LA's monthly meetings were held in London and from provincial members there were 'jeering references to the LA being in the hands of its "London Branch"'[3]. In consequence, a number of independent provincial societies were formed.

There were some early discussions about a branch structure for the Association – but when A.W. Pollard wrote[4] of *The Library Association and its branches* in 1907 he wrote only of England. And when, in 1911, LA Council adopted a tentative scheme of branch districts, the proposals were, again, for regional branches covering only England[2]. It was around the time of the 1931 union between the LA and the SLA that branches were established in Northern Ireland and in Wales; and not until 1949 could the LA's *Annual report* state proudly: 'The Branch organisation … now covers, for the first time in our history, the whole of Great Britain and Northern Ireland'[5].

However, although a number of other societies and associations may have been formed as a result of the 'disjunctive urge,' this does not seem to have been the case with the Scottish Library Association, established in October 1908. Alan Marchbank, reviewing the coverage in the *Library Association Record* of the establishment of the SLA[6] notes that 'no comment is passed on why a Scottish Association had been formed' but he implies that the reason was to do with a wider educational movement in Scotland to give greater emphasis to the study of Scottish history. Certainly, the SLA has always promoted Scottish heritage and culture. Robert Craig, writing on the occasion of the SLA's 75th anniversary in 1983, notes the strong liaison between the SLA and a range of 'organisations important in the political, educational and cultural life of Scotland'[7]. There are recent examples of SLA involvement in Scottish cultural activities, such as the award winning partnership with the Scottish Arts Council to promote Scottish writers, and the current engagement of the SLA and the Scottish Library and Information Council (SLIC) with work being done by the Scottish Executive to develop a national cultural strategy for Scotland. Craig also records that 'in the early years the majority view within the Association was that "having regard to the national character of the SLA the interests of Scottish librarians and libraries would be best served by the retention of its separate identity"'[7], suggesting that a related factor in the establishment of the SLA was a strong sense of a separate national Scottish identity.

A sense of separate history, culture and identity may have been behind the formation of the SLA, but in the years between 1908 and the union

Bob McKee

between the SLA and the LA in 1931, the main professional concerns of the two Associations were identical; public library legislation and the education and training of librarians. However an important distinction can be made. When it came to professional education, the topics studied at the autumn and summer schools arranged by the SLA in Edinburgh and Glasgow were the same as those studied at the School of Librarianship founded at University College London in 1919, or those studied at the summer schools in Aberystwyth which were also arranged during this period. As Craig notes[7], 'professional education has always been a major concern' of the SLA and the context of that professional education has always been a UK-wide approach to curriculum, examinations and qualifications. The SLA Review Working Party of 1993-94 notes the general agreement 'that a UK wide qualification and educational structure was essential, for example to ensure that members could move freely between employers in the UK'[8].

But when it came to public library legislation, the aim of the LA and the SLA may have been the same – the betterment of public libraries – but the legislative context was different. The LA focus was on public library legislation in England and Wales; specifically on the Public Library Act of 1919, which removed the rate limit and authorised adoption of the Public Library Acts by County Councils. The SLA focus was on the legislative position in Scotland where the Public Libraries (Scotland) Act of 1920 retained a rate limit which was not removed until the further Act of 1955.

It has often been said that for much of its history the LA has been dominated by public library interests. Certainly the different legislative and administrative context of public libraries in Scotland has been a major factor in the recognition that professional matters in Scotland sometimes need separate attention. In modern times, work on standards, local government reorganisation and public library legislation have all been carried on separately in Scotland (by the SLA) and in England (by the LA). This has been particularly true since the appointment of a full time Executive Secretary of the SLA in 1984 and the ensuing engagement of the SLA with Scottish political life: the development of close working relations between the SLA and the Convention of Scottish Local Authorities (COSLA), leading to the publication of the first COSLA public library standards in 1986; the formation of the Scottish Library and Information Council (SLIC) in 1991 and the subsequent sharing of resources between SLIC and SLA; and the recent establishment of a strong relationship between SLA, SLIC and the newly formed Scottish Executive.

The original basis of the modern relationship between the LA and the SLA was laid during what can be described as the LA's first era of unification between 1926 and 1931. In January 1927, LA Council adopted the recommendations put forward by the Special Development Committee established in 1926, on a motion proposed by E.A. Savage, 'to consider the constitutional and administrative reforms necessary to extend and strengthen the influence of the LA'[9]. At the heart of these recommendations was unification. The year 1927 marked the LA's fiftieth anniversary and Savage wrote in the *Record*[10]: 'If we neglect to consider sectional interests, and if the branches, sections and district associations ignore general interests, we may remain disunited for another half century'.

The move to unification was also given impetus by the Carnegie United Kingdom Trust which wrote to the LA in December 1927, offering grant-in-aid and also additional funding dependent on the LA attracting new members. A number of conditions were attached to the offer, including 'that the Association undertake in due course to make a considered effort to induce other library groups and associations to come within a single unit'[11].

To facilitate unification and other changes recommended by the Special Development Committee, the LA Byelaws were revised at the AGM in September 1928; the revision came into force, following approval by the Privy Council, from January 1929. The move towards unification began at once. Independent provincial societies like the Birmingham and District and the North Midlands Association amalgamated with the LA. The Association of Assistant Librarians (AAL) united with the LA as the result of an agreement signed in 1929. And, in the words of LA historian W.A. Munford, 'the Scottish LA became a branch as from January 1931, in accordance with the terms of an agreement providing for its own special and national status'[2].

What exactly was agreed between the LA and the SLA – or indeed between the LA and the AAL – is open to debate. Michael Ramsden, reviewing the history of the AAL[12], notes that the original intention of the Special Development Committee was to achieve greater unity through a federal approach rather than by amalgamation of the various other groupings into the LA. The report of the Special Development Committee noted that 'a federal union of the Societies would not be difficult to arrange, and when arranged, would give us a stronger and more permanent organisation. The Societies can preserve their own constitution and regulations and control their own finances and business, while joining together to forward common interests'.

Whether union means federation or amalgamation is at the heart of Robert Craig's comment that 'the SLA's relationship with the LA has been, over the years, curiously ambivalent'[7]. Munford, writing from the LA perspective[2], is clear that in 1931 the SLA 'became a branch' of the LA – albeit one with an agreement reflecting its 'special and national status'. This reflects the statement in the LA's *Annual report* for 1930 which anticipates the union with 'there is every prospect of the Scottish Library Association becoming a Branch of The Library Association as from the 1st January 1931'[13].

Bob McKee

However Alan Marchbank, writing from the SLA viewpoint[6], is equally unequivocal as he outlines a potted chronology of the SLA's first ninety years: '1928: SLA turns down invitation to become a Branch of The Library Association but agrees to examine the possibility of closer affiliation with the LA ... 1931: Affiliation with The Library Association'. From the SLA perspective the union with the LA has always been 'affiliation' rather than amalgamation. The SLA *Report of the Council 1929-30* states: 'The Council have considered very carefully the invitation to this Association to become a branch of The Library Association and, having regard to the obvious value of a co-ordinated body representative of the entire library service of the Kingdom, and to the fact that under the proposed agreement of union the SLA would retain its national identity, they have concluded that the interests of both the Scottish library service and the Association would be best served by the closest possible affiliation with the LA'[14]. The 1931 Agreement itself states that 'the SLA shall continue to be known as the Scottish Library Association (in affiliation with The Library Association) or by any other name selected by its members, provided always that the title chosen shall indicate the connection and/or union with the LA'[14]. Hence, ultimately, the new name for the newly created organisation, supported overwhelmingly in the ballot of 2001, of the Chartered Institute of Library and Information Professionals in Scotland.

Perhaps the difference, as Ramsden says of the relationship between the LA and the AAL, is that between a *de jure* amalgamation and a *de facto* affiliation. Looked at legalistically from the LA perspective, the SLA is a branch of the UK-wide Association. But in fact, and seen from the SLA perspective, the SLA operates in affiliation with, but independently of, the LA in many of its activities: and, in particular, in its relations with the political and administrative structure surrounding the delivery of library services in Scotland.

The reality behind the ambiguity of the 1931 agreement with its 'connection and/or union' is that the SLA is neither independent of the LA nor a dependency of the LA: the success of the relationship between the two associations is in their interdependence. As devolution gathers pace this interdependence – which is, in practice, very like the federal approach suggested by the Special Development Committee of 1926-27 – may well become the model for the relationship between the LA and the associations in each of the Home Nations; and may, in time, also become the model for relations with the English regional branches as they develop a strategic role in relation to the emerging regional agenda.

This state of interdependence does not mean that relations between the LA and the SLA since the union of 1931 have always been harmonious. On occasions there has been friction – usually because a document or policy has emanated from the LA in London without, in the view of the SLA, taking due account of the situation in Scotland.

There was early warning of this possibility. In 1938, the LA published *A survey of libraries: reports on a survey made by the LA during 1936-1937*. The SLA objected to that part of the survey which included South West Scotland and at the LA's AGM in June 1939, a motion on behalf of the SLA was proposed and carried repudiating this section of the *Survey* and instructing LA Council to publish and issue to all subscribers a new report supplemented by re-inspection of the area. In the event no further action was taken: a larger conflict intervened and the matter was dropped. But the implication was clear: the union of 1931 meant that proper attention had to be paid to the Scottish dimension of UK professional life.

In similar vein, the Minto Report *Public library services in the North of Scotland: their present condition and future development* (1948) was produced in response to the McColvin report of 1942 because the SLA Council felt that McColvin's proposals were 'unworkable in Scotland.'[7].

Recent instances have been handled more quietly without becoming a matter of public dissent. Friction over the LA's *The primary school library: guidelines*, published in 2000, was resolved by an explanatory preface noting that primary schools in Scotland should use the *Guidelines* as useful background information but should refer primarily to the COSLA *Standards for school library resource services in Scotland* and associated documents. Discussion of this issue also led to the decision that all reports to LA Council and committees should consider, as a standing item, the implications of regionalism and devolution.

More recently a degree of concern expressed by the SLA about the report of the LA's Policy Advisory Group on Regionalism and Devolution, published in 2001, has led to the proposal to establish a Home Nations Forum to consider issues related to devolution. Political devolution accentuates the need for the LA to be sensitive to the separate contexts of the individual Home Nations when framing policy statements and promotional campaigns. There was, for example, some unease in Scotland about the LA's promotional campaign in 2000 to celebrate 150 years of public libraries, bearing in mind that the legislation of 1850 covered only England and Wales.

Devolution – and in earlier decades the prospect of devolution – has concentrated attention on the precise nature of the relationship between the SLA and the LA. The foundations for the SLA's ability to respond positively and successfully to the challenge of devolution were laid in the 1980s and 1990s in three important ways, two of which have already been mentioned. One was the appointment in 1984 of Robert Craig as the first full-time Executive Secretary of the SLA, giving the SLA the beginnings of its current staff and office infrastructure. Another was the close working relationship between the SLA and COSLA in the 1980s and with SLIC in the 1990s, leading to the present position where the SLA and SLIC share

Bob McKee

resources to mutual benefit. And the third factor was the review of the relationship between the SLA and the LA carried out in the mid 1990s. The report of the SLA Review Working Party in 1994 and the introduction to that report by the then Chair of SLA Council, Andrew Miller, are both written from the standpoint of an organisation which sees itself as affiliated to, but independent of, the LA. As Miller reports, writing of the February 1994 SLA Council meeting 'Avril Johnston (the SLA representative on LA Council) ... emphasised that the SLA was an affiliated organisation and not a national Branch of The Library Association'[15]. And the Working Party itself describes the SLA's constitutional position as that of 'an independent association which had affiliated with the LA in 1931'[8].

The Working Party was clear that 'Scotland's unique legal and constitutional position and our clear sense of national identity required special treatment'[8]. Reflecting the distinction already made in this essay, the Working Party recognised the separate statutory underpinning of library services in Scotland but also acknowledged the need for a UK-wide structure of professional education and qualifications. Commonality of purpose between the SLA and the LA was also underlined by the Mission Statement and Statement of Purpose for the SLA recommended by the Working Party which had been drawn up in tandem with the parallel statements being prepared at the time by the LA.

The objective of the Working Party was 'to strengthen and formalise the relationship between the two professional bodies'[15] and the recommendation, agreed by the SLA Council, was that the '1931 affiliation agreement' should be renegotiated with two clear aims: to achieve 'devolution to the SLA of all policy, financial and operational matters relating to the SLA and library and information services in Scotland'; and to get agreement that 'the SLA would be responsible for the delivery of the functions and services of The Library Association in Scotland'[8].

The resultant agreement, signed by the LA and the SLA in January 1995, can be described, in best negotiating parlance, as a 'win-win' agreement for both parties. The Council of the SLA is responsible for all policy, financial and operational matters relating to the internal affairs of the SLA; and for those professional issues solely affecting the operation, development and promotion of library and information services in Scotland. The SLA is also responsible for delivery of those functions and services which are agreed (by the LA and the SLA) to need a distinctive or separate Scottish approach. But there is also the necessary *caveat* that SLA activities are ultimately subject to the provisions of the LA's Charter and Byelaws, and to any requirements arising from the Association's charitable status.

In addition, the agreement recognises that an important role of the SLA is to fulfil the functions of a branch of the LA in Scotland; that those policies, functions and services which are agreed should be delivered on a

UK-wide basis (such as the maintenance of the professional register) will continue to be discharged by the LA; and that LA members in Scotland have the right of full participation in professional activities on a UK-wide basis.

Two other important points were agreed during the negotiations. One was that the LA would provide full funding for its office infrastructure in Scotland. The other was that there would be twice-yearly meetings between the LA and the SLA to discuss issues of common interest. The first such meeting took place on 4 July 1995 and this essayist wonders if the choice of Independence Day was mischievously deliberate.

This process of renegotiation was helpful in creating a clearer framework for the partnership between the LA and the SLA. But while a written agreement provides a valuable framework for partnership, what matters in practice is the day-to-day interpretation of the framework and the maintenance of open lines of communication between the partners. At the time of writing, the LA and the SLA are in close dialogue, not the least in working through the implications of unification with the IIS and in planning the IFLA Conference in Glasgow in August 2002. This close dialogue is formalised through the meeting every six months between senior officers from the LA and the SLA; a meeting which is minuted and reported to the Policy and Resources Committees of both bodies. By keeping lines of communication open and by regular documented meetings, misunderstandings can be avoided and areas of difference can be more clearly identified, understood, and, if needed, resolved at an early stage. Areas of joint working and common purpose can also be identified and celebrated.

Every institution needs to reinvent itself, through evolution or transformation, in order to remain relevant and valuable in a changing society. So it is not surprising that the relationship between the LA and the SLA has evolved over time through several phases: from independence, through the ambiguity of 'connection and/or union', to interdependence, the current framework agreement, and a *de facto* devolved federalism.

What emerges then, from this reflection on the history of the relationship between the LA and the SLA?

One clear point is that, in the library and information profession, history repeats itself. Robert Craig, writing of the first 75 years of the SLA, notes that 'the history of the SLA is the story of the library movement in Scotland and it is a salutary experience to realise that the concerns of the 1980s are not peculiar to this decade but have concerned libraries virtually from their inception'[7]. Similarly the story of the professional association is one of perennial concerns – with, for example, a clear commonality between the first unification era of 1926-31 and the current process of unification between the LA and the IIS. One of those perennial issues is the exact nature of the relationship between the LA and the SLA – linked to the view in Scotland

Bob McKee

that 'throughout the seventy-five years of its life there has existed in the SLA the belief that, despite denials to the contrary, the LA has never really understood the situation in Scotland'[7].

The framework agreement of 1995 has helped, as has the establishment of processes of formal dialogue between the LA and the SLA, but there are still vestiges of the 'connection and/or union' ambiguity evident in some attitudes and documents (for example in the text of the SLA review report taken to SLA Council in March 2001) and a further review of the framework may be necessary – probably within the context of the sort of federal union envisaged by the LA's Special Development Committee of 1926-27.

One other point to emerge is the separateness of Scotland, at least in so far as public libraries are concerned. There is surprisingly little movement of professionals across the Border between England and Scotland but also – and unfortunately in terms of the important benefits of professional networking – there is little connection between the public librarians of the two nations. Few Scottish librarians make the trip to Harrogate or Torquay for the annual PLA Conference; and very few English librarians travel to Peebles for the annual SLA Conference. Both groups are missing out on a rich source of professional contact. Similarly, the Heads of Service of Scottish public libraries have no formal link with the Society of Chief Librarians (SCL) which is currently active in England and Wales. The SCL is currently in discussion with the Heads of Service in Northern Ireland; and it is to be hoped that similar discussion with the Scottish Heads of Service will follow to create a federated SCL for the whole of the UK.

Scotland is different. The different legislative and administrative context of libraries in Scotland is now underpinned by political devolution and the likelihood that, over time, the policy context of library services in Scotland – and in each of the Home Nations – will diverge from the policy context in England.

Devolution can be seen as a symptom of the strong feeling of separate identity felt by each of the Home Nations, and librarians in Scotland have always – like the SLA – promoted the culture and heritage of Scotland. Indeed cultural and historical links tie Scotland much more closely with the other Celtic countries and – through the 'Auld Alliance' – with France, than with England. It is significant that when the SLA Conference was held outside Scotland for the first time, in 1968, it was held in Portrush in co-operation with the Northern Ireland Branch of the LA (now LA-Northern Ireland, or LA-NI) and the Library Association of Ireland. That 'Celtic connection' has since been strengthened by the first Celtic Conference held in Peebles in 1996 involving the SLA, the Welsh Library Association, LA-NI and the Library Association of Ireland. The second Celtic Conference was held in Killarney in 2001 and the next, continuing the five year cycle, will be held in Wales in 2006. The 'Auld Alliance' was reflected in the SLA's joint conference with the French Library Association in 1992 and in a strong French presence at a number of recent SLA annual conferences.

Culture, heritage, identity, politics and administration all make Scotland different – and that difference has to be respected and celebrated if the allegation that 'the LA has never really understood the situation in Scotland' is finally to be laid to rest. But the difference has to be respected and celebrated within a framework of interdependent partnership.

Effective partnership working is not easy. It requires five critical success factors: common objectives; mutual respect and trust; compatible cultures; clear outcomes; and a willingness to 'let go' of entrenched positions for mutual benefit and the common good. The history of the relationship between the LA and the SLA has shown all these elements; and suggests that the partnership will remain robust and effective in handling the twin challenges of professional unification and political devolution.

A great deal has changed since the foundation of the LA in 1877 and the establishment of the SLA in 1908. But the fundamentals – of mission, purpose, value and values – do not change. These remain the powerful ties of common professional interest and ethos which have bound the LA and the SLA together in productive partnership; and which will continue to unite our professional activities.

A framework of *de facto* federalism, a clear sense of shared objectives, and open dialogue between stakeholders gives the professional partnership between the LA and the SLA every chance of continuing to move forward in a spirit of 'harmony and progress' into a shared and interdependent future: as the Chartered Institute of Library and Information Professionals; and the Chartered Institute of Library and Information Professionals in Scotland.

Acknowledgement

Thanks are due to Caroline Nolan of the Library Association's staff, who assisted the author with research for this essay.

References

1. Savage, E.A. *A librarian's memories*. Grafton, 1952
2. Munford, W.A. *A history of the Library Association*. Library Association, 1976
3. Olle, James G. The Library Association and the American Library Association: their first fifty years. *Journal of librarianship*, 9, 4, October 1977, p247-260
4. Pollard, Alfred W. *The Library Association and its branches*. North Western Branch of the Library Association, 1907

Bob McKee

5. Library Association. *Annual report of the Council for the year ending December 31st 1949*. Library Association, 1949

6. Marchbank, Alan. Scottish Library Association celebrates 90 years of service. *Scottish Libraries*, *12*, 5, September/October 1998, p11-14

7. Craig, Robert. The pace of change: SLA 1908 – 1983. *Scottish Library Association News*, 177, September/October 1983, p7, 9-12

8. Scottish Library Association. Scottish Library Association review; report of the SLA Working Group. *Scottish Libraries*, *8*, 2 (Issue 44), March/April 1994, p10-14

9. Library Association. Council notes. *Library Association Record*, *4*, 9, September 1926, p156-158

10. Savage, E. A. The new bye-laws and why they are necessary. *Library Association Record*, *6*, 12, December 1928, p264-267

11. Library Association. *Annual report of the Council for the year ending June 30th 1928*. Library Association, 1928

12. Ramsden, Michael J. *A history of the AAL 1895-1945*. FLA thesis, 1971

13. Library Association. *Annual report of the Council for the year ending June 30th 1930*. Library Association, 1930

14. Scottish Library Association. *Report of the Council 1929-30*. Scottish Library Association, 1930

15. Miller, Andrew. Scottish Library Association review: introduction to the Working Party report. *Scottish Libraries*, *8*, 2 (Issue 44), March/April 1994, p9

1 2

Serving the Scottish Library Association's membership

Rhona Arthur

At the time of the foundation of the Scottish Library Association (SLA) in 1908 there were some 65 members[1]. F. T. Barrett and his fellow founders cannot have envisaged the range of services which would one day be provided for members in Scotland by two full-time officers. The number of professionals has grown dramatically to around 2,300 but has varied little since 1984 when Robert Craig became the Association's first full-time paid officer. In 1984 libraries were under pressure with continued erosion of local government expenditure, while cuts to bookfunds of 83% in the Western Isles and 23% in Argyll and Bute meant that levels of provision were being reduced, especially in rural areas. At the same time, the Scottish Library Association and the Library and Information Services Committee (Scotland) were investigating service provision in schools and there were increasing concerns about the number of professional posts and levels of pay. There had been a campaign by the Scottish Library Association over a number of years to persuade the Library Association to establish a full-time professional post in Scotland. It was envisaged that the establishment of a permanent office in Scotland would bring fresh impetus to the work of the Association, especially in encouraging wider participation by the membership. The Library Association accepted the unique role which the Scottish Library Association performs and it is thanks to a number of officers of the SLA, particularly Alan White, for their tenacity and foresight, that the SLA has been enabled to develop rapidly since 1984[2].

On his appointment in 1984, Robert Craig envisaged that his role would fall into four main areas: servicing the Council and Committees, promotion of library and information services to other organisations, promotion of the Association to the membership and acting as a link between the SLA and the Library Association[3]. The role of promoting the Association to its members remains crucial to this day, since without a strong and active membership its effectiveness will always be limited. It is interesting that, as in 1984, the Council of 2001 asked for improvements to be made to communications in order to strengthen the links between the Council and Committees and the grass-roots membership.

The other fundamental principle that Robert Craig addressed was the establishment of a number of successful partnerships with key Scottish agencies, which contributed to the development of the Association. He felt strongly that the SLA Council could not effect change in isolation from external factors and that success lay through strong partnerships. Whilst the Scottish Library Association was established to provide services to the library and information community for the specific benefit of the individual member, many of the impressive list of successful activities run since that time have been achieved with the support of local and national government, national agencies, the private sector and key individuals.

Advocacy

The appointment of a full-time officer had a dramatic impact on the advocacy role of the Association. Over previous years, Honorary Secretaries wrote letters of concern and lobbied as best they could but it was only with a full-time officer that significant progress began to be made. In response to the concerns raised in the Western Isles and Argyll and Bute, both the SLA and the Library Association made strong protests to the authorities involved and in the case of both authorities significant improvements were made to the bookfunds. The levels of expenditure in rural services were still low enough to cause concern and the development of the first public library standards, identifying realistic and achievable levels of public library service provision, was initiated. All of the standards documents which the Association has produced have been developed with a broad-based working group including key partners from the particular sector, whether directors of finance, head teachers, elected members or college principals. This has helped to create ownership and credibility in the sector the initiative is aimed at. This has proved successful and avoids the development of unrealistic and unattainable recommendations in reports. The Scottish Library Association's major achievements have been the development of COSLA public library standards, 1986[4] and 1995[5], COSLA school library standards, 1999[6] and *Libraries in Scottish further education colleges: standards for performance and resourcing*[7], 1997. Other important reports include *Lights in the darkness*[8], an adult literacy report, and *Libraries and the arts*[9].

However, two areas where the Association was particularly effective were its support for the establishment of the Scottish Library and Information Council in 1991 and its work during the Scottish local government reorganisation in 1996. The creation of the Scottish Library and Information Council (SLIC) was the result of hard work developing support for a library advisory body in Scotland. SLIC was created to enhance the work done for libraries by the Scottish Library Association and to take on areas where the professional body was unable to be effective. Whilst it might have been thought that there would be a conflict of interest, SLIC and the SLA have formed an excellent working relationship for the benefits of their respective members, due in no small part to the joint directorship held by Robert Craig since 1991. During the run-up to the reorganisation of Scottish local government in 1996, the Association lobbied hard, working with other national agencies and local authorities, to secure a place for public library services within a cultural services grouping in local authorities. Concerned about the long-term viability of leisure and recreation departments in an era which saw contracting-out as government policy and equally anxious about the ability to protect library budgets if libraries were submerged in education services with their focus on funding classroom teaching, the Association secured the services of George Cunningham, a former MP and former Chief Executive of the Library Association, to advise on lobbying. The lobbying was successful but, over time, the position has been eroded, partly due to the pressure on local government funding, which has largely driven the move towards flatter structures. Library services have suffered as they have slipped down the local government structure but the People's Network initiative has ensured that they are now a key part of the government's strategy in delivering lifelong learning, digital inclusion and modernising government. The good working relationship formed between the New Opportunities Fund, the People's Network Team at Resource and the Scottish Library and Information Council ensured that information was shared and communicated to members, providing them with the necessary support to implement the radical changes required by the People's Network.

School libraries have seen vast changes over the last 30 years. There have been two reorganisations of local government. In 1975 the establishment of the regional councils created strong central support services and school libraries developed rapidly within this climate. The Scottish Library Association and the Library and Information Services Committee (Scotland) published two reports in 1985, *The school library resource service*[10] and *The curriculum and library and information services and resources for school education in Scotland*[11], which looked at the current provision. The Association campaigned vigorously for improvements to services. Writing in the *Times Educational Supplement*[12], Robert Craig identified the problems of low status and pay, high turnover of staff, a lack of understanding of the role of the school librarian in supporting learning and teaching and inappropriate deployment of staff time. Following strike action in Strathclyde Region in 1985 the situation began to change. Over recent years, the case for school libraries has been the focus of Association campaigning, resulting in the COSLA school library standards, *Taking a closer look at the school library resource centre*[13], the Scottish Writers Project, a deputation to the

Rhona Arthur

Scottish Parliament's Education Committee, and two revisions to HMI guidelines for the inspection of school libraries.

Quite apart from the development of the public library standards, the Scottish Library Association also had an interest in developing high-quality book promotions to raise the profile of reading and libraries with the Scottish public. Early promotions included the publication of a special Large Print Scottish Writers Series with Magna and the successful Quest for a Kelpie Book Trust Scotland project. Good relationships had been built up with the Scottish Arts Council and these have made it possible to develop reading promotions such as Now Read On, Readiscovery and the Scottish Writers Project. The Now Read On book promotion campaigns were the brainchild of Robert Craig and Walter Cairns, the then Director of Literature at the Scottish Arts Council. The idea was simple – users needed to be led to reading more widely and libraries needed to use more effective promotional material to do this. Libraries were given lists of 48 titles in four themed collections and were asked to buy multiple copies to ensure that the public was not drawn in by attractive promotion only to find an insufficient supply of books. Books had to be in paperback format and displayed 'face-on'. The Scottish Arts Council provided the budget for all the promotional materials, the Albany Book Company provided free display stands to hold all the books and Book Trust Scotland handled the administration. A committee decided the themes and titles and that started a very successful series of reading promotions. 1995 was a particularly fruitful year for reading promotion with Readiscovery: Scotland National Book Campaign and some wonderful innovations including the Readiscovery Book Bus, Now Read On 5, the National Poetry Day postcards and a plethora of imaginative posters.

The largest single book promotion was the Scottish Writers Project which was a £520,000 project promoting Scottish books to 14-16 year olds through school and public libraries. Similar in approach to Now Read On, school libraries contributed a small partnership fee in exchange for multiple copies of the paperbacks for promotion purposes, dump-bins and lots of attractive posters. The promotion used new technology and included a CD-ROM and website with a virtual writer in residence. Pupils in Scotland's schools were asked to nominate the books they would like and nearly 500 separate nominations were received from which the final 36 were drawn. The CD-ROM was nominated for a BAFTA Award for Innovation in Learning, a category that also included works from the studios of Steven Spielberg and George Lucas. The evaluation report states that 'the Project amply justified the investment of a large sum of public money by delivering a high-quality integrated resource'. Both Now Read On and the Scottish Writers Project attracted considerable political and media attention and significantly raised the profile of libraries in Scotland.

Whilst school and public librarians make up a significant percentage of the membership, the Scottish Library Association has also addressed the interests of members in other sectors. The structure of the SLA Committees was altered in 1982 to bring together members working in the education field. The Libraries in Education Committee was established to identify and act on concerns of members working in schools and higher and further education. Links were made with the Scottish Higher Education Funding Council, the Joint Funding Council's Library Review Group (Follett Report), the Dearing Enquiry into the Future of Education and the Scottish Further Education Unit. The 1993 and 1997 FE college library standards emanated from this committee. Prison, health sector and special libraries have also been the focus of SLA and SLIC efforts, with the production of *Enabling access to the knowledge base of healthcare* in 1998, a review of prison library funding and provision, and a special libraries campaign in 1999. More recently, the SLA and SLIC have encouraged cross-sectoral working through the establishment of cross-sectoral committees and SLIC grant aid. Other organisations like Aslib, the Scottish Health Information Network (SHINE), the Institute of Information Scientists (IIS) and the Scottish Law Librarians have been invited to attend SLA committees and to establish closer links with the SLA.

Participative governance

The membership of the Association has always been involved in both the governance of the Association and in supporting its development with a huge contribution from voluntary office bearers. These volunteers sustained the Association through much of its early existence and that rich resource is still a feature of the organisation today. At the time of Robert Craig's appointment, Gavin Drummond voiced concerns in his presidential introduction to the *Annual report* of 1985[14] that once a paid officer was in post the volunteers would melt away. This danger has not materialised and the contribution made by the voluntary element adds quality, ownership and strength to the SLA.

The operation of the Association has been developed and refined over the years, but has reached a significant point with unification with the Institute of Information Scientists. The membership of the Association has been able to play a role in its governance through direct election to the Scottish Library Association Council, or as a full voting member representing the branches and special interest groups. Unification with the IIS to form the Chartered Institute of Library and Information Professionals in Scotland resulted in a review of the Scottish Library Association to ensure that current practices are open to and inclusive of the whole membership. Members are welcome to attend Council meetings as observers and to raise issues of concern through their branches.

Rhona Arthur

Although the branches fulfil an important role delivering courses and providing a networking forum for librarians at local level, the most significant function they can perform is contributing to the policy-making process. The network of branches was reviewed in 1986 with a view to revitalising them. However, despite strenuous efforts by the Association, it has not been possible to sustain the West Branch which covered the biggest geographical area but which was disbanded in 1991. Other branches have been under pressure at various times – Central, North East and Tayside. The pressure in the workplace is great and it is increasingly difficult for branches to get the support at the level they need to function effectively. The development of cross-sectoral groupings of libraries in the late 1990s has been seen as a competitor but this need not necessarily be the case. Whilst many *ad-hoc* groups can organise training, participate in co-operative planning and project applications, they cannot develop policies which can be fed through a well-funded and effective advocacy body. This is an area where there is considerable scope for development.

Links to the Library Association

The Library Association and the Scottish Library Association have a long and interesting relationship reaching back to 1907 when the idea of a Scottish Library Association was conceived at a Library Association conference in Glasgow. In 1931, it was agreed that it was in the best interests of the Scottish Library Association to affiliate with the Library Association and to develop the closest possible links for the greater good. Reviews of the relationship have taken place at regular intervals over the last 70 years. All of the negotiations worked towards improving services to members in Scotland. The discussions have often been heated with firm stances taken on both sides. In 1994, relations entered a new phase with an agreement for bi-annual summit meetings alternating between Scotland and England. These meetings have brought a greater depth of understanding about the role of each partner and have improved relations significantly.

Services to members: professional development

The Scottish Library Association has run an Annual Conference for many years. The Conference provides members with an annual opportunity to come together and discuss current issues and matters of common concern. The Conference is the main source of income for the Association and has a well-deserved reputation for being financially successful, professionally relevant and a highly enjoyable event. Robert Craig worked with each President in turn to develop the theme and build a programme, which would appeal to the core support, public librarians who have supported the

Conference throughout its long history. Whilst efforts were made to focus on specific groups, such as academic librarians, there was a delicate balance to be achieved and the fear was that radical change would alienate the traditional supporters. Over time the Conference's target audience became chief librarians and elected members and, although this was successful in securing local political support for libraries, there was a perception that the Conference was a somewhat elitist event. It became increasingly important to broaden the appeal of the Conference whilst avoiding marginalising this core support. Efforts were made to attract greater support from other sectors by including papers on sectoral issues, but met with a limited response.

The answer lay with the branches and groups of the Association. Working in partnership with the special interest groups strengthened the links with the 'grass-roots' of the profession, improved the scope of the programme and quite probably secured the continuing success of the Conference. The first Branch and Group Day was held in 1993. The branches of the SLA and the special interest groups were asked to identify and invite speakers to speak on the Conference theme, whilst the Scottish Library Association offered financial assistance, organisational support and the venue. As the Conference was held in Peebles, with no main line railway station, further assistance was given by providing free bus transport from seven pick-up points across Scotland. Members embraced the opportunity to play a fuller part in the Conference through attendance at the Branch and Group Day and numbers attending have increased year on year. The Branch and Group Day is now the host to the Presidential Address, giving each President an opportunity to address a wide range of members. Thereafter members pursue their own interests and specialisms through a three or four strand programme of parallel sessions.

The Conference is widely recognised for its excellent professional programme and its balance of contributions from politicians and external organisations who bring their own perspective to user needs and library priorities.

Much of the financial success of the Conference is due to the exhibition and the close links, which have been developed over the years with library suppliers. Library suppliers have shaped the Conference and play an important part in the programming and have contributed much to the enjoyment and camaraderie of the occasion over the years.

Although the Annual Conference provided an opportunity to keep abreast of current initiatives, the establishment of a sustainable training programme was important to the future of the profession in Scotland. Continuing professional development had been a key concern for the Association from the days of the Summer and Weekend Schools, which ceased in the 1980s. The issue of access to training courses for the profession had to be addressed at a more local level. The branches and special interest

Rhona Arthur

groups ran events and courses of interest to the membership, but barriers of high costs for rural services and communication limited their success. The Association had Honorary Education Officers and courses were planned and delivered by them. The SLA Council accepted a report in 1991, which acknowledged that more could be done to support continuing professional development in Scotland. A second full-time officer was appointed in 1992 to establish a fuller short-courses programme, co-ordinate the courses run by the branches and groups and to improve communication in this area. The courses run by the branches and groups are vital to the Association, providing a geographical spread of venues and specialist courses in Scotland. Information was collated and circulated to Heads of Service on a six-monthly basis and regular bulletins were sent to secretaries to avoid duplication or over-crowding particular dates. This worked well initially but the branches and groups found it difficult to plan sufficiently far in advance and the introduction of the SLAINTE (Scottish Libraries Across the INTErnet) website saw the demise of the system.

In the early 1990s, the SLA's own courses proved very popular and trainers could be brought to Scotland to run a range of high-quality courses and special courses were commissioned. However, following re-organisation in 1996, the financial constraints on local authority budgets began to bite and it has been more difficult since then to sustain a programme of this nature.

Other initiatives to offer librarians an opportunity to participate in professional events have included the Scottish Library and Cultural Resources Exhibition, run in 1996 and 1998, in partnership with Library Resources Ltd. The most ambitious of all is the plan to bring the International Federation of Library Associations and Institutions (IFLA) Conference home to Scotland in 2002 to celebrate the 75th anniversary of its foundation. IFLA was founded at a Library Association Conference in Edinburgh in 1927. The last IFLA Conference to be held in the United Kingdom was at Brighton in 1987 and it was around this time that planning began to bring IFLA to Scotland in 2002. The Library Association and Scottish Library Association gave their full support to efforts to secure the Conference and, although Glasgow rather than Edinburgh became the accepted venue, Scotland will again be host to the world's librarians in August 2002. Visits to the venue took place by the IFLA headquarters staff and budgets and project plans were developed. The first meeting of the IFLA 'Start Up' Committee took place in May 1998 and this developed into a National Organising Committee. The Scottish representation on the Committee was strong and the Scottish Library Association took responsibility for the local planning process and volunteers. The SLA has been a supporter of IFLA for a number of years and has built up contacts with librarians in a number of different countries and this has proved very helpful during the run-up to the Conference. The planning process has been long and complex but there are rich rewards, in professional and financial terms, to be gained from hosting the largest gathering of librarians in the United Kingdom.

Services to members: communications

The Association's journal has been the main vehicle of communication with the membership over the years. The first issue appeared as a *Scottish Library Association News Sheet* in October 1950. The SLA Council soon saw that this was an important means of informing members about the activities and events run by the Association and started to publish a bi-monthly journal - *SLA News* - in 1956. *SLA News* and its successor, *Scottish Libraries*, have appeared under the editorship of various honorary editors since that time. Looking back over the early issues it is clear that the journal has not moved far from its original concept – it has never been a scholarly academic journal but focuses on news, events, people and innovation in the profession. The journal has changed in its appearance moving to an A4 size in 1987 and to the use of colour. Following a Council decision, a professional Editor was appointed in 1992 and the journal operates at arm's length from the SLA staff. The journal has never made a significant contribution to the Association's finances but it is very important, as for many members it is their main point of contact with the Association. The time has come for the Association to review the journal once more as it unifies with the IIS. The journal must reflect the issues that concern the membership and content, whilst dependent on contributions from the profession, is already under the scrutiny of the readers. Technology has advanced rapidly in recent years and it is now possible to investigate other means of communication. These might include moving to an electronic journal, regular e-mailed bulletins of news and other communication aimed at sections of the membership.

SLAINTE, the jointly run website of the Scottish Library Association and the Scottish Library and Information Council, was established in 1995. It has gone through some fundamental changes since its inception. Originally the website was developed as a result of another successful partnership including the involvement of the then Scottish Office and Dynix, a major supplier of library management systems. The successor company to Dynix, epixtech, is still closely involved with the website and although the early website was developed along traditional lines, the use of Dynix's NetPublisher to present information was the first in a series of radical approaches. Gradually the extensive lists of information held on multiple HTML pages caused management problems with enormous implications for currency and accuracy. Further migration to a robust database allowed greater flexibility for searching and retrieval. SLAINTE meets a broad range of international standards and is widely recognised as a successful model.

Rhona Arthur

The website is already an enormous asset to the Association's communications strategy, with a news section, directory information, minutes, support for special projects like the People's Network and a well-developed range of Scottish literature links. The website has the potential to offer access to information about the activities of the branches and special interest groups and discussion forums for members. All of these developments will need to be addressed as the Association improves its service for the new millennium.

In reviewing the way in which the Scottish Library Association serves its membership there have been many challenges in creating a balance between providing appropriate services for members, securing sound funding for the Association to enable it to deliver its agenda, and raising the profile of libraries. The Association has been more successful in some areas than others. The Association has not always been good at communicating to the wider membership about the range and depth of its advocacy and, consequently, members sometimes see no relevance to their daily concerns. But it is clear that there have been some notable successes. The concentration on advocacy and building productive partnerships, at a time when libraries elsewhere in the United Kingdom were being savagely cut back, has been effective in raising the profile of libraries across the sectors and improving standards.

References

1. Aitken, W.R. *A history of the public library movement in Scotland to 1955*. Scottish Library Association, 1971, p230

2. Scottish Library Association. *Annual report of the Council 1984*. Scottish Library Association, 1985

3. Profile: Robert Craig. *SLA News*, 187 (1985), p21-22

4. Convention of Scottish Local Authorities. *Standards for the public library service in Scotland: report by a working party appointed by the Arts and Recreation Committee of the Convention of Scottish Local Authorities*. COSLA, 1986

5. Convention of Scottish Local Authorities. *Standards for the public library service in Scotland: report by a working group appointed by the Arts and Recreation Committee of COSLA*. COSLA, 1995

6. Convention of Scottish Local Authorities. *Standards for school library resource services in Scotland: a framework for developing services. Report by a task group appointed by the Education and Cultural Services Forum of COSLA*. COSLA, 1999

7. Scottish Library and Information Council *and* the Scottish Library Association. *Libraries in Scottish further education colleges: standards for performance and resourcing.* SLIC, 1997

8. Craig, Robert *and* Gerver, Elisabeth, *eds. Lights in the darkness: Scottish libraries and adult education.* Scottish Institute of Adult Education, 1985

9. Scottish Library and Information Council *and* the Scottish Library Association. *Libraries and the arts: report of a working group.* Scottish Library Association, 1992

10. Scottish Library Association. *The school library resource service and the curriculum 'before five' to 'sixteen plus'.* Scottish Library Association, 1985

11. Library and Information Services Committee (Scotland). *Library services and resources for schools education in Scotland: report of a working party on current provision.* National Library of Scotland, 1985

12. Craig, Robert. The crisis facing Strathclyde. *The Times Educational Supplement (Scotland)*, 14 November 1986, p5

13. Scottish Office. *Taking a closer look at the school library resource centre: self-evaluation using performance indicators.* Scottish Consultative Council on the Curriculum, Scottish Library and Information Council, Scottish Library Association and HMI Audit Unit, 1999

14. Scottish Library Association. *Annual report of the Council 1985.* Scottish Library Association, 1986

Rhona Arthur

1 3

International liaison, advocacy and policy transfer

Ross Shimmon

Libraries are inherently international – or cross-national – in outlook. There must be very few libraries which do not include materials originating outside of the country in which they are based. Donald J. Urquhart, long-time critic of professional librarians and their professional practices, made the point more succinctly than most[1]:

> Libraries are concerned with collecting and making available the records of mankind. They are concerned with all types of records irrespective of how or where they are produced. They are concerned with all the techniques for promoting the use of their records. Inevitably librarians should have a world outlook on their problems for they are really the servants of mankind. To librarians national boundaries are handicaps to be overcome so they should be organised on a world basis.

True to his iconoclastic reputation, Urquhart went on to dismiss contemporary international organisations, such as the International Federation of Library Associations and Institutions (IFLA), the International Federation for Documentation (FID) and the International Council on Archives (ICA) as inadequate, proposing instead a single world-wide organisation, but without national representation. He argued that, because libraries dealt with information materials irrespective of country of origin, they did not need a world-wide organisation modelled on existing international political and economic institutions. The evolution of international organisations in the library and information field, despite his stricture, continues to mirror that of international organisations generally. They have tended to be federations of representatives of national organisations or of governments.

Before IFLA

The decision to establish what is now the only world-wide body representing the general interests of library and information services, the International Federation of Library Associations and Institutions, was taken during the 50th anniversary conference of the (British) Library Association, held in Edinburgh in 1927. There were, however, many earlier attempts to establish international liaison on a formal basis within the profession. Probably the first recorded international conference of librarians was held in New York in 1853, attended by 82 participants (all of whom were men, incidentally). Although sponsored by American librarians and publishers, papers were read by librarians from other countries, dealing with topics with an international flavour. For example, Alexandre Vattemare of France proposed the organisation of an international exchange of official publications issued in the countries of Europe and America. Another French speaker described the classification scheme used by the Bibliothèque nationale de France. The conference established a commission to prepare statutes for a librarians' union and for another conference, but nothing appears to have happened for another 23 years[2].

In 1876, the year of the centenary of American independence, a second conference of librarians was held, this time in Philadelphia. 103 people attended, including a delegation from Britain and several overseas guests. It was at this conference that the American Library Association (ALA), generally regarded as the first such professional body in the world, was established. J.W. Wallace, chairing the conference, said in his opening address[3] that he hoped the 1876 conference would be the first in a series of conferences of librarians from all parts of the world. The conference agreed that an international congress of librarians be held in the following year, 1877. A proposal from the British delegates to hold the conference in London was accepted. Also in 1876, the *American Library Journal* (now entitled *Library Journal*) was first published. In the first volume, Melvil Dewey wrote[4]:

> Through all the coming time 1876 will be looked upon as the most eventful year in the history of libraries – the year in which the librarian fairly claimed and received at the hands of the public his place among the recognised professions. Something of this feeling has spread not through this country alone, but in nearly all countries a new interest and activity in library matters is noted.

The first International Conference of Librarians with that name was held in London in 1877. It was attended by 219 delegates from nine countries:

Ross Shimmon

Austria, Belgium, Britain, Denmark, France, Germany, Greece, Italy and the USA. In his opening speech, the president of the conference, Professor Winter Jones, curator of the Library of the British Museum, stressed the international aspects of librarianship. Out of that conference came the decision to set up the Library Association of the United Kingdom, as it was originally called. Among the overseas speakers was Melvil Dewey who, for the first time in an international context, spoke about the decimal classification scheme he had developed.

Further international conferences of librarians were held in 1893 (Chicago), 1897 (London), 1898 (St Gallen, Switzerland), 1900 (Paris), 1904 (St Louis, USA), 1908 (Berlin), 1910 (Brussels), 1923 (Paris) and 1926 (Prague). Attendance rose from 305 in 1893, to 700 in 1923. Although delegates at these conferences were predominantly from European countries and the USA, representatives of Bolivia, Brazil, Ceylon, Costa Rica, Cuba, the Philippines and Venezuela attended some of the later conferences. Topics discussed included: the need for library legislation; how to set up library associations in countries where they did not yet exist; the international exchange of duplicates; international library statistics and uniform terminology. Margarita Rudomino, recording the prehistory of IFLA[2], laments:

> All international conferences held since 1853 generally elected a committee consisting of librarians from different countries, to organise liaison and preparatory work aimed at convening subsequent … conferences. However, at that period there did not yet exist essential organisational, economic and training facilities which could promote the establishment of an international library organisation. Differing attitudes of countries in respect to libraries did not contribute to the official unification of librarians of all states. Lastly, there were no library personalities capable of taking the initiative of organising a permanent library committee … it took more than half a century of joint efforts of the library community to set up a permanent international library organisation.

However, the main result of the Prague conference of 1926 was that an interim international committee of librarians was established. It was this group which in turn led to the establishment of IFLA in 1927, though not under that name.

Bibliographers

Meanwhile, bibliographers, as opposed to librarians, were also getting organised. In 1895, an international conference on bibliography was held in Brussels, sponsored by the Belgian government. The objectives of the conference were to establish the Institut Internationale de Bibliographie (IIB), to create a Répertoire Bibliographique Universel (RBU), classified according to the Dewey Decimal Classification Scheme, and to form an international bibliographic union. The IIB consisted initially of organisational and personal members. In the event, the development of the Universal Decimal Classification (UDC) became a prime interest of the founders of the IIB. The first complete edition of the UDC was published in French in 1895 under the title *Manuel du répertoire bibliographique universel*[5]. In 1924, the IIB was reorganised and became a federation with five national members: Belgium, France, Germany, the Netherlands and Switzerland. It eventually became the Fédération Internationale de Documentation (FID).

For the rest of the 20th century there were sporadic but ultimately unsuccessful attempts to bring together these two international organisations, which between them represented librarians and bibliographers and, latterly, documentalists.

After the First World War, there was a general impetus towards the promotion of co-operation and understanding across national frontiers. The establishment of the League of Nations was a major manifestation of that trend. In 1925, the League established its International Institute for Intellectual Co-operation (IIIC), which can now be seen as a forerunner of UNESCO. Regarded as the founder of IFLA, Gabriel Henriot, President of the Association des bibliothécaires français and Professor at the American Library School in Paris, originally proposed at the 1926 Prague conference the establishment of a standing international library committee to be based at the IIIC offices in Paris. Its remit would have been: to co-ordinate activities; to maintain contacts between national associations; to follow up resolutions adopted at international congresses; and to conduct the exchange of bibliographic information.

The establishment of IFLA

On 30 September 1927, the final day of the conference during which the 50th anniversary celebrations of the (British) Library Association were held, the resolution to establish what was to become IFLA was signed. Authorised delegates from 15 countries signed the resolution. One of the principal tasks of this new body was to organise, at intervals of between three to five years, large international conferences. The establishment of the International Library and Bibliographical Committee was officially declared in Rome in 1928, whilst the first constitution of the body was adopted at the first World Congress of Librarianship and Bibliography, also held in Rome.

The period from its inception until the outbreak of the Second World War saw steady, if unspectacular, growth. The first IFLA conference to be

Ross Shimmon

held outside Europe took place in Chicago in 1933. By 1936, membership had reached 41 associations from 31 countries and, although several of these were from beyond the founding regions of Europe and North America (for example, China, India, Japan, Mexico and the Philippines), the Federation could not yet truly claim to be a world wide organisation:

> Originally, IFLA was a meeting point for leading librarians from Europe and America and continued as such for a long time. In the early years notable personalities – true representatives of the profession – defined IFLA's profile. It became a kind of 'conference family', where personal friendships led to close co-operation in such areas as international loan and exchange, bibliographical standardisation and library education.[6]

Slow growth

The period immediately after the Second World War was one of slow growth, hampered by lack of resources and a permanent home. However, by 1958, membership had grown to 64 national associations from 42 countries. A major event was the International Conference on Cataloguing Principles, held in Paris in 1961, assisted by a grant to IFLA from the US Council on Library Resources of $20,000. This led to a new edition of the *Anglo-American Cataloguing Rules* and, in due course, to the International Standard Bibliographic Description (ISBD), both providing evidence of IFLA's long-term commitment to the development of standards of bibliographic control and exchange. In 1962, IFLA's first permanent secretariat was established with the help of a grant from UNESCO. Anthony Thompson became the first full-time Secretary General, based at his home in Sevenoaks, England. Gradually, despite minuscule financial resources, IFLA began to develop professional programmes and the capability of reacting to the issues of the day. The offices of a strengthened secretariat moved to The Hague in the Netherlands in 1971, with the support of the US Council on Library Resources. A new structure was adopted in 1976, together with a revised name, the International Federation of Library Associations and Institutions. The addition of 'institutions' to the title was to reflect the fact that libraries, departments of library and information studies and other related institutions were eligible for membership. The acronym IFLA was retained, however.

Into the twenty-first century

Further constitutional changes were adopted during the IFLA conference held in Jerusalem in 2000. These were intended to encourage wider participation in the work of the Federation by introducing postal elections (and provision for the introduction of electronic voting) for the post of President-elect and the membership of the Governing Board and by reducing the number of meetings which Board members had to attend.

What has become of the original vision of a truly international body to represent the interests of libraries and librarians? IFLA has developed well beyond being a gentleman's club for the leading librarians of Europe and America – a tendency which characterised its early years. With nearly 1,800 members in 153 countries it can fairly claim to be 'uniting libraries globally'. The new statutes have led to the election of Kay Raseroka, Chief Librarian of the University of Botswana, as President-elect. In 2003, she will be inducted as the first President of IFLA from Africa and, indeed, the first from outside Europe and the USA. The new Governing Board, which took office in 2002, has members from Argentina, Australia, Botswana, China, Malaysia and South Africa, as well as from countries in Europe and North America. Developing from the successful establishment of a staffed regional office in Kuala Lumpur, Malaysia in the 1970s, there are now three such offices, based in Africa (Dakar), Asia (Bangkok) and Latin America (Sao Paolo). These offices support the voluntary work of the three regional sections in an attempt to ensure that the interests of members in these regions are catered for adequately.

Clearly, IFLA is much more than just a conference, though the annual general conference remains the Federation's flagship event. It now regularly attracts upwards of 3,000 participants. At the Boston conference held in 2001, more than 5,000 participants from 150 countries attended. The conference itself is a kaleidoscope of activities with plenary sessions, council and business meetings, parallel professional sessions, workshops, a major trade exhibition, library visits and social and cultural events. It has become the largest international gathering of library and information professionals. During the business meetings, members of the numerous professional units (Sections and Discussion Groups) debate the need for standards, surveys, research, guidelines to best practice and other publications. This work is co-ordinated by a Professional Committee, which has established a set of professional priorities[7] intended to underpin the work of all the professional units of the Federation. Drafting standards and other statements, which are applicable in different cultures, political systems and language groups, is a demanding task. Successful adoption around the world of the end product is the ultimate reward of such work, frequently complemented by long-lasting friendships formed between librarians working in very different parts of the globe. A good example is the *IFLA/UNESCO public library manifesto*, which has been published in three editions, most recently in 1994[8]. It has been translated into more than twenty languages, partly with the help of UNESCO. The manifesto was then developed into guidelines, which have

Ross Shimmon

been published in three editions, latterly as *Public Libraries: IFLA/UNESCO guidelines for development*[9]. First published in August 2001, plans are in hand for translations in 12 languages. 46,000 copies in Russian are being prepared for distribution throughout the Russian Federation.

IFLA has five working languages: English, French, German, Russian and Spanish. Teams of volunteer interpreters are available to provide interpretation services at the major sessions at the annual conference. In recent years volunteers have also translated major documents and *IFLA Express*, the daily conference newspaper.

Core activities

IFLA's aspiration to become a truly world-wide federation has always been severely hampered by a lack of resources. Well over 80% of the organisation's income is derived from membership contributions. Its ability to carry out specific projects has usually been dependent on attracting funding from agencies such as UNESCO, the US Council on Library and Information Resources (CLIR) and the US National Council on Library and Information Services (NCLIS). In the late 1970s and 1980s, a series of 'core programmes' was established. The aim of the core programmes was to carry out that practical work which was beyond the capacity of the largely voluntary effort of the professional units of IFLA. A characteristic of these core programmes was that they were generously hosted by a national library or, in one case, by a university library. Additional funding came from a special fund based on contributions from a number of major libraries, again mainly national libraries, supplemented by income from sales of publications and research grants. Five core programmes were developed.

Advancement of Librarianship (ALP)

ALP is based at Uppsala University Library in Sweden. Its mission is to further the library and information profession in the developing countries of Africa, Asia and Oceania, and Latin America and the Caribbean. It does this by facilitating workshops, research projects and other initiatives. The bulk of its funding derives from grants from several Scandinavian government development agencies. ALP also administers the fellowships funded by DANIDA, the Danish development agency, to enable librarians from the developing world to attend IFLA conferences.

Preservation and Conservation (PAC)

PAC is based at the Bibliothèque nationale de France in Paris. It has a series of six decentralised regional centres around the world. It is concerned with all aspects of preservation and conservation of library materials, including research, training and publicity.

Universal Availability of Publications (UAP)

UAP is based at the British Library, Boston Spa. The objective of UAP is the widest possible availability of published material to intending users. To this end, it develops guidelines and standards, organises conferences and workshops and administers a cash-free international inter-lending voucher scheme.

Universal Bibliographic Control and International MARC (UBCIM)

UBCIM is based at Die Deutsche Bibliothek in Frankfurt. Its aim is to co-ordinate the development of standards for the international exchange of bibliographic data. UBCIM promotes the UNIMARC format and co-ordinates its development and maintenance. This aspect of its work is due to transfer to the National Library of Portugal in 2003.

Universal Dataflow and Telecommunications (UDT)

Based at the National Library of Canada, UDT aimed to facilitate the international and national exchange of electronic data by providing the library community with practical approaches to resource sharing. However, the programme concentrated increasingly on the development and maintenance of IFLA's website, IFLANET[10], and the related electronic services. IFLANET is in the process of moving from Canada to its new host at the Institut de l'Information Scientifique et Technique (INIST) in Vandroeuvre-lès-Nancy, France.

Advocacy

In recent years, IFLA has undertaken two other major initiatives: the Freedom of Access to Information and Freedom of Expression (FAIFE) Committee and its associated office in Copenhagen, and the Copyright and other Legal Matters (CLM) Committee, whose secretariat is located with UAP. FAIFE monitors the state of intellectual freedom in different countries, working with other agencies and responding on IFLA's behalf to violations of principles. CLM aims to ensure that the voices of the profession and of the users of libraries are heard in the international arenas determining copyright legislation and other regulations affecting library and information services.

These two initiatives, together with the original five core activities, are now known as IFLA's core activities. Although described as 'core activities', none of them receives significant funding from IFLA's central budget. All

Ross Shimmon

are heavily dependent on their host institutions and on money received from grant-giving agencies, supplemented by contributions from a special IFLA fund made up of donations from a small number of libraries. All are, therefore, vulnerable to changes to the policies of their hosts and donors.

The two functions, FAIFE and CLM, illustrate a trend in IFLA's work towards the adoption of a higher public profile and a greater emphasis on advocacy. The FAIFE Committee, for example, has made a number of pronouncements on the role of libraries in securing freedom of access to information[11]. It has also published a world report on libraries and intellectual freedom[12]. Current projects include the preparation of a manifesto on intellectual freedom and the Internet. CLM has similarly been active in making statements on copyright in the digital environment[13], licensing principles and developments within the World Trade Organisation[14], for example.

All these core activities exhibit features testifying to the challenges faced in international work in the library and information field, including a severe lack of resources. As with national professional bodies, the demands are virtually infinite, while the resources available to carry them out are strictly finite. With a small headquarters secretariat of less than nine full-time equivalent staff and a range of even smaller specialist and regional offices spread around the world, much of the work has to be undertaken by people with demanding day-time jobs, working in a great variety of circumstances.

Alliances

One response to this situation is to seek strategic alliances with like-minded organisations. Many attempts were made over the years to work more closely with the International Federation for Documentation (FID). The most recent initiative was the Global Information Alliance, formed in 1995, of information non-governmental organisations (NGOs), including FID, the International Council on Archives (ICA), IFLA and the Internet Society. The Alliance aimed to speak 'with blended voices' on major issues related to the development of the information society, including the ethical, human and social impacts of information technology and the growing gap between the information rich and the information poor. However, with the demise of FID in 2001, the Alliance has, in effect, ended, having achieved nothing of substance. Attempts by IFLA to help FID's professional programme to survive also came to nothing, leaving IFLA as the sole international NGO in the field. This puts a great onus on IFLA to try to ensure that it truly represents the whole spectrum of library and information services, since FID's membership reflected its greater interest in the information science end of the spectrum. It also challenges IFLA to encourage membership in regions where FID has traditionally been stronger, for example in South America and the Middle East.

A more successful example of inter-organisation co-operation is the International Committee for the Blue Shield. This is a joint initiative of IFLA with the International Council on Archives, the International Council on Museums and the International Council on Monuments and Sites (ICOMOS). Established with the help of UNESCO, its focus is on the protection of cultural property arising from the effects of natural and man-made disasters, including armed conflict. It takes its title from the blue shield adopted as the emblem of the 1954 Hague Convention on the Protection of Cultural Property in the Event of Armed Conflict. It aims to be a source of information and advice in both emergency relief and disaster preparedness. It encourages the establishment of national Blue Shield committees. Although modestly successful, it exhibits the typical situation of NGOs in the library and information field; plenty of work to do, but virtually no resources with which to do it.

International liaison in the library and information community has developed gradually, at times painfully slowly, from initial contacts at irregular conferences at which the emphasis was on the exchange of publications and descriptions of classification schemes, through the development of international standards and guidelines to best practice (which continues to this day), towards a much greater attempt at advocacy on behalf of libraries and their users on the world stage. Constant themes during this development have been the struggle for resources, gradually improving geographical representation and the need to identify priorities. The arrival of the Internet and electronic mail have revolutionised the management of international organisations such as IFLA and have enabled the drafting of statements and guidelines on a more timely basis. But, so far at least, it has not diminished the need for, or desirability of, face to face contact at conferences, workshops and seminars.

The future

In future, international activity will undoubtedly concentrate on securing sufficient resources to ensure an effective voice at international fora affecting the provision of effective library and information services. The issues for the next few years will be tackling the divide between those who have access to the knowledge they need and those who do not, and attempting to ensure that the power of technology is harnessed to that end.

References

1. Urquhart, Donald J. IFLA – a provocative view *in* Koops, Willem R. H. *and* Wieder, Joachim, *eds. IFLA's first fifty years: achievement and*

Ross Shimmon

challenge in international librarianship. (IFLA Publications 10) K. G. Saur, 1977, p133

2. Rudomino, Margarita I. The prehistory of IFLA (recalling the history of international library congresses) *in* Koops, Willem R. H. *and* Wieder, Joachim, eds. IFLA's first fifty years: achievement and challenge in international librarianship.* (IFLA Publications 10) K. G. Saur, 1977, p67

3. Wallace, J. W. Inaugural address. *Library Journal, 2,* 1877-78, p92-95. Quoted in Rudomino, Margarita I. *Ibid.* p67

4. Dewey, M. The American Library Association. *Library Journal, 1,* 1876-77, p245-246. Quoted in Rudomino, Margarita I. *Ibid.* p67

5. Keenan, Stella. International Federation for Documentation *in* Wedgeworth, Robert *ed. World encyclopedia of library and information services.* American Library Association, 3rd edition, 1993, p376

6. Henry, Carol. International Federation of Library Associations and Institutions *in* Wedgeworth, Robert *ed. World encyclopedia of library and information services.* American Library Association, 3rd edition, 1993, p378

7. The professional priorities are listed in a press release on the IFLANET website at http://www.ifla.org/V/press/pr02-01.htm

8. International Federation of Library Associations and Institutions *and* UNESCO. *IFLA-UNESCO public library manifesto.* IFLA, 1994

9. *The public library service: IFLA-UNESCO guidelines for development.* Edited for the (IFLA) Section of Public Libraries by Philip Gill *et al.* K. G. Saur, 2001

10. The IFLA website, IFLANET, can be found at http://www.ifla.org/

11. *See,* for example, the statement on libraries and intellectual freedom at http://www.ifla.org/V/press/pr990326.htm

12. *Libraries and intellectual freedom: IFLA-FAIFE world report.* IFLA-FAIFE Office, 2001

13. The IFLA position on copyright in the digital environment may be found at http://www.ifla.org/V/press/copydig.htm

14. The IFLA position on the World Trade Organisation (2001) may be found at http://www.ifla.org/III/clm/p1/wto-ifla.htm

Part Five

SCOTTISH LIBRARY AND INFORMATION SERVICE DEVELOPMENTS

I n recent years, cross-sectoral working and the forming of partnerships and consortia have characterised public sector activity, manifested in partnerships between the libraries of two or more universities, between groups of public libraries, between a university and a public library, to mention but a few. This has done much to restore confidence in the tradition of inter-library co-operation that suffered more than a little during the 1980s and 1990s, with their perhaps well-intentioned, but too narrow, emphasis on competition and 'bottom-line' measures of performance.

Arguably, the most important cross-sectoral development of Robert Craig's career, and one of his principal achievements, has been his ability to establish strong working relationships, not just between organisations, but between *professions* – librarians and other professionals, librarians and senior managers, librarians and politicians. He has brought into fruitful dialogue and collaboration, groups that had little tradition of working together in other than fairly monochrome superior-subordinate relationships. All library sectors in Scotland have benefited from his work and approach; he has used the overarching structure of their professional bodies as a means of getting librarians talking to politicians and senior managers in *their* overarching bodies (eg, COSLA, SFEU, Directors of Education, the Scottish Executive Health Department).

As Derek Law, President of the Chartered Institute of Library and Information Professionals in Scotland, notes in his foreword, the key has been Robert Craig's ability to make himself credible and approachable to senior people in management and government, both elected and executive. He has shown how libraries can contribute to issues on existing public, political and managerial agendas, by concentrating on practical achievements and getting things done. The success achieved has in turn enabled him to place other library issues on these same agendas and to gain support for their resolution.

The essays in this section deal with issues and developments in the public, school, further and higher education and special library sectors. In each case, much of the development has been facilitated and guided by Robert Craig.

1 4

Public libraries

Alan R.C. Hasson

The one universal constant in the public library sector since 1980 has been change. This change can be typified as having been driven by three, overlapping factors. These are: the breakdown of the post-war political consensus and its concomitant effects on society; administrative reorganisations; and technological advances, particularly within the information communications field.

Political and social context

Of these forces, the first is the most crucial to the public library service. The service derives its very existence from statute and hence from a shared political acceptance. The breakdown of consensus has been articulated on three main fronts. Firstly, the Conservative government and bodies closely associated with it, by adopting a consumerist analysis and justification for public services, challenged the one element that all the diverse public library services in the United Kingdom share - free access.

In Scotland, this challenge was never as formalised or as advanced as it was in England and Wales, where a Green Paper on charging was produced in 1987. However, the argument was alive. The opposing views were encapsulated in a debate in 1988 between Douglas Mason of the Adam Smith Institute and Jack McConnell, then of Stirling Council. Mason's argument and the government's was that:

> ....people should not expect other people to provide them with their pleasure, leisure and livelihood free of charge...it is a moral case that people should expect to pay for what they get and they should not expect other people to do it for them.[1]

McConnell's case was equally straightforward and just as purely based on a clear set of political and ethical values:

Alan R.C. Hasson

> What we are discussing is the issue of a free public library service which was fought for historically versus whatever form of charging was introduced, which would lead to some form of privatisation and would definitely exclude many sections of the population.[1]

Whilst the political argument for the maintenance of free services was won, the larger argument deriving from the consumerist analysis was not. The relative proportion of income available to local government for services that are not closely defined by statute (with the statute implying or setting out levels of funding) has fallen. This situation is much more insidious than the overt debate, in that it has led over the entire period to a fall in the resources available to public library services and hence to their ability to exploit the opportunities which the skills of their staff and the services they deploy potentially offer. This acceptance represents a second manner in which the breakdown of the post-war consensus affected public libraries.

For instance, in the period between 1987 and 2000 spending on all book and audio-visual material in Scottish public libraries rose from just over £8,500,000 to approximately £12,250,000. However, the value of this latter amount, using the Retail Price Index, at 1987 values was only £7,356,000, a decrease of 15%. The effect of this real fall is reflected in the amount of material acquired by public libraries, the total amount dropping from approximately 1,525,000 in 1987 to about 1,308,000 in 2000 or a decrease of c14.3%[2].

Even by 1986, the dangers were becoming apparent. Donald Dewar, speaking at the Scottish Library Association Conference warned:

> I know that there's always a theory that there's fat about; I know there's always a theory that we can manage somehow; but I think we are getting to a point where we really are going to pay a direct price.[3]

The statistics bear out his point, reflecting the tightening of resources: thus between 1986 and 1996 the annual issue of books per head of population in Scotland fell by almost 24%, reflecting the same problem that English and Welsh authorities faced, where falls ranged between 32% and 18.3%. The increase in audio-visual issues of approximately 4.7% between 1992 and 1996 on a much smaller scale of issues did nothing to compensate for the core business fall.

It should be noted, however, that the political divergence between Scotland and England mitigated the overall thrust of central government policy, with Scotland faring relatively better than authorities in the south. Thus, in 1994-95 the total amount spent per thousand of population in Scotland on library services was £17,525, whilst £12,658 was the equivalent figure for England and Wales[2].

The social situation facing public libraries was also changing. Thus, in Strathclyde Region, a centre of traditional industries, the overall unemployment rate was 16% in 1995, with 23% of families on income support and 44% of children receiving clothing grants[4]. But the situation was worse than this because such deprivation was not spread evenly. For instance, whilst in 1992-93 just under one in eight of the Region's school leavers went straight into unemployment, more than one in five did so in Glasgow, whilst in those parts of Glasgow designated as areas of acute deprivation, one in three went from school to unemployment[5].

Thus by the early to mid nineties, a situation existed where increasing social need for the learning, leisure and self-improvement opportunities provided by public libraries was coupled with a reduction in the resources available to libraries to fulfil that very role.

Even with these difficulties however, professionals and their councils in the public sector have continued and expanded the tradition of providing innovative and relevant services. Indeed, the imagination and thought which have been displayed have often far anticipated developments taken forward by national initiatives and relatively better funded sectors of local government. In a short paper of this type it is possible to highlight only a few high profile examples of this activity, but it should be remembered that these initiatives all arose from the work which had established libraries as neutral, well used, freely accessible, community based facilities.

Both the Yoker youth Library in Glasgow and Johnstone Information and Leisure Library (JILL) in Johnstone, Renfrewshire addressed the now central issue of social inclusion by targeting young people who were excluded from or had excluded themselves from learning and leisure activities. By the early nineties, it was possible for a police representative to tell an evaluation group from the Scottish Office visiting Yoker that in his view:

> ...better links have been formed with the youth of the area and
> without this facility (the Library) it was more than likely that the
> majority of youngsters would either fall into a life of crime or indulge
> in drug abuse. Now, by focusing their attentions on the library it gave
> them an opportunity to benefit in terms of education and learning
> new skills.[6]

It is unfortunately typical of the fragility of such projects that both Yoker and JILL have fallen to cuts in their library services' budgets.

In more traditional avenues, public libraries again turned an increasing amount of attention to lessening social exclusion. Thus activity has been directed at those with a physical disability which has historically prevented or lessened their access to library stock. As an example, in the case of visually

Alan R.C. Hasson

impaired people, the scale of services has developed from the simple provision of large-print books through the free provision of page magnifiers by, for example, East Lothian in 1977, to Cunninghame's production of a weekly talking newspaper by 1990 and Dundee's use of Braille guides to their spoken word collection by 1992.

By the early 1990s, both Edinburgh and Glasgow had a sophisticated matrix of provision for the visually impaired, including Kurzweill machines, on-line daily newspapers and print-to-voice facilities, with other authorities, such as Renfrew, having similar, if less integrated, provision. Again, funding was and remains the problem. For instance, a project in Scottish Borders targeting visually impaired unemployed people, seeking to address the improvement of ICT skills could only be established in 2001 with a grant from Scottish Enterprise.

In addition, throughout the period, collections of materials for ethnic minorities were increasingly established: Edinburgh, for instance, launched its collection in 1979, whilst that of Dundee, after advice from members of the target communities, was established by 1992. Glasgow's provision was perhaps the most comprehensive. It was based on a five year Urban Aid Grant of £110,000 for material, with personnel back-up, and involved both Urdu and Punjabi-speaking members of staff and community working, on much the same basis as Dundee's scheme. Glasgow's service, which it actively promoted via community venues such as mosques and Sikh temples, acted as a resource for other authorities throughout the west of Scotland.

In terms of 'joined-up government', public libraries have also been to the forefront. The island of Benbecula, where services have been physically brought together, can be used as an example. In 1991, Margaret Sked, then President of the Scottish Library Association, described Linaclaite as a 'superbly designed complex, blended together as school, community centre, museum and dual-purpose library'[7].

Similarly, in a concentration on joined-up service provision with the public library at its heart, Ferguslie Park in Paisley was only the most prominent of a number of similar initiatives. From the library, housed in a previously derelict shop, within an area of extreme social deprivation, a multi-disciplinary team operated. This team, led initially by a librarian, comprised professional and para-professional librarians, community workers, youth workers and teachers, hosting sessions with careers officers, community development staff and local activists and working on formal and informal sessions with social workers. In addition to anecdotal evidence from social workers and local teaching staff on improvements in literacy and social skills, the project recorded, in the late 1980s, an active membership of 66% of the local population. In effect, Ferguslie could be looked on as a progenitor of a community learning plan approach. Again however, this project, like many of its siblings, has greatly reduced in size under fiscal pressure.

A similar approach in Hamilton led to the setting up of the Whitehall Community Resource Unit. The justification for the project is indicative of the more ambitious and holistic approach to the work of public libraries which was being undertaken through the pressure of need and the support of committed councils. The basic rationale was stated to be:

> ... evidence in the area of low literacy levels, anti-social behaviour amongst young people, lack of communication between youth and the other sections of the community and poor use of existing library facilities.[8]

Amongst the stated aims of the project were:

> To provide a meeting place for all age groups within Whitehall A.P.T. which could be used as a planning and co-ordinating base for existing and new groups.
> To encourage community involvement with problems of vandalism, illiteracy ... and through parental involvement [encourage] a more constructive and educational input to their child's learning ...[8].

Similar multi-disciplinary work, utilising the public library as a community contact point, has been carried out. Examples include the former East Kilbride District Council's co-operation with the NHS in providing healthy living information; Renfrew's one-stop shop approach in Linfo; and the still-developing work involving community education and libraries in Dundee.

The third manner in which the consumerist ethos manifests itself, admittedly in concert with other drivers, is in the greater influence which central government seeks to exert in policy, delivery and 'efficiency' matters.

National benchmarks of provision, league tables of inputs and performance, nationally-set priorities for action and centrally-funded national initiatives, cutting across locally decided priorities, are now a fact of life. Audit Scotland's statutory performance indicators and the New Opportunities Fund (NOF) People's Network can be seen as examples of these. In the area of benchmarking, the public library sector has been well served by both the Scottish Library and Information Council (SLIC) and the Scottish Library Association (SLA), standing in marked contrast to other, related, publicly-funded sectors as pointed out in the National Cultural Strategy. The development of national standards of provision and their acceptance by Scottish central and local government is a prime example of the importance of the SLA and SLIC.

Alan R.C. Hasson

The bedrock of these developments lies in the three reports which attempted to set basic standards of provision and direction for the public library sector. The first of these, the Robertson Report of 1969, was followed by two reports produced under the aegis of the Convention of Scottish Local Authorities (COSLA), the first in 1986 with a second in 1995. The COSLA public library standards were successful in that they established, amongst other points, a minimum set of quantifiable inputs for each authority based on population, with some modifying factors such as rurality. Every Scottish authority has formally agreed to seek to meet these minimum targets; few have succeeded.

The search for greater efficiency still goes on through the Best Value Regime and the Performance Management and Planning (PMP) audit process. How these will and can be used to improve the diverse public library services nationally remains a moot point.

Essential for the sector in this area has been the work of SLIC and the SLA: for instance, by channelling funding from the Scottish Executive for innovative and transferable experimental projects and, more importantly, by establishing a credible, unified and consistent voice for the sector in its relation with the Executive. The role of SLIC in bringing together the library community in Scotland to speak with one authoritative voice is of real importance to public libraries, particularly given the lack of a body speaking solely on behalf of public libraries as does the Society of Chief Librarians in England.

Administrative change

The second of the factors affecting public libraries has been administrative change. In 1995, a re-organisation of local government took place, replacing the two-tier system established in 1974 with the unitary authorities which now exist throughout Scotland. The effect of this change has been central to the position of public library services and continues to develop and evolve, a process reinforced by the establishment of the Scottish Parliament. At this point in time, there are perhaps two significant elements which can be distinguished as directly due to this organisational change.

Firstly, in all councils where a single authority has replaced the former Region/District organisation, officers in charge of library services have found themselves further removed from policy presentation and, crudely, the arguing of the case for the library service. Instead of the head of library services holding a director-level post, the new structures take a multi-disciplinary approach, with library services coming under Leisure and Recreation, Cultural and Leisure Services, Lifelong Learning and variations on such themes, with the chief librarian at second to fourth tier. In principle, such organisational changes are not negative, in that the structural backing to co-operative and cross-disciplinary work can be synergistic. However, there is little evidence, yet, to support the view that service provision has actually benefited from organisational change. Instead, what evidence exists, such as in the *Public library expenditure statistics* formerly provided by the SLA and now produced by SLIC, shows a relative decrease in funding for public libraries and a continuing decline in the core business, lending books.

Secondly, coupled with the new multi-disciplinary departments has come a flatter organisational structure, where an increasing gap appears between the head of service, who requires to display skills in policy formulation, strategy and political understanding, and subordinate officers whose attention must largely be on tactical, professional and administrative duties. The virtual disappearance of posts of Assistant Chief Librarian raises the question of just how middle-ranking professionals are developed to lead a library service or the larger multi-disciplinary departments now existing. The problem is not confined to Scotland. Indeed, the most positive reaction to the emerging problem has been that put forward by the Society of Chief Librarians in England, who, with the assistance of the Library Association have held courses on preparing for leadership. The lack of such professional development in Scotland may be of central importance in the future.

Technological change

The third factor affecting the public library sector is technological change. It is difficult, from the standpoint of 2002, to remember just how far information and communications technology (ICT) has come in twenty years and how wrong the predictions for its growth have been. Thus in 1982, James Thompson could cite as distinguished a practitioner as Professor Michael Twyman, Head of Typography and Graphic Communications, University of Reading, speculating on the development of on-line databases and suggesting that:

> ... he [Professor Twyman] does not think that they will be in general use within ten years, if only because we are constricted by the deficiencies of the present systems, which cannot be replaced by anything much more sophisticated before around about the year 2050.[9]

In this area again, public libraries, on relatively meagre financial resources, showed innovation and ambition in trying to harness the new technology. By 1980, six public library authorities were participating in an on-line information retrieval pilot study, funded by the British Library. In 1983, five out of the six papers at the Annual Conference of the Scottish

Alan R.C. Hasson

Library Association which touched on public libraries had 'new technology' as a major theme. The use of computerised systems for management functions was already well established by 1980 and has continued to expand, although strangely for a sector increasingly dependent on ICT there remain public library authorities which have no such system.

Throughout the greater part of the period from 1980, there was no lack of understanding of the potential of ICT within public libraries, but neither was there substantial and sustained investment across the country. The situation mirrored the various services' responses to the social and political changes which had prevailed during the same period. These ranged from islands of innovative and ground-breaking activity, such as in South Ayrshire, Glasgow, Shetland, West Lothian and Fife to authorities who were content to (or lacked the political influence to do any more than) give the same services which had proved adequate for the 1960s. In effect, the very nature of local government worked against the consistent gaining of co-operative synergies which colleagues in the further and higher education sector were able to achieve through, for example, the establishment of the various metropolitan area networks (MANs). This has changed, and changed crucially, with the Labour government's direction of NOF resources to support the People's Network.

The funding provided by NOF and the guidelines set for the use of such funding have, for the first time, given public libraries the resources to exploit their potential as a local access point for connection to the wider opportunities offered by ICT. The funding is three fold: for staff training, for digitisation of content and for communication links and front-end equipment. Whilst all of these are of importance, the training of staff is especially crucial. NOF funding has recognised the role of library staff as facilitators and guides for users, a role which is unique and at the same time radical and firmly rooted in traditional public library service - providing access and assisting information retrieval.

Just as importantly, the commitment which all Scottish local authorities have individually agreed upon to provide free access to these resources means that there are no economic barriers to the acquisition of knowledge. The importance of this lack of a monetary barrier can be exemplified by the experience of Scottish Borders, where the removal of charges led to an increase of computer use of 370% in three months.

The public library sector currently stands at a crucial point. The investment in ICT gives it the opportunity to establish itself as a key provider in the government's vision for 21st Century Government, in the drive towards social inclusion and in the aspiration towards lifelong learning. The next few years will see if the sector can live up to the role Jack McConnell saw them as playing in 1988: 'the immediate access to the opportunity of gaining knowledge'.

The future

The quotation above from James Thompson shows the dangers of trying to predict the future. However, there are a number of themes and issues which, in 2002, seem prominent.

Firstly, the rate of change in ICT is exponential. Some of the opportunities which the technology offers can be seen but many cannot. We are, as Bill Bell, formerly of Glasgow Libraries, has said, like people who have invented the railroad, thinking that it will be useful for carrying goods and not realising that Mr Thomas Cook has a wee idea.

The influence of interactive satellite and cable technology, fed through the TV in each home may be immense. The provision of affordable broadband connection may change entire patterns of industry and service sector provision. Can electronic distance learning actually become a reality? Does book lending remain our core business? Is the Co-operative Academic Information Retrieval Network for Scotland (CAIRNS) the way forward? Do such developments put a premium on the skills of public library staff as organisers of knowledge, providers of local content, providers of advice?

Secondly, the current statutory basis of public libraries, coupled to the financial pressures on local government, is inadequate if the sector is to play a consistent and valuable role throughout Scotland. The inability of councils to reach the minimum standards set by COSLA shows that, even though Scottish councils have been, in UK terms, comparatively generous in funding, their priorities are, arguably by *force majeure*, elsewhere.

Should the People's Network be a success, it will surely be, at the very least, an argument for greater Scottish Executive direction in the ring fencing of expenditure for centrally-decided priorities. If lifelong learning is truly the ambition of the government and public libraries actually have a key role to play, then the directing and controlling role that the Executive plays in relation to primary and secondary education requires to be replicated for the public library service. It is possible that the National Cultural Strategy may provide such an opportunity. The experience of the period from 1980 shows that councils cannot and will not spend the amount they recognise as the minimum to provide an adequate public library service.

Several different courses of action are available. These include the establishment, openly, of a National Public Library Service, funded and managed by the Executive, giving consistency and perhaps more front line services as a result of economies of scale. As the real problem centres on the resources available to local government, another solution would be an increase in such resources, allowing public libraries to play the role which they have proven in the period since 1980 that they have the imagination and people skills to do.

Alan R.C. Hasson

Again, perhaps the provision of larger but fewer authorities would provide some leeway. The Executive's recent actions in directing social work departments to work in multi-authority units in relation to the Criminal Justice Act, is perhaps a pointer here.

The option to remain as the sector is at the moment, on its current funding base, offers the great danger of nothing but slow decline and marginalisation.

Perhaps the best way to sum up the challenges which are faced by public libraries is, conversely, to quote from the COSLA public library standards report of 1986, for the consistency of the change we face is striking:

> We believe that any assessment of, and recommendations on, stand-ards for the public library service made in 1986 must, in their ap-proach and format, reflect past changes and those likely to occur prior to the turn of the century. Among these changes are the ... consistently maintained levels of unemployment; the greater amount of leisure time available to members of the community, whether on a voluntary or involuntary basis, the developments which are occurring in the new technologies . . . the growing needs for and interest in adult and continuing education; . . . the growing awareness of the needs of the disabled; the needs of ethnic minorities.[10]

References

1. Dakers, Colin D. *ed. Progress through partnership: proceedings of the 74th annual conference of the Scottish Library Association.* Scottish Library Association, 1988

2. Spiller, David *and* Creaser, Claire. *LISU annual library statistics 1997.* Loughborough University, Library & Information Statistics Unit, 1997

3. Taylor, Alan F. *ed. In search of excellence: proceedings of the 72nd annual conference of the Scottish Library Association.* Scottish Library Association, 1987

4. *The Herald.* 1 May 1995, p7

5. Strathclyde Regional Council. *Moving on.* Strathclyde Regional Council, 1994, p4-15

6. Yoker Youth Library. *Yoker Youth Library: project review and annual report.* Yoker Youth Library, 1992. Appendix II, p2

7. Sked, Margaret. Presidential report. *Annual report of the Scottish Library Association.* Scottish Library Association, 1991, p3

8. Hamilton District Council, Urban programme application form. Unpublished internal document, 1991

9. Thompson, James. *The end of libraries.* Clive Bingley, 1982, p67

10. Convention of Scottish Local Authorities. *Standards for the public library service in Scotland.* COSLA, 1986

Alan R.C. Hasson

1 5

Libraries and information services in schools

Liz Knowles

In *Teaching children to think*[1], Robert Fisher puts information at the heart of learning:

> Changes in society are accelerating so rapidly that it is difficult to assess what factual knowledge will be needed for the future. The educational implications of this are that we should focus on teaching skills essential to the gaining, organising and using of information. To be prepared for the challenge of the future, children will need skills that will give them control over their lives and their learning, for of their learning there will be no end.

Learning is increasingly recognised as life-long and 'lifelong learning' has become a useful catch phrase as recent government initiatives in public library networking and strategic planning for community learning have again brought a focus to the role of public libraries and community education in supporting learning in local communities.

Schools are a crucial influence in the lives of young people and can determine their learning habits for life. The current standards for the development of school library resource centres in Scotland[2], derived as they are from a statement of learner entitlement, focus on the role of the school library in developing and supporting learners during the important school years. Supporting the needs of the individual learner together with the needs of the school as a learning organisation are today accepted as core functions of any school library and information service.

Lifelong learning is easy to say – but much more difficult to achieve. This essay reviews the position of school libraries in Scotland within the context of formal education initiatives and the lifelong learning debate. It also considers their possible future in the development of learning communities.

Beginnings

The first major reports on school libraries in Scotland were published in 1985 by the Scottish Library Association[3] (SLA) and the then Library and Information Services Committee (Scotland)[4] (LISC(S)). They clearly set the role of school libraries in the whole-school context and made a strong and clear case for their importance in learning to be valued, recognised and developed within the core activities of schools education. They challenged local authorities, schools and individuals to think creatively about the purpose of school libraries and provided a framework for their development within both the formal and informal school curricula. They were key documents, led and promoted by key figures in school librarianship and in education, and strongly supported by the Scottish Library Association and the Library and Information Services Committee (Scotland). They displayed an understanding of educational needs and confidence in the ability of libraries to support those needs.

With hindsight, it is perhaps significant that these reports were published during a period of substantial growth within the school library sector and at a time of relative stability in local government, mid-way between the reorganisations of 1975 and 1996. The 1970s and 1980s saw an increase in the numbers of qualified librarians in schools in Scotland, rising to 229 in 1985. They also saw significant development in local authority-based central resource services. These services provided strong central support to schools and their librarians and also provided strategic direction, leadership, training and development at local authority level. The reports offered a blueprint for development and, in reviewing the quality of provision across Scotland, argued for all authorities to begin to move towards improving provision where possible.

With the exception of five regional and island council authorities, school libraries and their support services were largely managed, in the local government structures of the time, within the education functions of the regional authorities, while public libraries were the responsibility of the district authorities. It was generally recognised that the strongest services were those clearly integrated into the education department, where management of the service was focussed on supporting education initiatives.

Now, in 2002, 17 years after the publication of these reports and more than 25 years after qualified librarians were first appointed to schools, the pressure to demonstrate clearly the added value that school library and information services bring to schools education is still with us. Indeed, it is greater than ever. The extent to which school libraries are consistently integrated into curriculum development and support for learners across schools in Scotland is still open to question. It is important that we should ask why this is the case.

Liz Knowles

The current context

We can perhaps identify three main reasons: the impact of the most recent re-structuring of local government in 1996; the move towards more devolved school management, with its subsequent change in the role of the centre; and the developing climate and culture of performance monitoring and review in local authority services.

In 1996, regional and district authorities were re-structured to form 32 smaller unitary authorities carrying out combined functions. The regional education resource services were disaggregated, their staff and resources split and re-allocated, service functions re-thought and re-configured. It was a difficult time and demoralising for those who had worked so hard on the development of strong central support services. Many have had to return to fighting for the continuing provision of services once thought to be well established. Re-structuring continues today at service level and, of the 32 authorities, 15 now manage both school and public libraries from within one department, compared to only five, six years ago. The pace and extent of change has inevitably affected development.

In addition, it has been government policy to devolve more and more decision-making and budget management to school level. Greater control over how education is delivered now rests with the school and its community of young people, staff, parents and carers. While strategic policy development and quality assurance may still lie with the authority's management team, the responsibility for the delivery of services in schools and for the quality of provision increasingly rests with the school management and the individual school librarian. While this approach now seems entirely appropriate, we should not underestimate the shift in thinking it represents and the additional responsibilities it places on school librarians. In some authorities, the role of central staff has diminished, impacting on policy, leadership and development at authority level.

Similarly, the government agenda to increase accountability in local authorities and to secure improvement in education has led to many initiatives relating to the review of performance. This approach inevitably leads to a need to evaluate and review performance in libraries. There is, however, little documented hard evidence available that school libraries in Scotland have indeed impacted on pupils' learning.

Recognising the need to support the changing position, SLA and the Scottish Library and Information Council (SLIC) initiated a number of projects to refocus attention upon the role of school libraries.

Firstly, they recommended the publication of national standards which could provide a guide and benchmark for local authorities and schools in taking forward development. The standards were published in 1999[2] and were based on recognised effective practice across the country. The task group was keen to ensure that the standards were not only aspirational, but also attainable. In many ways, the standards re-emphasised the role outlined in the reports of 1985, but they also made clear recommendations relating to provision in schools and at authority level. While the document may have brought little to the debate that was revolutionary, its significance lay in its publication by COSLA, and in the involvement of politicians, educationists and school library staff in its production. It was hoped that this collaboration, together with the endorsement of COSLA, would secure a place for school libraries in planning at both local authority and school level. While no national review of the impact of the standards has yet been undertaken, the extent to which this has been the case is still debatable. Increasing the level of provision has also been difficult at a time when local authority budgets are constantly under review.

Secondly, a group of school library service staff began to develop performance indicators which would link the evaluation of school libraries to school evaluation as outlined in *How good is our school?*[5], focusing especially on seven key areas of activity. The work undertaken built on earlier performance measures identified by regional authorities and the initiative received strong support from SLA and SLIC. It was again a feature of the resulting publication[6] that it was supported by key educational organisations, namely, the Scottish Consultative Council on the Curriculum (now Learning and Teaching Scotland) and the Audit Unit of Her Majesty's Inspectorate (HMI).

Authorities and schools have been working to take forward both the standards and the use of performance indicators and the Scottish Library Association has played a major role in promoting them nationally. It might be argued, however, that the key to the real development of school libraries lies in the recognition by the Scottish Executive and by HMI that school libraries matter and are worthy of the concern, scrutiny and debate which surround other areas of school life. It is important to note now that the performance indicators are being used by HMI when inspecting schools and that the inspection of school libraries is to be more rigorous. Some early evidence, albeit anecdotal, suggests that this approach is already raising the profile of the library in some schools. It will be interesting to see any longer term impact of such inspection on the future quality and development of school libraries.

Thirdly, statutory status was sought for school libraries. As the establishment of the Scottish Parliament in 1999 brought the governance of schools education at national level much closer to home, the opportunity to influence the national position of school libraries was taken. In 2000, the Scottish Executive published the *Standards in Scotland's Schools etc Act*. The Act created a statutory framework for schools education that requires education authorities and schools to plan, monitor and report on improvement in education. During the committee stages of the Bill, SLA and SLIC made efforts to secure statutory status for school libraries; this had been a recommendation of the COSLA standards. While the efforts were ultimately unsuccessful, school libraries were given a further platform for debate at national level.

The importance of these varied initiatives should be recognised.

The inability to secure statutory status may reflect a view that the important issue in school improvement is *what* is achieved, not *how* it is achieved. The question is – 'Is there a unique contribution that libraries make to the learning of young people?'

The Scottish Executive has now identified five National Priorities for schools education. These were approved by the Scottish Parliament in December 2000 and will give emphasis and direction to the approaches to monitoring and reporting on progress contained within the improvement framework of the Standards Act. Recent guidance to education authorities on the implications of implementing the Priorities confirms that their focus will be on outcomes. Delivery will be the responsibility of local authorities and schools, and both authority plans and school plans will identify how the Priorities will be implemented in their areas.

It will be important, therefore, to ensure that the role of school libraries in supporting learners within the context of the National Priorities is clearly understood at both school and local authority level if school libraries are to figure in the improvement planning framework. Inclusion in that framework will, however, mean contributing to the delivery of measurable outcomes linked to identified targets and performance indicators. Some may argue that the work of school libraries is not just about measuring outcomes and that impact on learning is difficult to evaluate. That is of course true, but it is important to be realistic about the context within which school libraries currently work. The improvement agenda is here to stay; school libraries must contribute to it and be seen to contribute to it, or they will be marginalised.

We should not underestimate the task that lies ahead for school library staff. Numbers working in schools have increased since 1985. Over 300 qualified librarians are now based in schools within the secondary sector. The demands made on them have increased steadily since the early 1970s, yet the majority still work on their own, managing increasingly complex resources and working with young people and staff with increasingly diverse needs. Their responsibilities for planning, developing and monitoring progress in the school library have increased substantially, while at the same time they are expected to effectively communicate their role in learning and teaching and to work collaboratively with teachers, young people and parents. The core function of supporting learners remains a major challenge in itself.

The National Priorities

The National Priorities provide a framework for considering the nature of the task of supporting learners and how it is currently being addressed. The focus is inevitably on secondary schools, where the majority of specialist staff are located, but we should recognise the fundamental need for library support in primary and nursery schools where the foundations of learning are laid. Five Priorities are identified; they are described below.

Achievement and attainment – to raise standards in literacy and numeracy and to achieve better levels in national measures of achievement including examination results.

School libraries have always had a strong role in the development of literacy skills. There is significant evidence across Scotland of the development of support for reading in its widest forms. Initiatives involving book groups, reading clubs, parental workshops, reading promotions, paired reading and writing workshops with authors are varied and legion. Many schools and local authorities have developed interesting and innovative projects with outside agencies such as Book Trust Scotland and Education Extra, and with public libraries.

In this regard, it is interesting to note some recent action research published by the Scottish Council for Research in Education[7] which focused on the issue of raising attainment in literacy for boys. The research, based in a school resource centre, has led to an intervention programme for boys in S1 and S2. Evidence now suggests that reading habits have changed and there is a noticeable increase in the breadth of their project work.

Libraries also have a continuing role in providing information and resource support for curriculum development. As sources of information become more varied and complex, the importance of identifying resources appropriate to the needs of pupils and staff is crucial to effective learning. An ability to understand the nature of that need is vital.

Framework for learning – to support and develop the skills of teachers, the self discipline of pupils and to enhance school environments so that they are conducive to learning and teaching.

School libraries have always sought to provide a supportive and structured environment for learning. Work with young people on developing study skills and structured approaches to tackling project work has been an important aspect of the librarian's role. It is hoped that librarians will contribute significantly to core skills delivery as the National Qualifications are introduced. Similarly, librarians can work with staff to enhance teacher understanding of generic information and study skills. Research in the USA[8,9,10] has shown this role to be important in raising pupil attainment. The recent building developments through public-private partnerships will give many schools new, well-designed libraries, providing a basis for further

Liz Knowles

development of services and an opportunity to enhance pupil learning experiences.

Inclusion and equality – to promote equality and help every pupil benefit from education. Particular emphasis will be placed on pupils with disabilities and special needs, and to Gaelic and other lesser used languages.

School libraries are inclusive by their nature. They are available to all, whether within the framework of the curriculum or for the pursuit of personal interests. They provide access to information and communications technology (ICT), resources and tutor support not always available to all at home and they have supported the recent growth in homework and study clubs and out of school hours learning initiatives.

Values and citizenship – to work with parents to teach pupils respect for self and one another and their interdependence with other members of their neighbourhood and society and to teach them the duties and responsibilities of citizenship in a democratic society.

School libraries have been involved in schools for many years in promoting a positive ethos and are ideally placed to encourage young people to take responsibility for learning and become involved in wider social issues, as they are often important reference points for young people outwith the formal curriculum. There will obviously also be opportunities for school and public libraries to work together to ensure good access to national and local information and to support initiatives in youth and pupil councils.

Learning for life – to equip pupils with the foundation skills, attitudes and expectations necessary to prosper in a changing society and to encourage creativity and ambition

For school libraries, this is perhaps the most fundamental issue and the area in which the direct involvement of library staff can have most impact. The developments in the use of ICT have been highly significant over the last three years. The government initiative of the National Grid for Learning, supported by Excellence Fund monies for equipment and infrastructure and New Opportunities Fund monies for training, has had a major impact on schools and many school library staff have been at the forefront of developments. In addition to using ICT for information searching and library management, they are engaged in developing pupil and teacher skills in accessing the Internet, searching the World Wide Web, handling and presenting information and using a wide variety of software. Increasingly, librarians are also taking responsibility for intranet development and management, for network administration and for Web authoring and design. Access to the wide range of information available over the Internet has again raised issues about the suitability and appropriateness of information, together with the need for pupils to be taught information search and analysis skills. The application of ICT in learning and information provision has now become a major focus for library staff, bringing with it a level of excitement and interest from young people that is obviously encouraging. There are many good examples of the genuine involvement of young people in creative and imaginative ICT developments within the library.

Within this priority, there is also opportunity for school library staff to work with staff in other sectors to bring greater coherence to the network of library and information services available to young people. This applies whether these young people use the network as school pupils, students, members of a community group, or members of the public. There are, of course, individual initiatives at local level, but links between the school, FE, HE and public sectors could now be more overtly strengthened, particularly in the light of recent government initiatives in public library networking, community learning and new community schools.

We can, therefore, point to many examples of the contribution school libraries can make to learning and teaching in delivering the national priorities. Will this guarantee a central place for school libraries in the learning communities of the future? A number of factors might be considered.

Demonstrating libraries' impact on learning

As noted earlier, hard, quantifiable evidence that school libraries do indeed have an impact on pupil attainment and achievement is negligible. While we have many instances of success at local level, there is no national picture of the impact of school libraries in Scotland. Research in the United States, specifically in Colorado, Pennsylvania and Alaska[8,9,10] claims to show that there is a direct relationship between good school libraries or media centres and student results in examinations. In brief, and as an example, the US findings suggest that student test scores increase when librarians:

- plan and teach co-operatively with teachers;
- teach information literacy skills to students;
- provide in-service training to teachers;
- serve on school standards and curriculum committees;
- manage information technology networks which allow library information and materials to reach beyond the library;
- identify appropriate materials for teachers.

And when libraries:

- are open longer hours;
- have a co-operative relationship with the public library;

Liz Knowles

- provide access to local, national and world-wide information on-line;
- have well selected and adequately resourced collections.

While the findings of the research might be questioned, we can learn from the way in which the information can be used to promote the value of school libraries and media centres in raising student attainment.

Research was also undertaken recently in Scotland by the Robert Gordon University on behalf of Resource: the Council for Museums, Archives and Libraries[11]. It looked for evidence of the impact of the school library resource centre on learning in ten secondary schools across Scotland, all of which were involved in focus group discussions but only six of which went on to participate in the case study phase of the project. While recognising the potential impact of libraries and resource centres on a wide variety of aspects of learning, the research makes no direct correlation between school libraries and pupil attainment. It does, however, highlight certain key issues which remain to be resolved if school libraries are to make an effective impact on learning:

- need for better collaborative planning and decision-making - joint planning between librarians and teachers is limited;
- lack of understanding of the factors which influence effective learning;
- need for more understanding of the use of skills involved in information handling - outcomes concentrate on product rather than process;
- need for mutual understanding of the respective roles of librarian and teacher;
- need to look beyond the school library for impact – recognising that the library is one part of the process;
- need to be clear about the outcomes teachers and librarians are looking for.

It is a matter of concern that these are still key issues 25 years after the first appointment of qualified librarians to schools.

Understanding what librarians do

Despite all the developments identified, local authorities seem to have failed to fully understand the nature of the work that school librarians do. Staffing levels are still low and, in general, support for primary schools is still limited and provided mainly by staff who are based centrally, rather than in-school. There is a problem with recruitment, a result of both a poor profile within the profession and low salary grades. The McCrone agreement on Scottish teachers' pay and conditions is now being implemented and will further distance librarians, in salary terms at least, from the teachers with whom they work and collaborate on a daily basis. This undoubtedly has an impact on motivation and morale.

It is important, therefore, that we engage in real debate about the future role of school libraries and their staff. Are we sure librarians are trained appropriately for the range of tasks now demanded of them? Do they teach, mentor, tutor or instruct? Are they information providers or ICT managers? Do we expect them to lead and guide developments in school, or to be directed? Do they need to be in or out of the library to be most effective? And to most of these questions may be added the supplementary query – Or both? Perhaps we need to think a little more radically about the support schools really need and re-shape our libraries and staffing structures accordingly.

Co-ordination between library sectors

Library support for lifelong learning is still compartmentalised and much remains to be achieved in bringing sectors closer together. Are we prepared to develop libraries and resource centres which will work across school, public and community learning activities, with links to further and higher education? There are examples of this approach in some rural areas, but perhaps we should now be looking more closely at taking further opportunities for cross-sectoral working where it might be most effective. The Fryer Report, *Learning for the twenty-first century*[12], outlined a vision of the development of an integrated network of local learning centres, including schools, libraries, museums, study centres and community facilities. School libraries of the future could be a critical element of such a network, but only if they are fully integrated into learning developments. We need confident, motivated, well-qualified and properly trained staff to take this forward, and strong leadership at national and local authority levels to fully realise a partnership approach to supporting lifelong learning.

There is some way to go to achieve this vision, but librarians can begin to network, technologically and personally, to bring support to learners wherever and whenever it is needed most. It is no longer appropriate to consider education only in its statutory form, but change is difficult, not least within the more formal structures of school and curriculum, and school libraries work within these structures.

Developing and supporting lifelong learners remains a challenge for all of us. The future shape of schools education is to be debated nationally yet again during 2002. Perhaps there will be real opportunities for change and real

Liz Knowles

opportunities for school librarians and local authority staff to be instrumental in that change. If there are such opportunities – we should take them!

References

1. Fisher, Robert. *Teaching children to think*. Blackwell, 1990

2. Convention of Scottish Local Authorities. *Standards for school library resource services in Scotland: a framework for developing services. Report of a task group appointed by the Education and Cultural Services Forum of COSLA*. COSLA, 1999

3. Scottish Library Association. *The school library resource service and the curriculum*. SLA, 1985

4. Library and Information Services Committee (Scotland). *Library services and resources for schools education in Scotland*. LISC(S), 1985

5. Scottish Office Education and Industry Department. *How good is our school?: self-evaluation using performance indicators*. SOEID, 1996

6. Scottish Consultative Council on the Curriculum *et al. Taking a closer look at the school library resource centre: self-evaluation using performance indicators*. Scottish CCC, 1999

7. Simmons, J. *Raising the standard of boys' achievement in literacy*. Scottish Council for Research in Education, 2001

8. Lance, K. C., Hamilton-Pennell, C. *and* Rodney, M. J. *Information empowered: the school librarian as an agent of academic achievement in Alaska schools*. Alaska State Library, 1999

9. Lance, K. C., Hamilton-Pennell, C. *and* Rodney, M. J. *Measuring up to standards: the impact of school library programs and information literacy in Pennsylvania schools*. Pennsylvania Citizens for Better Libraries, 2000

10. Lance, K. C., Rodney, M. J. *and* Hamilton-Pennell C. *How school librarians help kids achieve standards: the second Colorado study*. Hi Willow Research and Publishing, 2000

11. Williams, D. *and* Wavell, C. *The impact of the school library resource centre on learning*. (Library and Information Commission, Research Report 112.) The Robert Gordon University, 2001

12. National Advisory Group for Continuing Education and Lifelong Learning. *Learning for the twenty first century*. NAGCELL, 1997

16

Libraries and information services in further and higher education

Stuart James

As with so many aspects of Scottish life, education has always had a UK and international dimension as well as a uniquely Scottish character and structure. A post-devolution decision to abolish tuition fees unilaterally in Scotland indicates a potential for political and practical divergence, but Scottish higher education (HE) and further education (FE) enjoy fruitful relations with their UK (and EU and international) colleagues, while still operating within a specifically Scottish administrative structure and context.

In 1992 and 1993, with the closure of the 'binary divide', the eight Scottish universities were joined in university status by the five large, multi-disciplinary central institutions. Subsequently, there have been further additions to the number of HE institutions, including specialist and monotechnic establishments. The former colleges of education have all merged with existing universities and nursing colleges have, since 1996, been absorbed into HE institutions. Further education comprises a seeming plethora of colleges across the country, from large to small, including some specialist colleges. The pattern is uneven geographically, with larger colleges to be found in Edinburgh and Dundee especially; subsequent mergers have produced similar sizes of college in Glasgow, but those in areas and towns apart from the major cities tend still to be relatively small, albeit active and locally significant institutions.

Higher education policy is a distinctly Scottish responsibility, with the Scottish Higher Education Funding Council[1] (SHEFC) acting as the executive and funding arm of the Scottish Executive. In 1999, responsibility for the financing of FE colleges moved away from local authorities to the Further Education Funding Council[2]. But a significant United Kingdom context remains, through the Joint Information Systems Committee (JISC) and the Combined Higher Education Software Team (CHEST) for example, while research libraries in Scotland, notably those of Glasgow[3] and Edinburgh Universities, are major partners in the Consortium of University Research Libraries (CURL)[4], as well as players in a European context.

Stuart James

When government expanded the size of the university sector in 1992, it was made clear that the roles of the new universities were to remain unchanged from those they had held as polytechnics and (in Scotland) as central institutions. Initially, this brought great diversity to the sector, especially when set alongside the activities of FE colleges. The aim was to offer students a broad choice of types of course as well as of subjects, all validated to the same standards of quality. Library services would also continue to develop with different emphases to support the several missions of their parent bodies. The FE and HE library sectors have benefited from ranges of outlooks and experience, encompassing areas and attitudes as diverse as advanced research support, outreach to local communities, collaboration with other sectors, and close student support.

SHEFC has always reckoned to support the diversity of the HE sector in Scotland, but its formulaic distribution of funds has tended to lead to an increasing homogeneity across the sector, if on very unequal terms. In libraries, this leaves everybody unsatisfied: the larger ancient universities find it increasingly difficult to acquire the materials they need to help keep their institutions on the world stage, while the new universities see an historical funding and resource gap which cannot be bridged by present means or present resources. Still, innovation is in evidence: in Dumfries, Glasgow and Paisley Universities, in collaboration with the local FE college and other local providers, have established a new university campus[5] designed specifically for the region. This shows one path for the future. Another example is the University of the Highlands and Islands[6], which takes the distributed electronic learning concept to another large and generally remote region, while also involving local colleges for local delivery.

Following the creation of so many new universities in 1992, the funding councils sought a review of university library provision. The Joint Funding Councils' Libraries Review ('Follett') Group had significant Scottish presence with the late Henry Heaney of Glasgow University and Professor Michael Anderson of Edinburgh University. The resulting Follett Report[7] was published in December 1993. The Group concentrated on practical outcomes based on an assessment of trends over the next ten years. It singled out for comment and recommendation six main topics:

- the management of the library in the institution;
- library resources;
- library provision in support of teaching;
- library provision in support of research;
- information technology (IT);
- copyright.

Some of these issues are considered below in their Scottish context, but, as Rennie McElroy pointed out[8], there was nothing peculiarly Scottish in the report and its recommendations, or in the accompanying survey papers[9,10] and the two follow-up reports[11,12]. The issues were all common across the United Kingdom, although the implementation of the recommendations would be expected to have a different flavour in Scotland, with its distinct administrative system.

Despite the publication, mentioned above, of a separate report on library provision for research, no parallel report on library support for teaching and learning was ever commissioned. The Follett Report itself reproduced some futuristic visions of learners in libraries, but did not address learning needs as thoroughly as it did some other matters. Learning has developed its own agenda, especially arising out of the influential MacFarlane Report[13] and a continuing raft of research and application projects into teaching and learning developments. Together, these place library and information services, if they are to remain relevant to students' needs, in a context wider even than that envisaged by the Follett Report.

This point and other issues discussed below indicate the various agendas that different university libraries have developed in recent years. It is obviously nonsense to suggest that teaching and research orientations are wholly separate alternatives for any institution: the best endowed research libraries have strong teaching agendas, while the new universities already had, and have subsequently developed further, a range of specialist research collections. But tensions arise in funding terms between the needs of research-oriented libraries and the libraries of more teaching-based institutions. The SHEFC formulae address only imperfectly many underlying problems related to the missions of particular institutions. Libraries with large collections claim the need to be recompensed for granting access to external users; a process is now in place, as a result of the Anderson Committee's report[12]. But teaching-oriented universities believe that their needs for greater support for 'disadvantaged' students are not adequately met. In a period of diminishing units of resource, neither can expect satisfaction.

Pivotal in the progress of HE libraries in Scotland, certainly since 1992, is the Scottish Confederation of University and Research Libraries (SCURL)[14], a sub-committee of the Board of Trustees of the National Library of Scotland (NLS). SCURL's enlargement after 1992 into thirteen university libraries, plus the NLS and the city libraries of Glasgow and Edinburgh, gave it an impetus to develop into a more formal organisation. Subsequently, membership has been extended further, to embrace the libraries of all SHEFC-funded institutions. SCURL's meetings are also attended by observers from the FE sector, from SHEFC and from the Scottish Library and Information Council (SLIC). As a result of pressure from the varied agenda it needs to pursue and from the broadening of membership, SCURL

Stuart James

has recently established a Business Committee to carry its work forward. The Business Committee has executive powers delegated to it, but the principles of plenary decision making and voluntary collaboration remain central to SCURL's vision.

SCURL is focused on practical co-operation and among various projects completed or still running under its auspices are:

- CAIRNS; Co-operative Academic Information Retrieval Network for Scotland (a means of searching the online catalogues of several university libraries)[15];

- SCONE; the Scottish Collections Network Extension[16];

- SALSER; Scottish Academic Libraries Serials (an online directory of serials holdings)[17];

- SPIS; Shared Preservation In Scotland[18];

- SAPIENS; Scottish Academic Periodicals, Implementing an Effective Networked Service (an enabling service for Scottish periodicals to be published electronically)[19];

- CASS; Collaborative Academic Store for Scotland[20];

- the successful digitisation and publishing (within Edinburgh University's EDINA service) of the texts of the first and second *Statistical Accounts of Scotland* [21].

Some projects raise new issues: SALSER led inexorably to greater mutual access for researchers at all levels between Scottish HE libraries. The *Statistical Accounts* database started as an HE initiative but, in raising questions of funding for its sustainability, has broadened into a wider consortium. CASS will raise questions of enormous significance for the joint operation of HE (and potentially other) libraries as a Scottish, rather than just a local, resource. While much consortium purchasing, especially of electronic materials, is more effectively carried out at a UK level, SCURL has also negotiated some consortium contracts.

The opportunity to have all HE libraries in Scotland use the same automated system was lost in the early days, as each institution developed and invested at its own pace, or that of its paymasters. However, it remains possible that with re-procurements, the range of systems in use might be reduced to three or four. Edinburgh University Library and the NLS carried out a joint procurement of their new system, although this lead has not been followed elsewhere in Scotland. FE college libraries have acquired generally PC-based systems, while a few remain without automated systems altogether.

Both the UK government and the Scottish Executive have a strong agenda for widening access to higher and further education[22,23,24]. This forms a significant part of a social inclusion policy. Scotland already had higher take-up rates for further and higher education than England and these have increased further under the Scottish Executive's policy. The newer universities, in particular Abertay Dundee, Glasgow Caledonian and Paisley, had strong records in taking, and – more significantly – successfully educating, students from social classes C and D and from postcode areas defined as areas of social deprivation. In addition, the policy has led to more mature students entering HE: Paisley University pioneered a Credit Accumulation and Transfer Scheme which proved enormously successful and has been followed by other (mainly, but not exclusively, new) universities.

These students bring different attitudes and requirements to library use: they may have low IT skills, little or no experience of education or library use for many years and a host of personal circumstances. Of these last, not least for most students, even after the abolition of tuition fees in Scotland, is the need to take part-time or full-time employment to finance themselves through university or college. Universities may adjust to accommodate these needs, with knock-on effects on the pattern of use made of libraries. The impact of the wider access policy and its implications for library support has parallels with work in FE in the 1960s and 1970s. Then, college libraries tackled similar issues with pioneering work which has subsequently influenced most HE libraries; the concepts of the tutor librarian and of embedding the library in the taught curriculum were largely pioneered in FE college libraries. Coming from a background more influenced by FE, nursing students in HE libraries have demanded a greater adoption of patterns of service from that sector.

More recently again, the Scottish Executive's lifelong learning agenda[22] has led universities, and their libraries, into new patterns of delivery and to increases in open and distance learning provision, as presaged by the MacFarlane Report[13]. Distance learning was initially developed by various universities in addressing the overseas market: many Scottish universities have established successful courses by distance learning in many subject areas and in various parts of the world. It was then an obvious step to use the same materials for students geographically closer to home, whether as the primary means of course delivery or as support material.

Libraries may, or may not, have found themselves closely involved in the development of open and distance learning programmes, and in the virtual learning and managed learning environments which are now being widely established across both the HE and FE sectors. Their involvement in the delivery of services, however, is crucial and the implications for new and evolving kinds of library support, whether in collaboration with others, by postal loans, by remote electronic access (all adding up to the 'library without walls') or other means, pose major questions, but open up major opportunities. The closer integration of library and teaching and learning

Stuart James

services is a variable process both between and within institutions. There are examples of close involvement, but one clear benefit for all concerned is the greater efficiency in provision and use of library stock. Automated reading list systems, for example, encourage students to use a range of materials and also help the library to identify materials that need to be made available in optimum numbers at certain times. Problems with the availability of library materials when and where students require them is usually one of the major complaints concerning library services: automated approaches to learning, including electronic provision of information, offer solutions to the problem.

University management itself varies between individual institutions, with corporate management approaches sitting sometimes uneasily alongside traditional academic democracy. Combinations of closer financial scrutiny, set against decreasing units of resource, and ranges of policies for higher and further education emanating from the Scottish Executive, impose a greater requirement for centralised management and strategic planning within institutions. This has led to a range of administrative and budgetary models for library services across Scottish HE and FE institutions, including the use in some instances of service level agreements for library services to faculties or departments. No clear pattern has been established, even among like institutions.

This is in turn reflected in the management of library and information services, one of the topics specifically discussed in the Follett Report[7] (pages 27-36). It identified three areas for consideration:

- strategic planning and the context in which this needs to take place;
- the development and use of performance indicators;
- staff management.

Strategic planning places library and information services at the heart of university policy, both for teaching and for research. Institutions were encouraged to develop holistic information policies[25], although by no means all have done so. One pilot study for an information strategy was conducted in Glasgow University[26]. Again, the pattern and impact of information strategies is uneven; a few universities which have such strategies find they have inherent flaws, some being process-based rather than outcome-based. But whether or not fully-developed strategies were produced, the effect was to bring out the importance of managing information resources across an institution and encourage the significant and constant investments required for library and IT provision to be geared to the institution's aims and policies.

In many, but by no means all, universities and colleges this led to at least an administrative convergence between library and IT services. In some universities, especially for example, Abertay Dundee and Stirling, it developed into a full integration of services; some, especially but not uniquely larger, universities have decided not to follow this route, while in others again, convergence has been partial, or addressed by a single appointment at senior management level. In some cases, this has produced clear institutional policies and action derived from them, such as at Strathclyde and Abertay Dundee; but local circumstances and personalities play a significant role in the success or otherwise of converged services and coherent, or incoherent, information strategies.

Performance indicators were under development for several years prior to the Follett Report. The Standing Conference of National and University Libraries (Sconul), for the university sector, and the Council of Polytechnic Librarians (Copol), for the former polytechnics and central institutions, produced detailed annual statistics based on returns from individual libraries. From these began to evolve, not only the raw statistics themselves, but measures based on them. Working parties have considered performance indicators in depth and in 2000 Sconul produced a first *Benchmarking manual*[27].

Sconul has now produced a first edition of analysis of library management statistics[28]. The Sconul statistics produce a wide range of data and permit benchmarking against a sophisticated range of indicators, so that the very limited range of indicators presented for a single year seems rather basic:

- total library expenditure/full time equivalent (FTE) students;
- expenditure on information provision/FTE;
- expenditure on library staffing/FTE;
- seat hours per week/FTE;
- loans/FTE;
- inter-library loans (ILLs) as percentage of loans.

The actual use of such data then becomes a matter for each university and library. There are instances of comparative data being used to support resource or other cases internally, so to that extent at least, the production and publication of performance indicators has a positive effect in improving services. On a wider basis, comparison with similar libraries has encouraged a better understanding of trends and helped identify areas within particular libraries where improvement could most profitably be sought.

These exercises are carried on most valuably on a UK-wide basis. This must continue, but it does highlight the fact that data specifically on Scotland

Stuart James

and Scottish institutions must be extracted as a separate exercise. The Library and Information Statistics Unit (LISU) of Loughborough University[29] produces wider annual statistics for UK libraries across sectors, but Scotland information does not always feature clearly in this exercise. Given the fact of devolution and funding across the sectors from the Scottish Executive, the collection and analysis of Scottish library statistics seems to be essential.

Staffing of HE libraries was addressed by a report separate from the main Follett Report. The Fielden Report[11] addressed the barriers between grades of staff within university libraries and called for more flexible working arrangements. Developed expertise would be needed in teaching and learning skills, electronic services, customer care and team working. The role of library staff and their closer integration with teaching and learning service delivery was highlighted; the extension of staff appraisal schemes to library staff urged, and to inform and enable all these changes, a much higher and more intense level of staff training and development was called for. Coupled with financial pressures and the reduced staff establishments resulting from them, flatter staffing structures have generally evolved, or have been put in place, and there has been an ever greater requirement for university librarians to adopt standard business management practices to deal with the issues which arise.

Inevitably, the level of progress towards these aims differed widely between individual institutions. Staff training and development had been taken forward by the Scottish Academic Libraries Co-Operative Training Group (SALCTG)[30], founded in 1986. It has organised, and continues to organise, a wide range of courses on professional topics, including a series of management training courses which were well supported and highly effective. Some attempts have also been made through SALCTG to provide training for non-professional staff, although with limited effect. SALCTG's training, and that of other providers, has lacked overall co-ordination. There has been a good and regular response to identified training needs, but the HE (and FE) library community has never formally identified training requirements on an ongoing basis, so that the response of providers must always be largely opportunistic. National Vocational Qualifications (NVQs) have made little impact in HE libraries, although rather more in FE[31], and it remains to be seen whether renewed activity through the Information Services National Training Organisation (isNTO)[32] will lead to greater consistency of training across all levels of staff. But HE, and most FE, libraries have taken the training message seriously and used the range of available courses, from greatly increased levels of in-house training within institutions, through all the providers up to the level of formal qualifications.

During the period under review, one of the most fundamental and dramatic changes has been in the nature of the raw materials libraries are dealing with. Electronic publishing has affected every library and the concept quickly developed of the hybrid library, where printed and electronic materials are managed jointly, in most cases in conjunction with research databases and newly developed learning materials. This forms a significant part of the developing concept of the virtual campus. Increasingly, access to special collections, both through catalogues and by digitisation of the materials themselves, is being enhanced through library websites; Edinburgh University Library has recently developed an outstanding digital gallery of treasures from its collections[33].

From Follett stemmed a wide-ranging eLib programme, comprising a great variety of types of project across the UK, which helped to inform libraries. One Scottish-based project of note was Heron[34]. Heron evolving out of an initial on-demand publishing and electronic reserve collection project[35], run jointly by Stirling and Napier University Libraries. This established a service to provide electronic copies of materials for short-loan collections, in particular addressing the copyright issues which the Follett Report had identified as an area of significance. Copyright in physical materials is covered by legislation, by agreements from the Copyright Licensing Agency and by other arrangements which, while far from ideal, give a legal basis for library activity in this area. But the question of electronic copyright remains a contentious issue whose legal and commercial implications seem to be understood imperfectly, if at all, by any party.

Economic constraints, within a context of rapidly burgeoning and frequently costly, but highly desirable, electronic services, continue to place huge burdens on university libraries. Some have proceeded rapidly to almost all-electronic provision of journal literature, but models for subscription and access, and future costings, remain unpredictable. One of the defining aspects of the hybrid library was a supposed divergence between holdings and access strategies: in reality, all libraries pursue both, albeit with differing emphases. The ancient universities have historic collections which are now being supplemented (and in the case of journals frequently replaced) by electronic publications. The new universities have tended to rely on more immediately user-focussed collections and on access to information from external sources. Heriot Watt University Library pioneered an engineering subject portal, Edinburgh Engineering Virtual Library (EEVL)[36], a model copied in numerous subject areas by other university (and increasingly FE) libraries.

Collaboration both in housing materials and in content creation by digitisation of holdings, especially within special collections, is an obvious step, and one which has been taken and is being further pursued by various bodies. Access then becomes centrally controlled and, over the years, barriers to researchers and other categories of users, including undergraduates and the general public, have begun to be broken down, especially at local level, through initiatives such as Glasgow Area Libraries Together (GALT), but

Stuart James

also with some national success through SCURL. Important and ground-breaking work in identifying collections (as opposed to individual items) within all types of library is being undertaken in the University of Strathclyde's Centre for Digital Library Research's (CDLR) SCONE Project[16]. This, again, highlights the question of cross-institutional and wider public access.

Despite the proposal in the Atkinson Report[37] for the self-renewing library, that concept was never practical, at least in the absolute terms then proposed. New university library buildings were erected at Abertay Dundee (the building won an architectural award for the quality of its development on a restricted site), Glasgow Caledonian and Paisley Universities[38], and a site library integrated into a new campus building at Garthdee for the Robert Gordon University. Other libraries made extensions to existing premises, most notably at Glasgow University where a new floor was added on top of the existing high-rise building. Such examples apart, the most dramatic changes in library premises, both in HE and FE, have been internal. Increasing numbers of students have demanded increased numbers of workspaces, and those workspaces have to be in large part equipped with IT, and with staff to support students using it. Libraries have also had to cater for students requiring spaces both for quiet individual study and for group work. But as remote access and virtual campus concepts take effect, there is already evidence in many institutions of decline in actual visits to the library; this is a fluid situation, difficult to assess until more reliable means of measuring 'virtual' visits are established.

Prior to 1992, the polytechnic and FE sectors had both been subject to regular external reviews of quality of courses, teaching and student support; library services were haphazardly included, to greater or (usually) lesser extents. Government policy after 1992 has been to seek closer, more regular and consistent quality reviews. This led to the Quality Assurance Agency, which has been working across the HE sector, although not without controversy and some outright hostility in certain quarters. Again, the inclusion of library services in subject reviews, and the level of understanding of the role of library and information services by the reviewers themselves, can most kindly be described as variable. Thus, the impact of these reviews on improving services to students remains minimal. FE libraries continue to be subject to review by Her Majesty's Inspectors (HMIs) within college appraisals. A more effective approach, although by no means universal, is for internal departmental reviews, which take more informed and realistic views of services and lead to more specific recommendations which can, in a regular cycle, be shown to have led to service improvements.

Further education has seen the creation of the SFEFC and its ever closer working relationship with SHEFC. FE colleges in Scotland remain for the most part much smaller than their counterparts south of the Border.

Library provision, too, varies enormously from college to college. It had been hoped that some standardisation to a higher level of provision might have resulted from the publication of the report of a SLIC working party[39] chaired by T.J. Burness, Principal of Glenrothes College. Disappointingly, the management of many FE colleges appear to have failed to formulate any coherent picture of how library and information services can serve their college's mission and fit with their teaching and learning functions. Library services in FE have had to support a wide range of 'initiatives', including NVQs and changes to the Scottish standard and higher grade systems. At the same time, they have been subject to very similar influences as those affecting HE. Library provision in some FE colleges remains at best basic. But there are also examples of innovative practice: a project such as the Glasgow Telecolleges Network[40], linking and sharing learning resource materials across a number of colleges, and linking with the National Grid for Learning[41], should signal an exciting future for FE information and library services.

In the last two or three years especially, library and information services across the sectors have come closer together. Many of the 'new' universities have been working closely with FE. The incorporation of nurse education into HE has brought more university libraries and health libraries into partnerships, adding to existing partnerships formed by older universities containing medical schools. At the same time, a number of FE colleges were offering courses in health-related areas. All of this has drawn the HE, FE and NHS library sectors into a range of local partnerships. The University of Paisley Library pioneered collaboration with public libraries across West and South West Scotland with a loan support service to lifelong learners matched by localised support to the University's own students. Napier, Dundee Abertay and Glasgow Caledonian University Libraries are pursuing similar paths, and all university libraries now play some role in cross-sectoral collaboration.

These activities have led to the creation of a number of truly cross-sectoral regional library partnerships. Grampian Information[42] had been operating for many years. Tayside and Fife produced a library and information plan[43] (Tayside Chief Librarians' Group 1994) which led to the formation of Tayside and Fife Library and Information Network (TAFLIN)[44]. The Ayrshire Libraries Forum[45] was set up in 1998, and similar bodies now cover Edinburgh, the Lothians and the Borders, and Glasgow, with still others in embryonic stages.

Since its establishment in 1991, SLIC has provided guidance and direction. All Scottish HE and FE libraries are members. It is fair to say that most of SLIC's agendas have not been directed specifically at university libraries, although in the developing era of cross-sectoral collaboration they increasingly are addressed by them. Influence on FE libraries has been more

Stuart James

direct, especially through the Burness Report. Much has been achieved through project work, and, since its establishment in 1999, the Centre for Digital Library Research (CDLR) at the University of Strathclyde[46] has taken on a pivotal role in devising and carrying out various projects. Many such projects are cross-sectoral, directed at the whole library community, but they are also central to HE and FE libraries and rely heavily upon them for their development.

HE and FE libraries have changed dramatically in the period reviewed, from primarily book-based services restricted to particular sites, to today's hybrid libraries. They retain on-site service, but they also combine printed materials delivered co-operatively through local libraries, with remote access to electronic library and information services from the student's residence or workplace anywhere in the world. Such services are free from physical restrictions and so are available 24 hours a day, 365 days a year. Once operating almost as independent fiefdoms of powerful university librarians in some institutions, libraries in both HE and FE, with a few lamentable exceptions mainly in FE colleges, now find themselves closely integrated within corporate structures and, at best, equally closely integrated with teaching and research activities. Much of this development was inevitable, driven by social, economic and technological factors both within and outside the professional field; the activities of the Follett and other committees served to identify if not actually direct these developments.

At the same time, libraries have come closer together and will continue to do so, both within and between sectors, and across domains, with increasing collaboration with, for example, museums and archives. Through the Scottish Executive and SHEFC it may be that a University of Scotland comes closer to realisation. A University Library of Scotland is a closer prospect, not through any formal mergers of institutions, but by increasing access agreements, collaborative acquisition, storage, inter-library loans, and through development of consortial access to electronic materials and collaborative digitisation of materials. But from another perspective, both HE and FE libraries form cornerstones, with public and other libraries, of regional library and information services evolving out of cross-sectoral activities. Again, this might not come about as a conscious formal entity, but will evolve from co-operating bodies as they address their mutual agendas of lifelong learning, wider access and equal opportunity in response to the clear policies of the Scottish Parliament and Executive.

If libraries are to change over the next ten years as fundamentally as they have over the last ten, great and exciting developments are in store. In ten years time, in addition to attending traditional, full-time courses at college or university, the citizens of Scotland will be able to dip into modules from universities and colleges (and other agencies in both public and private sectors – if that distinction remains valid), as they proceed through formal, yet seamless, levels of qualification. They will, equally automatically, have rights of access to a distributed national electronic library and information service, backed up by physical delivery of material, where appropriate, from any library in Scotland. They might gather for tutorial and/or social purposes at a convenient local place, whether university, college, community building, or public library, where they will also be able to access services and materials. Support will come both online and from staff at all these locations. The issues involved in getting the library-information profession to that stage are all recognised today and are all being addressed, as they have been during the last ten years to bring us to the interim state in which we find today's HE and FE library and information services.

References

1. The SHEFC (Scottish Higher Education Funding Council) website is www.shefc.ac.uk

2. The SFEFC (Scottish Further Education Funding Council) website is www.sfefc.ac.uk

3. Hobbs, Timothy. Research collections in a digital age: the development of special collections in Glasgow 1977-97. *Library Review, vol.47*, 5/6, 1998, p 290-295

4. The CURL (Consortium of University Research Libraries) website is www.curl.ac.uk

5. The Crichton campus (of Glasgow and Paisley Universities), Dumfries website is www.crichton.ac.uk

6. The University of the Highlands and Islands website is www.uhi.ac.uk

7. Joint Funding Councils' Libraries Review Group. *Report*. (Chairman, Sir Brian Follett). HEFC England, with SHEFC, HEFC Wales, and the Department. of Education, Northern Ireland, 1993

8. McElroy, A.Rennie. Follett: one view from Scotland. *British Journal of Academic Librarianship, vol.9*, 1/2, 1994, p83-90

9. Information Technology Sub-Committee. *Libraries and IT: working papers of the Information Technology Sub-Committee of the HEFCE's Libraries Review.* UKOLN, 1993

10. Sumsion, John. *Survey of resources & uses in higher education libraries, UK 1993.* (Occasional Paper No.6) Loughborough University, Library and Information Statistics Unit, 1994

11. John Fielden Consultancy. *Supporting expansion: a report on human resource management in academic libraries, for the Joint Funding Councils' Libraries Review Group.* HEFC England, 1993

Stuart James

12. Group on National/Regional Strategy for Library Provision for Researchers. *Report.* (Chairman, Professor Michael Anderson). HEFC England, 1995

13. Working Party of the Committee of Scottish University Principals. *Teaching and learning in an expanding higher education system.* (Chairman, Professor A. G. J. MacFarlane). CSUP, 1992

14. The SCURL (Scottish Confederation of University and Research Libraries) website is www.scurl.ac.uk

15. Information about CAIRNS (Co-operative Academic Information Retrieval Network for Scotland) is on the website http://cairns.lib.gla.ac.uk

16. Information about SCONE (Scottish Collections Network Extension) is on the website http://scone.strath.ac.uk

17. SALSER (Scottish Academic Libraries Serials) is on the website http://edina.ed.ac.uk/salser

18. Information about SPIS (Shared Preservation In Scotland) is on the website http://scurl.ac.uk/projects/spis/index.html

19. Information about SAPIENS (Scottish Academic Periodicals, Implementing an Effective Networked Service) is on the website http://sapiens.cdlr.strath.ac.uk

20. Information about CASS (Collaborative Academic Store for Scotland) is on the website http://scurl.ac.uk/projects/cass/index.html

21. Information about the first and second *Statistical Accounts of Scotland* is on the website http://edina.ac.uk/StatAcc

22. Secretary of State for Scotland. *Opportunity Scotland: a paper on lifelong learning.* (Cm 4048). The Stationery Office, 1998

23. Scottish Executive. *Scottish University for Industry: the shortest route to learning.* Scottish Executive, 1999

24. Joint Lifelong Learning Group. *Learning for life: a joined-up approach.* (Chair, Janet Lowe). SFEFC, SHEFC, Highlands & Islands Enterprise and Scottish Enterprise, 2000

25. Joint Information Systems Committee. *Guidelines for developing an information strategy.* JISC, 1995

26. Joint Information Systems Committee. *The University of Glasgow: case study: developing an information strategy.* JISC, 1998

27. Sconul. *Benchmarking manual.* Standing Conference of National and University Libraries, 2000

28. Sconul. *UK higher education library management statistics 1999-2000.* Sconul and Higher Education Colleges Learning Research Group, 2001

29. The LISU (Library and Information Statistics Unit, Loughborough University) website is www.lboro.ac.uk/departments/dils/lisu/lisuhp.html

30. Information about SALCTG (Scottish Academic Libraries Co-operative Training Group) is on the website www.jiscmail.ac.uk/files/LIS-SALCTG/welcome.html

31. Shackleton, Jenny. NVQs and their effect upon colleges: curriculum and resource implications in McElroy, A.Rennie, *ed. The changing face of further and higher education libraries in the 1990s*, p23-26. Library Association Colleges of Further and Higher Education Group, 1992

32. The isNTO (Information Services National Training Organisation) website is www.isnto.org.uk

33. Edinburgh University Library's digital gallery of treasures from its collections can be found at the website www.lib.ed.ac.uk/lib/about/bgallery/Gallery/researchcoll/index.html

34. The Heron (Higher Education Resources ON demand) website is www.heron.ac.uk

35. Halliday, Leah. *The impact of on-demand publishing and electronic reserve on students, teaching and libraries in higher education in the UK.* Library Information Technology Centre, South Bank University, 1997

36. The EEVL (Edinburgh Engineering Virtual Library) website is www.eevl.ac.uk

37. University Grants Committee. *Capital provision for university libraries.* (The Atkinson Report). UGC, 1976

38. James, Stuart. Design of the new library and learning resources centre for the University of Paisley. *New Library World, vol.98,* 1135, 1997, p132-140

39. Working Party on Libraries in Scottish Further Education Colleges. *Libraries in Scottish further education colleges: standards for performance and resourcing.* (Chairman, T.J. Burness). Scottish Library and Information Council and Scottish Library Association, 1993

40. The Glasgow Telecolleges Network website is www.glasgowcolleges.ac.uk/GTN/GTN.htm

41. The NGfL (National Grid for Learning) website is www.ngfl.gov.uk

42. The Grampian Information website is www.grampianinfo.co.uk

43. Tayside Chief Librarians' Group. *The Tayside local information plan.* The Group, 1994

44. Information about TAFLIN (Tayside and Fife Library and Information Network) is on the website www.dundeecity.gov.uk/taflin/about.htm

Stuart James

45. Information about Ayrshire Libraries Forum is on the website www.slainte.org.uk/alf/alfohome.htm

46. The CDLR (Centre for Digital Library Research) website is http://cdlr.strath.ac.uk

Disclaimer

The views expressed in this essay are those of the author and may not be representative of organisations with which he is associated.

1 7

Libraries and information services in healthcare

Graham Buckley and Mary Lakie

Healthcare in Scotland is supported by library and information resources which are rich in total, but highly fragmented. Parent organisations range from large to very small, from broadly based to highly specialised. They include universities and colleges, professional bodies and the Royal Colleges, research organisations, voluntary organisations and the National Health Service in Scotland's (NHS Scotland) Trusts and Health Boards. The authors of this essay would like to be able to report that each organisation contributes library and information resources within an integrated strategic framework which allows all of their personnel access to resources appropriate for their needs. While this is not so at present, it is an achievable vision. The barriers to such integrated delivery are substantial, but none is insurmountable.

The belief that such a vision is achievable is based on the many stimuli for change taking effect at present: developments in education for health professionals; pressure to ensure that healthcare is based on evidence of best practice; emphasis on lifelong professional development; evolution of specialist patient and family advisory and support groups; all serve to highlight the need for more access to the knowledge base of healthcare. Patients are also seeking personal access to information on disease states, potential treatments and sources of advice. Demand increases year on year, yet most libraries are under constant pressure to contain, or even reduce expenditure.

The NHS Scotland context

In 1996, the Scottish Library and Information Council (SLIC) commissioned a multi-disciplinary group to review library and information services in NHS Scotland. Its report and recommendations, *Enabling access to the knowledge base of healthcare*[1], were accepted by the Health Minister in 1998. SLIC's recommendations were subsequently embodied in *Learning together, a strategy for education, training and lifelong learning*[2], as part of a plan to modernise NHS Scotland and improve healthcare. The dovetailing

Graham Buckley and Mary Lakie

of the recommendations of *Enabling access* with the objectives for *Learning together* provides a framework, for the first time, for developing library and information services for all staff in NHS Scotland.

NHS services in Scotland are delivered by 15 regional Health Boards (eg NHS Grampian, NHS Fife), together incorporating 28 Trusts. In addition, several Special Health Boards are responsible for Scotland-wide specialist services, eg the Clinical Standards Board, Health Technology Board and NHS Education. Of the last, more later. Each region includes several library and information units, often small and stand-alone, managed variously by Health Boards and/or Trusts, and addressing some of the needs of staff in hospitals, primary care, public health and health education. Nine of the thirteen Scottish universities have service level agreements with Trusts or Health Boards to provide library services.

In addition, a myriad professional bodies, the Royal Colleges and voluntary organisations provide library and information services addressing the specialised information and educational needs of their members. In as much as NHS Scotland personnel are members of these professions and organisations and use their services, NHS Scotland benefits from access to their resources. Many patients and their families depend on information, advice and support from specialist organisations and voluntary bodies, in parallel with treatment and support from NHS Scotland. NHS Scotland personnel engaged in work-related projects and continuing education may also draw on these resources.

Although rich in total, these resources are distributed in such a way that, for most individual seekers of healthcare information, access is limited and unsupported. Value and efficiency are lost because there is no way of aggregating and integrating the whole.

Perceived problems

The patchy provision of information services across NHS Scotland reflects the lack of a clear information strategy. At a national level, there have been difficulties in influencing policy development in relation to meeting information needs, because there has been no clear managerial or communication route for the views, advice and insights of library staff to reach the Management Board of the Scottish Executive Health Department. *Enabling access*[1] was consequently of crucial importance, filling an information and policy vacuum. But although its recommendations were incorporated into *Learning together*[2], the problem of providing expert advice on a continuing basis to the Scottish Executive and to Trusts and Boards on the development of information services remains. Many NHS Scotland libraries are small, staffed by relatively junior people who do not carry weight with senior management.

This essay will comment more than once upon the relationship between NHS Scotland and higher education in the field of library and information services. The relationship is a force for good, to be valued as such. To criticise it and identify some shortcomings is not to assign fault or blame. Rather, it is to indicate how the relationship can and should be improved, to the benefit of all. Improvement will be achieved by the two sectors working in constructive partnership, each cognisant of and respecting its own and the other's needs and interests.

The long-standing, intimate relationships of university medical schools and their libraries with the teaching hospitals, and the more recent incorporation of nursing colleges into higher education, mean that, for many NHS health professionals, their library of first resort is in higher education, not the NHS. Others perceive the library of their professional body as their library of first resort, since postgraduate training and continuing professional development is undertaken under the aegis of that body. But for others in NHS Scotland, especially those in disciplines other than medicine and nursing, there has been no library of first resort.

Higher education institutions have contributed much to library and information services for the NHS. They have naturally focused primarily on their own enrolled staff and students. In areas without a medical school or nursing college, provision has been patchy at best and, frankly, often poor. In all locations, it can be difficult for anyone – even doctors and nurses – not formally linked to a higher education institution to access services.

The tradition of library provision from higher education has resulted in NHS Scotland feeling little need to develop expertise of its own in the strategic development and delivery of library and information services. This may explain why many NHS Scotland libraries have no clear and logical place within their parent Trust or Board. Only if NHS Scotland develops its own capacity to analyse and design what it needs, can it deliver, manage and evaluate information services properly.

Good access to high quality healthcare information depends on ready access to a robust electronic communications network. The shift from print to electronic provision has already had a major impact in all library and information services. The availability of comprehensive bibliographic databases and the rapid growth, especially since the late 1990s, of electronic journals in all disciplines, is revolutionising the way students use library services. As a result, graduate staff enter the NHS with an expectation of continuing to access library and information resources in this manner and almost all staff have some capability in using the Internet. Electronic networks significantly lower some of the barriers to providing an effective, equitable library and information service, especially in remote and rural areas.

Most, but not yet all, NHS locations are linked UK-wide by NHSnet, a national concept dependent on local development support. Consistent

Graham Buckley and Mary Lakie

development has been impeded by the autonomous nature of NHS organisations, local funding priorities, absence of nationally agreed standards for developing intranets and local decisions on levels of authorisation to use the network. Access to a high-speed broadband communications network is needed and should be available to all NHS staff, in order to support the efficient sharing of distributed resources and encourage their effective use.

For higher education, the Joint Information Systems Committee (JISC) has made central investment over many years, to develop the Joint Academic Network (JANET) and create the current enviable UK-wide capacity. JANET is an open network designed to enable students and staff to share resources located anywhere on the network or the Internet and to exchange resources created in-house. NHSnet is a closed network, designed primarily to hold financial and patient data securely. It permits closely controlled access to that data and offers a limited capacity for general communication usage. Overriding NHS concerns for data security are preventing direct network connection between JANET and NHSnet. Thus, university staff and students working within the NHS cannot reach resources on JANET from NHSnet or *vice versa*. They can, however, share resources held in common on the Internet.

Funding for library and information resources within the NHS comes from a variety of sources and is difficult to identify or untangle from other budget streams. Many categories of staff (again, especially those in disciplines other than medicine and nursing) have no identifiable funds allocated to ensure provision of and access to information. There is no consistency in source or amount of funding, much of which is non-recurrent. Effective services cannot be developed on this basis.

Higher education, the NHS and public libraries are all substantial providers of library and information services. These services are, in the main, developed in isolation from each other, resulting both in duplication and in gaps in provision for healthcare in Scotland. Provision could be much enhanced, even within the current spend, through enhanced cross-sectoral collaborations. However, funding streams derive from three separate Scottish Executive departments and there is, at present, no genuinely cross-sectoral body with the authority and credibility to negotiate for all on a collaborative basis. While there are many potential advantages of cross-sectoral collaborative purchasing, there is no place for a 'one size fits all' approach. Different sectors have different strategic objectives, network capabilities, service policies and organisational cultures. Collaborative requirements need to be negotiated by personnel closely familiar with their own sectoral strategies and policies, influential within their parent organisation, yet committed to seeking creative solutions to shared need. Library and information personnel in NHS Scotland see potential in such collaborations and will welcome progress on these lines.

This raises the devolution question – 'If one advocates cross-sectoral collaboration in Scotland to improve the depth and delivery of services, why not spread the net even more widely to work on a whole-UK basis?' The users' needs, the capacities of the technology and the economics of the marketplace all lead in this direction. However, one can only say that, currently at least, governmental structures effectively preclude an all-UK approach.

Differential pricing structures and publishers' resistance to the sharing of resources characterise the market in electronic information resources. This tends to obstruct potentially fruitful collaborations among the libraries of different types of organisations, even within healthcare itself. Some suppliers are becoming more flexible as they perceive the market opportunities that may flow from improving access and thus extending the user base.

Implementing 'Learning together'

An interdisciplinary and cross-sectoral Learning Resources Project Group (LRPG) was formed by the Scottish Executive Health Department in 2000 as part of a multi-faceted plan to implement Learning together[2]. Learning together synthesises thinking about the nature and purpose of lifelong learning in NHS Scotland, identifying high quality patient care as the focus for its educational strategy. Clearly, it is essential for healthcare practitioners to keep up-to-date and develop their skills throughout their careers. Staff will be encouraged to take more responsibility for their own learning and, in turn, can expect appropriate support from their employer, which acknowledges its responsibility to foster and support staff development. A key theme of the lifelong learning strategy is improved access to information and training for all staff. The development and maintenance of an NHS Scotland e-library is a critical element in the improvement programme.

The remit for LRPG included a specific charge to negotiate electronic access to databases and journals for all NHS Scotland staff. The initial objective was to obtain better value for NHS Scotland through collaborative purchasing of core resources. The support required from Chief Executives, information management and information technology managers and other Trust and Board managers to implement these objectives provided valuable opportunities to advocate the role and potential contribution of library and information services in a learning environment. This groundwork makes it possible to build future information services in NHS Scotland.

Graham Buckley and Mary Lakie

NHS Scotland e-library project

Requirements for the electronic access to information project were drawn from the recommendations of *Enabling access* and the objectives of *Learning together*. The broad objective was that all NHS Scotland personnel should have equitable and reliable access to the same core set of information resources, irrespective of their discipline or location. The concept of access for all staff was entirely new; previously, provision had been made for specific groups, most frequently medical and nursing staff.

This Scotland-wide project benefited from the lead taken by libraries within Greater Glasgow Health Board. In effect, Glasgow piloted a collaborative purchasing agreement upon which they built the Glasgow e-library[3]. Their success was based on a clear vision of what could be achieved, close and continuing consultation amongst all interested parties, imaginative solutions to funding and operational issues, lively relationships with providers and, to a considerable extent, a fortuitous coalition of library and information professionals who worked together effectively. Their product is efficient, highly effective and much appreciated by their user community. Each successful step in the Glasgow project made ground for LRPG by reducing the time required for formulating and presenting arguments and lobbying for support. The LRPG project was also supported by librarians in Grampian, where long-standing, informal co-operation (Grampian Health Information Network) has lowered many barriers to cross-sectoral provision.

In October 2001, the NHS Scotland e-library was launched, providing access to four major databases and 160 full-text journals. The library is accessible from any PC, from workplace or home, subject only to the user obtaining identification and a password from their local NHS Scotland library. Access is provided from each NHS Trust or Board intranet as part of the local library and information service, but an NHS Scotland e-library portal has also been established within the Scottish Health On the Web (SHOW) website[4]. This portal can be accessed from any location, whether inside NHSnet or not, requiring only user identification and password.

Electronic access to resources on the Internet allows NHS Scotland libraries to provide equitable access for all staff, whether located close to or distant from the library, thus overcoming some of the difficulties of provision for remote and rural areas. The SHOW portal provides easy access for those NHS Scotland personnel who are still not authorised to access the Internet directly from work.

Immediate and longer term outcomes

The negotiation for electronic access to library resources was initiated by LRPG with central funding for the first year of a contract but without provision for continuation funding, or an obvious locus of ownership for the contract. The Scottish Library and Information Council (SLIC) provided professional advisory and project management support for LRPG. The Clinical Research and Guidelines (CRAG) group in the Scottish Executive Health Department actively supported and promoted the e-library development among clinical practitioners. LRPG was chaired by the Chief Executive of the Scottish Council for Postgraduate Medical and Dental Education (SCPMDE) and that organisation provided administrative support and a locus for the project. The ultimate success of the project is due in no small measure to close collaboration among these organisations and their combined influence in the healthcare community in Scotland. An immediate and most valuable consequence of this collaboration was the agreement that SCPMDE would take ownership of the contract and provide continuation funding to maintain the e-library following initial pump-priming by the Scottish Executive.

The early success of the Glasgow and NHS Scotland e-libraries has raised expectations for improved information services, delivered by means of further collaborative purchasing. There is a need to identify more resources, based on actual needs, rather than custom and practice. A new purchasing model is required to achieve top-up facilities; some Boards or Trusts generate higher demands for certain resources than can be sustained by the core. Specialty interests across Scotland also need to be catered for, even though user numbers may be low.

The thinking in *Learning together* was sustained and reinforced in the health plan for Scotland, *Our national health*[5, 6], published in 2000 and in the later NHS Scotland *Performance assessment framework*[7]. As a result, and for the first time, a requirement to report to the Scottish Executive annually on the educational performance of NHS Scotland Trusts and Boards has been established, as part of an open accountability process.

Linked to this development was the decision by the Scottish Executive to create a new Special Health Board for Education. The Scottish Council for Postgraduate Medical and Dental Education (SCPMDE) was founded as a Special Health Board in 1993 to ensure continuing investment in the postgraduate training of doctors and dentists in Scotland. Its achievements and the corresponding success of the National Board for Nursing in Scotland and the Post Qualification Education Board for Pharmacy led to a decision to merge all of their responsibilities in the new Special Health Board for Education from April 2002. Its remit will expand to cover all the health professions and, possibly, the whole of the staff of NHS Scotland.

In future, co-ordinated planning and investment will be applied to the lifelong learning and training of all health workers in NHS Scotland. This decision sends a strong signal that maintaining a well-informed workforce in NHS Scotland now has a high priority for both politicians and managers.

Graham Buckley and Mary Lakie

The creation of a robust library and information service across the whole of NHS Scotland will be a vital component of these educational goals.

Implications for NHS Scotland staff

The drivers for change in healthcare practice are social, as well as professional. Individuals are now less deferential in their approach to professional advisors; doctors, nurses and other health professionals no longer have a monopoly on information and the rising expectations of an increasingly well-informed public are changing traditional relationships between patients and healthcare providers. Thanks in great part to the Internet, patients may be better informed about certain aspects of their disease than their doctors and nurses. The trust and confidence that lie at the heart of a therapeutic relationship depend upon clear explanations, given by health worker to patient, and based on explicit evidence and manifest competence. Maintaining that trust and confidence is the main aim of the move by health professions to require maintenance of registration through formal re-certification. This process encompasses participation in clinical audit, as well as continuing education. Evidence-based practice is the phrase that best describes the shift in approach required of clinicians. Previous practice was also based on evidence, but this was usually implicit, with the strength of evidence for treatment decisions not shared with patients. The demand for detailed, relevant information and evidence to support clinical practice brings library and information services into the front line of NHS Scotland service delivery.

As improved information services come on stream for NHS Scotland staff, what are likely to be the early implications? For busy clinicians, improved access to information alone is unlikely to be enough to change behaviour. However, for the many NHS Scotland staff who previously had patchy or no access to library and information resources, the opportunities are perhaps more obvious. For those in primary care, there is now ready access to the same information resources and services that are available in large hospitals. Staff moving between hospitals and Trusts as part of their training and career progression, and also in day to day service, can expect access to the same level of service, utilising uniform search facilities and techniques.

Evidence from clinical guideline implementation studies and other studies of adult learning demonstrate a number of key principles that will need to be addressed if improved access to information is to lead to effective learning and better healthcare. The educational needs of individuals and teams of staff must be identified accurately, by means of thorough clinical audit. Learning must be stimulated by a balance between support and challenge, underpinned by a direct link between learning needs and the information provided to address them, and explicitly valued by employers and the professions. Information itself must be reliable, readily available in the workplace, clearly relevant to immediate concerns about patient care and packaged so that it may be assimilated readily.

Implications for library and information service staff

The above formulation of the linkage between education, information and patient care implies a more proactive role for librarians and information officers in the new NHS Scotland. Devising ways of meeting the information needs of all healthcare practitioners and managers will require library and information staff to establish much closer working relationships with these groups. Efficient custodianship of collections is not enough. Understanding the working patterns of other professionals in the NHS and working with them to design information services that truly meet their needs is the challenge. Simply improving access via electronic media will create information overload unless library and information staff apply their professional expertise to enable their colleagues to seek out, evaluate and filter information effectively.

Most people are now familiar with the Internet and the use of search engines. Many perceive Google and other search engines as 'quality assured', believing that ranking of information sources by popularity is good enough for their purposes. Here is Plutchak's problem of the 'satisfied inept'[8], discussed elsewhere in this book by Derek Law[9]. How are librarians to help information users to be aware of the relative value of different types of sources for different purposes? How are librarians to help them to search with real efficiency and effectiveness? What new and traditional skills should be brought to bear, to exploit and add value to web-based resources, grey literature and ephemera?

While the work of LRPG was in process, SLIC, SCPMDE and CRAG were collaborating over the need for a strategic and policy framework for library and information services in NHS Scotland. As a result, it has been possible to create a new post of Advisor, Library and Information Services within the new Special Health Board for Education, to guide the development of coherent, equitable and relevant library and information services for NHS Scotland. This is an exciting development, full of potential. It is particularly significant for existing library and information staff, as a highly visible commitment designed to address issues of low status and professional frustration.

To date, there has been little evidence of support for the professional development of library and information service personnel. However, NHS Scotland librarians have managed to create effective professional and service networks, notably through the Scottish Health Information Network[10]

Graham Buckley and Mary Lakie

(SHINE). They are justifiably proud of the efficiency and cost-effectiveness of their inter-library lending scheme, which allows informal sharing of scarce resources. Their networking for professional advice and support, training activities and collaborative development projects make a substantial, if currently silent, contribution to operational effectiveness. How much more can they achieve now, with the prospect of strategic leadership and informed support at a senior management level?

The *Learning together* objectives for education, training and development apply to library and information staff, as to all other NHS Scotland personnel. Working with colleagues from other disciplines to identify the information requirements that arise from specific learning needs and an increased need to teach users how to seek out and evaluate information sources for themselves, rather than simply conducting searches for them, will offer many personal development opportunities. Knowledge management, leadership and project management skills demonstrated in the library and information environment may also lead to broader career opportunities in NHS Scotland.

Implications for patients

The Wanless report[11] commissioned by the Treasury analyses the societal shifts that are influencing expectations and demand for health services. The report compares the UK with other developed countries and documents and predicts trends in this country. An intriguing aspect of its analysis and conclusions is the increasing demand for choice in the style of services provided in healthcare. Linked to this, there is evidence of a developing segmentation of society into three, roughly equal-sized, groups:

- active managers and seekers of health and healthcare;
- dependent and compliant recipients of care;
- stoic avoiders of formal healthcare.

The information and healthcare strategies required to meet the needs of these groups differ markedly.

The challenge in meeting the needs of the first group is to translate information into understanding. Downloading poor quality information from the Internet is more likely to swell the ranks of the 'worried well' than to improve health. Readily understood quality markers or 'kitemarks' are needed, to help people make sense of the information that is now available electronically. In future, the review journal *Clinical Evidence* may have the public, rather than doctors, as its principal market.

For the second main group within the population, guided access to relevant information at the time it is needed is likely to be of most value.

This will be delivered through personal contact with health professionals, but will also be available through new telephone services such as NHS 24[12], the Scottish service analogous to NHS Direct[13]. As well as providing immediate advice, NHS 24 has the potential to provide targeted follow-up to help the individual. The educational literature suggests that this could have significant positive effects in encouraging behavioural change towards healthier lifestyles.

For the third group, the stoic avoiders, the mass media channels employed by the Health Education Board for Scotland[14] are the main communication techniques used at present. Even here, segmentation of the market may provide additional opportunities. Selective advertising on the proposed Scottish Premier League soccer channel may prove to be the most effective way of communicating effectively with young men, who are otherwise notoriously difficult to reach.

Today, people expect to know more and to be told more about healthcare in general and their individual conditions in particular; many use the Internet, but may be poorly placed to assess the quality of the information they find. It is in NHS Scotland's interest to acknowledge and address this expectation of being informed, by providing patients with ready access to quality assured information.

Looking to the future

Much has been achieved since SLIC and SCPMDE began to investigate healthcare libraries and information services in 1996. The essence of that achievement is that the issues have been clarified, a way forward identified and a strong start made. The political and organisational environments are favourable to further development. But much remains to be done; the NHS Scotland Advisor, Library and Information Services will lack neither challenges nor opportunities. The present authors hesitate to prescribe these too closely, but, given that this essay dwells to a considerable extent upon achievement, it will be well to finish with – not an overview, but a selection – of what may be in the in-tray.

Learning together, with its objective of equal access to learning opportunity for all NHS Scotland staff, brings into the learning and information environment new groups of people who have not previously had library and information service provision made specifically for them. Library and information service staff must promote information services to these new client groups (indeed, they might help to identify and define them in the first place) and persuade them of the positive contribution that effective use of information can make to job performance and personal development. Library and information service staff must also help these client groups to identify their information needs in fairly precise terms.

Graham Buckley and Mary Lakie

To accomplish this, they will need to develop and apply promotional and teaching skills of a high order. Developing and applying such skills will be critical. The essence of electronic information delivery is direct access by the end user in the workplace. So, the full benefit of electronic library and information services will not be realised until users are taught to search effectively for themselves and gain a fair degree of independence in doing so. The practice of librarians undertaking searches for users was valuable – an essential element of professional library service – but it may now be dysfunctional, because overtaken by technology. End users need not learn to search like library and information professionals; the latter will retain more sophisticated search skills and these will always be required as back up and in cases of particular complexity. But all users should be taught to search efficiently, and well enough to be confident of a successful outcome. Clearly, library and information professionals should do the teaching. Interestingly, library staff in higher education are currently improving their skills in these areas and seem well placed to assist colleagues in NHS Scotland via collaborative staff development and training programmes.

New client groups mean higher levels of demand and increased pressure on resources and, while significant improvements in provision can be achieved within existing spending by astute, and collaborative, purchasing, there remains a need for some new money to provide new materials. At time of writing (January 2002), such new money is not yet available, or at least not at individual library level in Boards and Trusts.

Learning together enunciates a policy of providing equally for all NHS Scotland staff, but anecdotal evidence indicates that guidelines still in force (or at least, still pursued) in some locations assign higher priority to some groups of staff, typically doctors and nurses, the established beneficiaries of healthcare library and information services. The implication is that the 'new' client groups cannot be provided for until the needs of existing groups are fully met and this is a barrier to providing for new groups. Clearly, some work remains to be done in translating policy securely and coherently into practice and in updating existing, but obsolete, guidelines.

All of the above strengthens the case for more collaborative (locally advised, centrally executed) planning, purchasing and provision. There is a need for a cross-sectoral forum to negotiate both collaborative purchases and collaborative access to information resources. To be effective, any such body should represent the healthcare, education and local authority sectors ('healthcare' is used in the widest sense, encompassing NHS Scotland, the Royal Colleges, medical schools, voluntary organisations *et al*). All participants need to be able to negotiate and buy into an agreement at some affordable level and all need to be able to formulate and enunciate their strategic needs and immediate priorities securely and confidently. At an all-Scotland level, SLIC's cross-sectoral experience and responsibilities may make it the logical starting point for such activity. A Scottish pilot project should be achievable in the near term, because in Scotland's relatively intimate professional community, the potential participants already know each other. One logical extension of such a pilot project would be to investigate and experiment with connectivity and access between the electronic networks of each participating sector. Library and information professionals are well disposed to such a project; the real challenge is to influence the respective funding bodies to support it.

But the above are subordinate to strategic responsibilities: promoting library and information services to the Scottish Executive Health Department and to senior managers in Health Boards and Trusts; setting standards and monitoring performance; leading the further development of the NHS Scotland e-library and other information services, local and national. Such strategic and networking activity is likely to account for most of the energies of the Advisor, Library and Information Services, and it is by the degree of success achieved here that he or she will ultimately be judged. All library and information professionals in NHS Scotland will need to support the Advisor, by taking a long-term, strategic view of issues, even at the expense of short-term local interest.

In conclusion

The post of Advisor, Library and Information Services has been created, but all the development work remains to be done. As *Learning together*[2] (p7) emphasises:

> As in all walks of life the NHS in Scotland is challenged by change. The public expects more and better healthcare, new techniques and new technology are constantly being developed, and staff have changing needs and aspirations. NHS Scotland is modernising to meet these challenges. Some will find the demands of modernisation difficult. Others will find them refreshing. All involved will have to adapt and develop, and to do this they will need to learn and keep learning. The core theme of Learning together is that learning is vital to delivering modern, high quality, responsive health care.

Besides traditional library and information skills, practitioners need to develop effective communication, teaching, organisational and interpersonal skills. They must be flexible when moving between project and core work, and willing to think strategically and 'see the big picture', albeit sometimes at the expense of parochial self-interest and territory. These challenges are seriously demanding and cannot be achieved without support. Significant

Graham Buckley and Mary Lakie

investment in staff development and training will be critical if transitions are to be successful; this is the employer-support element of *Learning together*. However, the most important aspect for the future of the library and information profession will be the extent to which practitioners are willing to take responsibility for their own development and that of their services, and then seek creative, collaborative ways of achieving it.

Library and information staff in NHS Scotland are not alone in being challenged to step up to a new role. For some, the very uncertainties of change will offer refreshing opportunities; for others, it may be just another nightmare. But change there will be.

Postscript

This review of healthcare library and information issues demonstrates one of Robert Craig's strongest suits. He has the enviable knack of working with other people, organisations and sectors to address *their* aims and issues on *their* agenda; and of doing so by harnessing the potential of library and information services to progress these aims and issues. In the process, the library and information service sector is itself enhanced. Ultimately, the real beneficiary is the end user. Which is what libraries are about, is it not?

References

1. Scottish Library and Information Council. *Enabling access to the knowledge base of healthcare*. SLIC, 1998

2. National Health Service in Scotland. *Learning together – a strategy for education, training and lifelong learning for all staff in the NHS in Scotland*. NHS Scotland, 2000

3. The Glasgow e-library is at the website www.northglashealthinfo.org.uk/electroniclibrary.htm

4. The NHS Scotland SHOW website is at www.show.scot.nhs.uk/elibrary

5. Scottish Executive Health Department. *Our national health: a plan for action, a plan for change*. The Department, 2000. The document can be found at the website www.scotland.gov.uk/library3/health/onh.pdf

6. Scottish Executive Health Department. *Our national health: delivering change*. The Department, 2001. The document can be found at the website www.scotland.gov.uk/library3/health/onhdc.pdf

7. Scottish Executive Health Department. *Performance assessment framework*. The Department, 2001. The document can be found at the website www.scotland.gov.uk/library3/health/PAFaletterOB.PDF

8. Plutchak, T.S. On the satisfied and inept end user. *Medical Reference Services Quarterly*, *8*, 1, Spring 1989, p45-48

9. Law, Derek. Developments in information technology, networks and services in McElroy, Rennie *et al, eds. Advocating libraries*. Chartered Institute of Library and Information Professionals in Scotland, 2002

10. The Scottish Health Information Network (SHINE) website is www.shinelib.org.uk

11. H.M. Treasury. *Securing our future health: taking a long-term view. An interim report*. (Chairman, Derek Wanless) H.M. Treasury, November 2001. The report can be found at the website www.hm-treasury.gov.uk/Consultations_and_Legislation/wanless/consult_wanless_index.cfm

12. Information about NHS 24 can be found at the website www.nhs24.com

13. Information about NHS Direct can be found at the website www.nhsdirect.nhs.uk/

14. The Health Education Board for Scotland (HEBS) website is www.hebs.scot.nhs.uk/

Graham Buckley and Mary Lakie

CONTRIBUTORS AND EDITORS

Rhona Arthur

Rhona Arthur, BA, FCLIP, has served as Assistant Director of the Chartered Institute of Library and Information Professionals in Scotland (formerly the Scottish Library Association) and of the Scottish Library and Information Council since 1997. She is an Associate Assessor with Her Majesty's Inspectorate of Education. Previously, she worked as School Librarian, Blantyre High School, 1980-87; Librarian-in-Charge at a Pre-Five Resource Centre in Glasgow, 1987-92; and Professional Officer, the Scottish Library Association, 1992-97. Professional interests include school libraries, reader development, information and communications technology (ICT) training, and continuing professional development. She chaired the New Opportunities Fund ICT Training Plan Assessment, Scottish Panel. She has served on the COSLA School Library Standards Working Party, the IFLA National Organising Committee, the Scottish Executive Education Department Innovative Practice Group. She was responsible for the BAFTA-nominated Scottish Writers project.

Jenny Brown

Jenny Brown has been Head of Literature at the Scottish Arts Council since 1996. She was previously Director of the Edinburgh Book Festival, 1982-91; National Co-ordinator of the Readiscovery campaign, 1994-96; and presenter of Scottish Television's book programmes, 1989-94. She was a Commissioner of the Press Complaints Commission, 1993-97.

Janey Buchan

Janey Buchan was Labour Member of the European Parliament for Glasgow, 1979-94; previously, Member of Strathclyde Regional Council, 1974-79. Housewife, socialist, defender of individuals' freedom of action, occasional scriptwriter and journalist. Honorary Member of the Scottish Library Association. Recreations include books, music, theatre and television.

Graham Buckley

Dr Graham Buckley, MD, FRCP(Ed), FRCGP, FRCS(Ed), is Chief Executive, NHS Education for Scotland, and was Chief Executive of the Scottish Council for Postgraduate Medical and Dental Education, 1993-2002. During that time he chaired the Scottish Library and Information Council's review of library and information services to the National Health Service in Scotland. His earlier career combined general medical practice in Livingston with hospital work in the care of the elderly, and postgraduate teaching. He was editor of *British Journal of General Practice*, 1983-91 and of *Medical Education*, 1993-98.

Loudon Craig

James Loudon Craig, BA, MCLIP, was Director of Community and Leisure Services, Falkirk, 1995-98. His career in local government began with Lanark County Libraries in 1963 and included the posts of Assistant District Librarian, East Kilbride, 1975-80; Depute Director of Libraries and Museums, Falkirk, 1980-90; Depute Director of Leisure Services, Falkirk, 1990-94; and Acting Director of Leisure Services, Falkirk, 1994-95. He married Jennifer in 1969 and has two grown-up daughters, Louisa and Amy. A voracious reader, he is also a lover of music, the theatre, cinema, the concert hall, long lunches and good conversation. He exercises by dining out as often as possible and travelling with his wife at home and abroad.

George Cunningham

George Cunningham, BA, Hon FCLIP, started his career in diplomatic service at home and abroad but, finding the political itch too strong, he joined the staff of the Labour Party as a specialist in international affairs. He was Labour and later Social Democratic Party Member of Parliament for South Islington from 1970 until 1983, serving on many House of Commons committees, acting as a Labour spokesman on Home Affairs and doing a brief spell in the European Parliament. He was appointed Chief Executive of the Library Association in 1984, retiring in 1992. He is an Honorary Member of the Scottish Library Association. He is President of the Study of Parliament Group and spends some time monitoring elections in far-flung places like Kosovo and Lesotho. He is an amateur, and very imperfect, bookbinder.

Gavin Drummond

Gavin Drummond, MBE, MCLIP, worked in the library services of Dunfermline, Perth and Kinross, Perth City, Bedfordshire and Aberdeenshire before moving to Angus as County Librarian in 1973. There, he held the posts of Director of Libraries and Museums, then Director of Cultural Services, before retiring in 2000. He served on the Scottish Library Association Council from 1974 onwards. He was President of the Scottish Library Association in 1985 and then became the Association's Honorary Treasurer. He chaired the Library and Information Services Committee (Scotland) for three years and was Company Secretary of the Scottish Library and Information Council when it was formed. He served as Library Advisor to the Convention of Scottish Local Authorities from 1982. He is involved in Rotary, is an elder of St Margaret's Church in Forfar and enjoys wayward golf and geriatric squash.

Judith Elkin

Professor Judith Elkin, BA, PhD, FCLIP, AcSS, is Dean of the Faculty of Computing, Information and English at the University of Central England in Birmingham. She heads a team of academics and researchers concerned with communication in its widest sense, highlighting the importance of access to information and information-handling in the world today. Her major concern is to enhance the quality of teaching and research throughout the Faculty. Her particular interest is raising the profile of information professionals, by attracting high quality students to undergraduate and masters courses, offering better opportunities for continuing professional development and creating a sound research base. She was a member of the Library and Information Commission and its Research Committee throughout its existence, from 1995 to 2000. She served on the Library Association Council. She has recently chaired the Higher Education Funding Council's 2001 Research Assessment Exercise Panel for Library and Information Management. She is the editor of a number of anthologies of children's literature and poetry and has recently co-edited, with Derek Law, *Managing Information* (Open University, 2000).

Lorraine Fannin

Lorraine Fannin, BA, DipEd, has been Director of the Scottish Publishers Association since 1987 and is also Board director of the distribution company, BookSource. Previously, she owned a children's book business, Glowworm (1978-88) and was a partner in the children's audio

Contributors and editors

publisher, Whigmaleerie. Earlier work included teaching modern languages to reluctant pupils, freelance journalism for *The Scotsman* and broadcasting with BBC Radio Scotland. She is a Trustee of the National Library of Scotland and an Honorary Member of the Scottish Library Association. She has served on the British Council's Publishers' Advisory Committee and the Council of the Institute of Publishing. Recreations include going to the theatre, to art galleries and to auctions, and, of course, reading.

Elaine Fulton

Elaine Fulton, BA, MCLIP, has been Assistant Director of the Scottish Library and Information Council (SLIC) since 1998. Before then, she worked in public libraries, holding posts including Support Services Librarian, Strathkelvin, and Operations Librarian, East Dunbartonshire. She spent a short time working with a library automated systems supplier. The development of information and communications technology (ICT) systems and services in libraries has been a mainstay of her professional work and continues to be a major part of her remit at SLIC. Current professional responsibilities include inter-operability and access standards, ICT networking and services, Best Value, co-operation and co-ordination. Committee member, Community Services Group (Scotland), 1982-84; Committee member, Association of Assistant Librarians (Scotland), 1986-89 and Secretary, 1989-90; SLIC Network Forum member, 1995-96; Member of Scottish Library Association Council, 1996-98.

Alan R. C. Hasson

Alan R. C. Hasson, MA, MBA, DipLib, MCLIP, is Head of Cultural and Interpretive Services, Scottish Borders Council. He was previously Chief Librarian for Cumbernauld and Kilsyth Council, and for East Ayrshire Council. Member, Scottish Library Association (SLA) Council, 1994 to 2002 and now a Member of the Council of the Chartered Institute of Library and Information Professionals in Scotland; Chair of SLA Council, 1999-2000; Scottish Representative, Public Libraries Group, 1994-97; Editor, *Public Library Journal*, 1997-99; Member of Management Committee, Scottish Library and Information Council, 1997 to date. Professional interests include public sector management, the development of information and communications technology services and the role of public libraries in lifelong learning. Recreations include golf, hill-walking and travel.

Stuart James

Stuart James, BA, FCLIP, FRSA, has been Chief Librarian of the University of Paisley (formerly Paisley College) since 1989, having previously been Deputy Librarian since 1978. President of the Scottish Library Association, 2001. In 2001, elected Vice-Chairman of SCURL (the Scottish Confederation of University and Research Libraries) and so *ex officio* Chairman of its Business Committee. Editor of *Library Review*, 1986-2002 and of *Reference Reviews*, 1990-2002. Chairman of the *Information for Scotland* Conference Planning Committee since its inception in 1993; and of the Ayrshire Libraries Forum since its foundation in 1998. Recreations include the history of aviation, book collecting and caring for grandchildren.

Liz Knowles

Liz Knowles, MA, DipLib, MCLIP, is Service Manager, Quality Development, Education and Children's Services, Perth and Kinross Council. She was formerly Regional Schools Librarian, Tayside; Senior Resource Librarian, Lanark Division; and School Librarian, Dalziel High School, Motherwell. She was President of the Scottish Library Association in 1999 and previously, a Member of the Scottish Library Association Council and of a range of professional working groups, including COSLA's School Library Standards Working Party. Professional interests focus on the role of libraries in education in schools, particularly in fostering independent learners; she is committed to working for the development and recognition of that role. Personal interests include travelling, the cinema, eating out and sailing – in calm and warm waters only!

Mary Lakie

Mary Lakie, MBA, MRPharmS, MCLIP, is a consultant in project management, change management and team-building. She was Program Director (Change Management), Syntex Research Division, 1992-95; and Manager of Scientific Information Services, Syntex Research Europe, 1981-92. Formerly, a Member of Library Association Council, Scottish Library Association Council and the Management Committee of the Scottish Library and Information Council. Professional interests include management education, coaching support in project management, and information management and delivery, principally in healthcare and the life sciences. Recreations include bird watching, gardening, reading, travelling, and good food and wine.

Contributors and editors

Derek Law

Professor Derek G. Law, MA, DUniv, FCLIP, FKC, FRSE, has been Head of Information Resources at the University of Strathclyde since 1998, having previously worked at the Universities of Edinburgh, Glasgow and St Andrews. He is responsible for the Centre for Digital Library Research at Strathclyde and holds a chair in the Department of Computing and Information Science. He was the last President of the Scottish Library Association, January to March 2002, and became the first President of the Chartered Institute of Library and Information Professionals in Scotland when that body came into being on 1st April 2002. He is Treasurer of the International Federation of Library Associations and Institutions (IFLA). Professional interests include electronic libraries and networked information, information strategy and policy, and the management of change. Recreations include naval history, travel and a perennial attempt to hold the world record for committee memberships.

Rennie McElroy

Professor Rennie McElroy, MA, MBA, FCLIP, was University Librarian, Napier University, 1984-98 and previously, Depute Librarian and Tutor Librarian at Napier. Member of the Scottish Library Association Council, 1976-99; President of the Scottish Library Association, 1989; Member of the Scottish Library and Information Council's Management Committee, 1991-96; and of its predecessor, the Library and Information Services Committee (Scotland), 1982-91; Chairman, the Library Association's Colleges of Technology and Further Education Group (CoFHE), 1983-88. Author and editor of several books, articles and reports about aspects of librarianship and education. Professional interests include the role of libraries in education, education for library-information work, standards for library provision and performance, and distance and open learning. Recreations include bird watching, golf, reading, travelling, especially in Scotland, France and the western US, and good food and wine.

Bob McKee

Dr Bob McKee, PhD, MCLIP, FRSA, is Chief Executive of the Chartered Institute of Library and Information Professionals, formerly Chief Executive of the Library Association. He was previously Director of Libraries and Arts, then Assistant Chief Executive, with Solihull Metropolitan Borough Council. He spent the earlier part of his career in community librarianship, teaching and the ICT industry. As a member of the Library Association, he has served on the West Midlands Branch Committee, on Library Association Council and on the Board of Library Association Publishing. He is a former President of the Association of Assistant Librarians. As a policy advisor to government, he served on the Library and Information Services Council for England and on the Library and Information Commission; he also advised the Local Government Association. He enjoys sports, music, reading and evenings in convivial company.

Andrew Miller

Andrew Miller, MA, FCLIP, was Glasgow's Director of Libraries and Archives, 1996-98, having been Director of Libraries, 1981-96, and Depute Director, 1974-81. He was Depute Burgh Librarian, Motherwell and Wishaw, 1965-74, with earlier service in The Mitchell Library and Hamilton Public Libraries. He was a long-serving Member of the Scottish Library Association Council, serving as Treasurer and being Chairman, 1990-98. He was President of the Scottish Library Association in 1984 and was appointed an Honorary Vice-President in 2001. From its inception until 1996, he was a member of the Management Committee of the Scottish Library and Information Council (SLIC), acting initially as Chairman to the infant organisation; currently he is SLIC's Company Secretary. He is a Past President and former Secretary of INTAMEL (International Association of Metropolitan Libraries); he was the second Chairman of SCURL (Scottish Confederation of University and Research Libraries); and Secretary of COCRIL (Council of City Reference and Information Libraries). Since 1995, he has been the Library Association's Official Orator. His recreations include gardening, motoring, public speaking, socialising with friends and travelling – but not necessarily in that order.

Ian R. M. Mowat

Ian R. M. Mowat, MA, BPhil, FRSA, FCLIP, FRSE, is Librarian to the University of Edinburgh, having served previously as Librarian of the University of Newcastle upon Tyne, 1992-97, and of the University of Hull, 1986-91. He has served on many bodies nationally and internationally, including, currently, the Chairmanship of the Scottish Confederation of University and Research Libraries, the Board of the Consortium of University Research Libraries and the Members' Council of OCLC. His work has been published in eight countries, in five languages.

Brian D. Osborne

Brian D. Osborne, BA, MCLIP, FSA(Scot), was District Librarian of Midlothian from 1983 to 1989 and Chief Officer, Libraries and Museums in Strathkelvin from 1989 to 1995, when he retired to concentrate on writing. Publications include *The Ingenious Mr Bell*, *The Last of the Chiefs* and *The Clyde at War* (the last, with Ronald Armstrong). Other collaborations with Ronald Armstrong include various Scottish literary anthologies and two plays produced at The Byre Theatre, St Andrews and Perth Theatre. He was President of the Scottish Library Association in 1992 and has carried out free-lance and consultancy work in the library field since retirement.

Alan Reid

Alan Reid, MA, MCLIP, is Library Services Manager with Midlothian Council. From 1991 to 2002, he was Honorary Publications Officer of the Scottish Library Association. He now holds the corresponding post with its successor, the Chartered Institute of Library and Information Professionals in Scotland. In 1997, he edited *Discovering Scottish Writers* in partnership with Brian D. Osborne; the book was published by the Scottish Library Association and Scottish Cultural Press. He was made an Honorary Member of the Scottish Library Association in 2000. Alan is active in a number of local organisations in Midlothian, including Penicuik Community Arts Association and the Midlothian World History Society.

Ross Shimmon

Ross Shimmon, OBE, Hon FCLIP, FCLIP, is Secretary General, International Federation of Library Associations and Institutions (IFLA), The Hague, Netherlands. Previous posts include Chief Executive of the Library Association, 1992-99, and various posts with the Library Association, the Administrative College of Papua New Guinea, Preston Polytechnic, the College of Librarianship Wales, the Department of Education and Science and several public libraries. Member, British Library Advisory Council, 1993-99; British Council Library and Information Advisory Committee, 1997-99; Book Aid International Council, 1992-99; Founder President, European Bureau of Library, Information and Documentation Associations (EBLIDA), 1991-95. Interests include cricket, photography and steam railways.

Alan G. D. White

Alan G. D. White, FCLIP, was formerly Assistant City Librarian, Edinburgh. Member of Scottish Library Association (SLA) Council, 1962-94; Honorary Editor, *SLA News*, 1966-76; Honorary Secretary, SLA Summer School, 1966-76; President, Association of Assistant Librarians, 1972; Chair, Public Libraries Group, 1978; President of the Scottish Library Association, 1980; SLA Representative to Library Association Council, 1984-92; President, the Library Association, 1989. Member, National Library of Scotland, Library Co-operation Committee, 1976-93. Many writings and reports on aspects of Scottish libraries. Professional interests include professional organisations and their role, library architecture, mobile library services, reference work. Hobbies include model making and collecting, motor sport, listening to jazz and (as other contributors to this book!) good food and wine.